Twayne's Filmmakers Series

Warren French
EDITOR

New German Cinema:
From Oberhausen to Hamburg

A scene from Deutschland im Herbst (Germany in Autumn, 1978) *Courtesy of New Line Cinema*

New German Cinema: From Oberhausen to Hamburg

JAMES FRANKLIN

BOSTON

Twayne Publishers

1983

New German Cinema

is first published in 1983 by Twayne Publishers,
A Division of G. K. Hall & Company

Copyright © 1983 by G. K. Hall & Company

Printed on permanent/durable acid-free paper and bound
in the United States of America

First Printing, April 1983

Book Production by John Amburg

Library of Congress Cataloging in Publication Data

Franklin, James C., 1943–
New German cinema.

(Twayne's filmmakers series)
Bibliography: p. 185
Includes index.
1. Moving-pictures—any (West)—History
2. Moving-picture plays—History and criticism.
3. Moving-picture producers and directors—Germany
(West)   I. Title.   II. Series
PN1993.5.G3F7   791.43'0943   82-6192
ISBN 0-8057-9288-0   AACRS

For my children and for me.

Contents

About the Author

JAMES FRANKLIN is a cynical man who finds that German film is right up his alley. Educated at Ohio University (B.A., 1965), the Free University of West Berlin, and Case Western Reserve University (M.A., Ph.D., 1972), he has taught courses in German language, literature, culture, and film at the University of South Carolina and Purdue University. A cofounder of the Purdue University Annual Conference on Film and of *Film Studies Annual*, he is a past chairman of the Purdue University Film Studies Program. He is the author of a monograph on the revelatory poetry of a thirteenth-century German mystic, Mechthild von Magdeburg, and has written articles on German literature and film for *Literature/Film Quarterly, German Quarterly, Mosaic, Die Unterrichtspraxis,* and *Quarterly Review of Film Studies.*

Editor's Foreword

THE NEW CINEMA of West Germany has probably been the most important movement in international cinema during the 1970s. Leadership in expanding the boundaries of Western cinema (to which these remarks are limited) has constantly changed hands since the advent of the feature film, usually—curiously—about the turn of each decade. Before World War I, D. W. Griffith in the United States set the pattern for the feature with *The Birth of a Nation* and then, in *Intolerance*, transcended it in a manner rarely equalled since. With the rise to power of the conservative major studios in the United States after World War I, leadership shifted to filmmakers in two defeated powers that began experimenting with new forms of film even as they were experimenting with new forms of government. Germany divided its efforts between Expressionist and "Street" films, while Soviet Russia concentrated on agitprop "montage" films.

With the rise of Naziism in Germany and the Kremlin purges in Russia, both industries lost their vitality. The lead shifted, during the first decade of talking pictures, to France, where "The Golden Age" saw great works of Jean Renoir, René Clair, Marcel Pagnol, Jean Vigo, Sacha Guitry, Marcel Carné, and others, between 1930 and the outbreak of World War II in 1939.

The war allowed little time for experiment anywhere, although Orson Welles's *Citizen Kane* seemed to promise a new American era that the studio masters quickly frustrated. After the war, another defeated nation, Italy, produced the neorealism that led to the masterpieces of Federico Fellini, Michelangelo Antonioni, and Luchino Visconti and influenced the development of *film noir* everywhere. Then suddenly in 1959, Francois Truffaut and Jean-Luc Godard restored the glory of French cinema with their "New Wave" trailblazers, *The 400 Blows* and *Breathless*, which, along with Alain Resnais's films, influenced the creation of the New German Cinema during the next decade.

The history of this New Cinema needs no summary here, for that is provided by James Franklin's account of what has happened in West Germany since the promulgation of the Oberhausen Manifesto in 1962. Here I wish only to explain some features of this book that distinguish it from others in the series. Since this is the account of a large movement involving many artists—a subject too large and complex to treat fully in a single volume—this book begins with a short history of the New German Cinema, followed by seven chapters on those directors whose work has so far received the widest distribution in the United States. The general chronology lists only those dates that mark important stages in the movement; chronologies of the works of individual filmmakers head the subsequent chapters about them. The bibliography lists general works about the movement and writings about the specific directors considered. In the most unusual departure from our standard format, however, the Filmography provides details not only of the films of these directors, but also of all feature films by directors associated with the New Cinema that were being distributed in the United States in 16mm. when this book went to press. Although these films constitute only a small part of the work of this productive movement, Mr. Franklin's study should prove useful for those planning American programs studying the New German Cinema.

Within the chapters about individual directors, James Franklin has not rushed through a film-by-film analysis of their works, but has rather analyzed the distinctive features of the whole body of work by each and explained their particular aims as filmmakers. These accounts are drawn largely from the filmmakers' own words in interviews in which they discussed their private visions of film.

This Introduction may appear, as the author suggests, at a time when the movement in West Germany has already peaked. The filmmakers discussed here are beginning to receive recognition that indicates that their once outrageous novelties have been assimilated: Schlondorff's *The Tin Drum* has won an American Academy Award as best foreign film, crowds lined a cold New York Street to press in to see Fassbinder's *The Marriage of Maria Braun*, Wim Wenders has been invited to Hollywood. More ominously, as Franklin points out, most of the films reaching the United States from West Germany today are the work of those who began their careers as feature filmmakers between 1965 and 1970. It is becoming increasingly difficult for young, inexperienced filmmakers to find the kind of subsidies that enabled this "older generation" to get started.

Even if the lead may shift elsewhere, however, American audiences beyond the reach of film festivals, the New York art-theater circuit, and campus film programs are just beginning to become acquainted with the work of Fassbinder, Werner Herzog, and their contemporaries. In this compact guide, James Franklin has provided the perspective needed in this country to understand the nature and impact of the New German Cinema that has dominated a decade marked throughout the Western film world by the rapid breakdown of old taboos concerning language, subject matter, and narrative techniques.

W. F.

Preface

AMERICANS VIEW German and, more generally, European affairs as if through a telescope held the wrong way round. Major figures and significant events tend to grow smaller when viewed from an American perspective. This book too, by necessity, views the New German Cinema from afar; it is a portrait of the most significant West German filmmakers as seen from the cornfields of Indiana. Details have doubtless been overlooked. But distance also offers a desirable objectivity, and objectivity is a quality that has frequently been lacking in the evaluation of West German directors within the Federal Republic itself. Until quite recently these directors have been artists without honor in their own land, winning respect in Paris, Rome, London, and New York but remaining relatively unknown to the average German moviegoer. Even now the scarcely concealed suspicion lingers in German society and especially among German academics and intellectuals that all German films remain trivial and frivolous. Praise has been grudging. May this book and others like it, as evidence of foreign esteem, help convince these filmmakers' skeptical countrymen.

I further hope that this book, which devotes most of its attention to a limited number of filmmakers, will not be interpreted as a slighting of other sensitive and creative West German directors. This work is an examination, a chronicle, of the growth to maturity of the New German Cinema during the 1960s and 1970s. The subtitle, "From Oberhausen to Hamburg," is a chronological, not a geographical, designation referring to the preeminent figures in West German film between 1962, the year in which New German Cinema was initiated by the signing of the Oberhausen Manifesto, and 1979, when post-Oberhausen achievements of the 1960s and 1970s were affirmed and new directions for the 1980s were outlined at a gathering of filmmakers in Hamburg. The few directors portrayed here in *New German*

Cinema represent only the most recognized of West German directors, but it is precisely the recognition they have received which has created the West German film scene of 1980. Later books can chronicle the maturing successors of Kluge, Straub/Huillet, Schlöndorff, Herzog, Fassbinder, Wenders, and Syberberg.

In portraying the directors treated at length in this book, I have tried to rely primarily on the words of the directors themselves as found in their writings or, more often, in interviews. One of the intended services of this book is to bring these words and ideas to an American public. In so doing I have avoided, for the most part, commentary by film critics in favor of direct quotes from the directors themselves. I have also favored German–language writings and interviews, since these materials are otherwise unavailable to most Americans. Unless otherwise noted, all translations are mine. German interviews frequently contain long run-on sentences that translate badly into English, so linguistic clumsiness may at times require the reader's indulgence. I have tried to do justice to my sources and have thus tended to strive for literalness rather than eloquence.

I want to acknowledge my debt—and the debt of the New German Cinema—to the late Jan Dawson. Known to me only through her writings, Jan Dawson was one of the earliest, most consistently perceptive, and liveliest observers of West German films during the 1970s. She once described film criticism as "an act of love followed by an autopsy." I wish my writing contained even half her acuity and wit.

I am grateful to Nancy Franklin for emotional support, to David B. Richards for his helpful comments on the manuscript, to Deborra Callis for her work typing the manuscript, and to Warren French and Twayne Publishers for their patience and editorial advice.

James Franklin

Acknowledgments

CHAPTER SIX first appeared, in an earlier form, as "The Films of Fassbinder: Form and Formula," in *Quarterly Review of Film Studies* 5, no. 3 (Spring 1980).

Stills have been generously provided by The Liberty Company, the Film Center of the Art Institute of Chicago, the Museum of Modern Art, New Line Cinema, New Yorker Films, and Zoetrope.

Chronology

1962	Alexander Kluge and twenty-five other young filmmakers sign a Manifesto at the Oberhausen Short Film Festival, February 26.
1964	*Kuratorium junger deutscher Film* established to promote first works by young filmmakers.
1965	Hans-Jürgen Syberberg's first feature film, *Fritz Kortner Rehearses Kabale und Liebe.*
1966	Kluge's first feature film, *Yesterday Girl,* and Volker Schlöndorff's first feature film, *Young Törless.*
1967	Jean-Marie Straub and Danièle Huillet release their first feature film, *The Chronicle of Anna Magdalena Bach;* Werner Herzog releases his first feature film, *Signs of Life;* Kluge's *Yesterday Girl* and Schlöndorff's *Young Törless* shown at New York Film Festival (first American recognition of the new cinema).
1968	*Kuratorium junger deutscher Film* placed under control of individual West German states; Film subsidies Board created to provide federal subsidies program.
1969	Rainer Werner Fassbinder's first feature film, *Love is Colder than Death.*
1970	Wim Wenders's first feature film, *Summer in the Cities.*
1974	Film/Television Agreement provides funds for coproductions.
1977	Syberberg's seven-hour *Hitler: A Film from Germany,* most ambitious production of the new cinema, released.
1978	Kluge, Schlöndorff, Fassbinder, and six other directors collaborate on *Germany in Autumn (Deutschland im Herbst).*

1979   Film/Television Agreement revised; one-hundred film makers sign Hamburg Declaration at Hamburg Film Festival in September.

1980   Schlöndorff's *The Tin Drum* becomes the first post-World War II German film to receive an American Academy Award as best foreign film.

Individual chronologies of the lives and works of the filmmakers discussed in separate chapters appear at the head of each of these chapters.

1

Introduction: The New West German Cinema from Oberhausen to Hamburg

The New Cinema in the New World: American Reception of West German Films in the 1970s

BORN IN 1962, the New German Cinema did not exist for most Americans until the mid-1970s, because nothing truly exists until it has been recognized by *Time* and *Newsweek* or—for a smaller, slightly more sophisticated audience—by the *New York Times* and the *Village Voice*. New York City is and was the focus of American cinematic awareness; new waves break first on our Eastern shores. Although West German films had been consistently present since 1967 at the annual New York Film Festival, they remained neglected even by New Yorkers.

The Program Director of the New York Film Festival, Richard Roud, was the author of the earliest monograph on the films of Jean-Marie Straub and Danièle Huillet and was also the earliest important patron of New German films in America. Roud brought to the Festival in the late 1960s and early 1970s films by the most interesting members of a new generation of German directors: Alexander Kluge's *Yesterday Girl* and Volker Schlöndorff's *Young Törless* in 1967; Kluge's *Artists Under the Big Top: Perplexed*, Straub/Huillet's *Chronicle of Anna Magdalena Bach*, and Werner Herzog's *Signs of Life* in 1968; Herzog's *Even Dwarfs Started Small* and Straub/Huillet's *Othon* in 1970; Herzog's *Fata Morgana* and Rainer Werner Fassbinder's *Pioneers in Ingolstadt* in 1971. For the most part these stark and intellectually demanding films fell on deaf ears and met with blind eyes, even among reviewers who later came to appreciate and to praise the young German filmmakers. Although the majority of these films had been well received at other major interna-

21

tional film festivals, the New York reviewers were either bored or repelled by the low–budget, black-and-white, coolly and ironically distanced films of the West Germans.

Compared with the poignant comedies and warm dramas of the Italians, of the French, and of the even more fashionable Czechoslovakians, the West German films of the late 1960s were found to be clumsy, bleak and, worst of all, humorless. The first of the West German films to be reviewed by the *New York Times* was described in this way: "Whatever *Yesterday Girl* symbolizes, Mr. Kluge applies his camera like a clouded microscope, side-stepping simple compassion for bland, clinical detachment."[1] A basically positive review of *Young Törless* unenticingly reported, "it is cold, hard, gray and monotonous in pictorial tone and quality."[2] A puzzled reviewer referred to *Chronicle of Anna Magdalena Bach* as "static in its stylization, and some will find it deadly dull."[3] *Artists Under the Big Top: Perplexed* perplexed its *New York Times* reviewer: at the conclusion of "this West German-made whatzit . . . an actor stoically looks at the camera and begins outlining the plot of *Il Trovatore*. That one we know. Good old Verdi!"[4] It was not only the *New York Times'* reviewers who yearned for simpler cinematic pleasures. After the 1970 Festival, for example, *Newsweek* used words like "obnoxious," "revolting," and "atrocity" in its review of *Even Dwarfs Started Small*[5] and after the 1971 Festival referred to *Fata Morgana* as "meaningless meanderings around junk piles in the Sahara" and to *Pioneers in Ingolstadt* as "the clumsiest, most mannered movie ever made about soldiers and their girls."[6]

While such comments typify most early critical response to West German film, beginning in 1972 there came a gradual change, a new awareness that West German films were not only acceptable but even laudable. In 1972 Fassbinder's *Merchant of Four Seasons* was shown at the New York Film Festival, drawing a favorable response from, among others, Andrew Sarris, the senior film critic of the *Village Voice*, and Roger Greenspun of the *New York Times*. Greenspun referred to the film's "imaginative freedom" and called Fassbinder's work "very exciting."[7] Sarris placed *Merchant of Four Seasons* at the very top of his ten-best film list and called Fassbinder "the most important new director of the past decade."[8] Even more responsible, probably, for the deepening of American interest in West German film was an extensive series of feature-length and short films shown at New York's Museum of Modern Art in spring 1972. This series generated favorable reviews in the New York press not only for Fassbinder but for other young West German directors, who displayed a cinematic earnestness, sophistication, and diversity that took New York critics by surprise. What had been "dull" was now perceived as "serious," "coldness" was now seen to be "integrity."

With the screening of other, even more accomplished films at subsequent New York Film Festivals, the New German Cinema received still greater acclaim. In 1973 came Fassbinder's *The Bitter Tears of Petra von Kant*, Straub/Huillet's *History Lessons*, and Herzog's *Land of Silence and Darkness*; in 1974 Wim Wenders's *Alice in the Cities*, Fassbinder's *Fear Eats the Soul: Ali*, Peter Lilienthal's *La Paloma*, and Kluge's *Occasional Work of a Female Slave*; and in 1975 Herzog's Kaspar Hauser film *Every Man for Himself and God Against All*, Fassbinder's *Fox and his Friends*, Schlöndorff and Margarethe von Trotta's *The Lost Honor of Katharina Blum*, and Straub/Huillet's *Moses and Aron*. Several of these films—especially Fassbinder's *Fear Eats the Soul: Ali* and Herzog's *Every Man for Himself*—arrived in America with the blessing of highly respected prizes from Cannes festival juries and won positive comment from even more grudging critics. By the end of 1975 critical admiration for New German Cinema had become an accomplished fact. Long, laudatory articles on Fassbinder and/or New German Cinema appeared in *New Times* (Arthur Lubow, "Cinema's New Wunderkinder," 14 November 1975), the *Village Voice* (Andrew Sarris, "The Germans Are Coming! The Germans are Coming!," 27 October 1975), and *Film Comment* (a series of articles by or about Fassbinder, November/December 1975).

Not all commentary was positive, even for Fassbinder and Herzog. Pauline Kael's *New Yorker* review of *Every Man for Himself* ("Metaphysical Tarzan," 20 October 1975), while admitting to Herzog's gifts as a director, said that the film was "a garbled, pop–abstract enigma," accused Herzog of "priggishness," and ended with a subjective and unconvinced assessment that Herzog's "goodness saps our strength." Frank Rich's *New York Post* review of *Every Man for Himself* bore as its title: "Herzog's Insult to Intelligence" (30 September 1975). In a *New York* article titled "Cinematic Illiterates" (25 October 1975), John Simon assailed both *Every Man for Himself* and Straub/Huillet's *Moses and Aron*, calling the former "choppy," "capricious," "ponderous," "attitudinizing," and "an offense against God and man," and referring to Straub as, with the possible exceptions of Andy Warhol and Marguerite Duras, "the dullest film-maker not only in Germany but in the whole world."

Better to be reviled than ignored: if nothing else, such reviews demonstrate that these German films and filmmakers were being taken seriously and—in the case of Kael and Simon at least—may also have helped to generate sympathetic support. Certainly for Fassbinder, for Herzog, for Wenders, and somewhat less enthusiastically for Schlöndorff, the last years of the 1970s turned out to be a period of recurring American acclaim, so that by the end of 1978 interviews or thorough profiles of Herzog, Fassbinder, Wenders, and Schlöndorff had appeared in the *New York Times, Film Comment, Film Quarterly, Rolling Stone,* or the *Village Voice.* New German Cinema had established itself as being, in the view of most "serious" American critics, the most exciting and innovative of any foreign cinema. In a series of articles during 1977, occasioned by Fassbinder and New German retrospectives in New York City, Vincent Canby, the *New York Times's* chief reviewer and thus a major influence upon American cinematic tastes, praised Fassbinder as "the most original talent since Godard" (6 March 1977) and wrote of "the long-awaited renaissance of the German film" (11 December 1977). Early in 1978 *Time,* with characteristic hyperbole, reported that "the 70's belong to the Germans," ("Seeking Planets That Do Not Exist," 20 March 1978). Finally as word spread from the Eastern press to more somnolent academic circles, several scholarly American film journals including *Literature/Film Quarterly, Wide Angle,* and *Quarterly Review of Film Studies* published special issues on New German Cinema during 1979 and 1980.

Clearly the ultimate test of success in the film world, where art comes with an extremely high price tag, is money spent by an audience at the box office. And here recent West German films have had their greatest failures. In 1973 Andrew Sarris chided New Yorkers for being "studiously indifferent to German movies,"[9] and Vincent Canby noted at the end of 1977 that "none of the young Germans has made much of a dent at theater box offices"[10] despite the enthusiasm of film critics. Even in this respect, however, the New German Cinema seems finally to have come to life. Early in 1980 a *Variety* article by Ronald Holloway (23 January 1980) noted the likelihood that Fassbinder's *The Marriage of Maria Braun* or Schlöndorff's *The Tin Drum* would finally manage a financial breakthrough by surpassing a watermark $1 million in U.S. box-office receipts, which did in fact occur early in 1980 with both films. This is a paltry sum by *Star Wars* standards ($175 million) but a clear measure of success for any non–American film.

Perhaps the New German Cinema truly came of age in America in spring 1980. Schlöndorff's *The Tin Drum* received an Oscar as the Outstanding Foreign Language Film of 1979, the first German film—East or West, pre– or post–Nazi—to receive the award. Even

(top) David Bennent in Volker Schlöndorff's The Tin Drum. *Courtesy of The Museum of Modern Art/Film Stills Archive; (bottom) Hanna Schygulla in Rainer Werner Fassbinder's* The Marriage of Maria Braun. *Courtesy of New Yorker Films.*

those who denigrate the value of the Academy Awards, finding them representative only of lowbrow taste and Hollywood hype, would have to acknowledge at least the symbolic significance of Schlöndorff's victorious appearance in Hollywood and on American television. Memories are long and anti-German hostility dies hard: part of the audience booed as Schlöndorff accepted the Oscar and as he alluded to the great German films of the Weimar period and to the influence of exiled German filmmakers on American films. Despite lingering antagonisms, the New German Cinema finally arrived through *The Tin Drum*'s acceptance by the American film establishment, a continent—if not worlds—away from the New York film critics.

"Oberhausen and the Decline of the 'Old' German Cinema"

Schlöndorff's *The Tin Drum* could hardly be more different from the early works of the New German Cinema. The budget for *The Tin Drum* was DM6 million (nearly $3 million), relatively modest by Hollywood standards but an enormous sum in comparison with most other recent West German films for which budgets have seldom exceeded DM1 million. Schlöndorff's own debut film *Young Törless* had cost less than DM900,000. Many other first features had cost far less: Herzog's *Signs of Life* DM400,000, Straub/Huillet's *Not Reconciled* DM117,000, Fassbinder's *Love is Colder Than Death* DM95,000. Such bare budgets obviously affected the final product; the elaborate costumes, sets, and historical verisimilitude of *The Tin Drum* cannot be paid for, nor could they be paid for in the 1960s, with DM1 million.

It is not only in their final appearance that *The Tin Drum* or Fassbinder's *Despair* or Herzog's *Nosferatu* differs from the early films of the New German Cinema, however. What is called "New" German Cinema is in fact by 1980 hardly new any longer, having originated almost twenty years ago at the 1962 Oberhausen Short Film Festival. A group of young West German filmmakers, mostly born in the 1930s, resolved to break with the prevailing, ailing, even disastrously moribund commercial German film industry. These twenty-six filmmakers formulated and signed a manifesto, a declaration that the German cinema of the first two post–Hitler decades was dead, that a new German film was about to be born, a phoenix rising from the ashes of "Papa's cinema":

The collapse of the conventional German film industry has finally removed the economic basis of an intellectual attitude that we reject. Thereby the new film has a chance to come alive.

In the last few years German short films by young authors, directors, and producers have received a large number of prizes at international festivals and have found international critical recognition. These works and their success show that the future of the German cinema lies with those who have proven they speak a new cinematic language.

In Germany as in other countries the short film has become the school and experimental laboratory for the feature film.

We declare our intention of creating the new German feature film.

This new film needs new freedoms: freedom from the conventions of the commercial film industry. Freedom from influence by commercial partners. Freedom from domination by special interest groups.

We have concrete artistic, formal, and economic conceptions about the production of the new German film. We are collectively prepared to bear the economic risks.

The old film is dead. We believe in the new.

Oberhausen, 28 February 1962

The "old film" whose death the Oberhausen group proclaimed in its manifesto was the commercial cinema that had grown up in the wake of World War II. The Oberhausen proclamation of the end of this cinema was, unquestionably, premature. The "old" film industry retained its dominance over West German filmmaking at least until the end of the 1960s and in fact still exists, although with ever diminishing significance as the younger filmmakers (and television and Hollywood) have usurped more and more of the traditional film audience and, as a consequence, of filmmaking capital.

The decline in West German filmmaking during the late 1950s and 1960s was in part a reflection of a more general decline in filmmaking throughout the world brought about by the rise of television.[11] West German cinema also faced unique problems that exacerbated the growing reluctance of the film audience to leave their homes and the free entertainment provided by their televisions.

The laudable (although always financially weak) German film industry of the Weimar Republic had, under Hitler and Goebbels, been nationalized, Nazified, and isolated between 1933 and 1945. With the collapse of the Nazi regime there came a simultaneous collapse in the apparatus of film production. After 1945 the major German film studios in Berlin-Babelsberg wound up within East German territory, leaving West Germany without a central film production facility. Even today, although Munich and secondarily

West Berlin are filmmaking centers, there is no true West German film capital.

After the Allied de-Nazification proceedings of the late 1940s production was begun again in West Germany but under a set of conditions inimical to the establishment of a healthy and durable film industry. In response to Allied regulations, the first impetus in cinematic reconstruction was given to the rebuilding of film theaters and of distributing companies to the detriment of actual film production.

Throughout the fifties, sixties, and seventies, film distribution has been the dominant factor in the triad of production–distribution–exhibition, and film distribution in West Germany has been effectively controlled by American companies. Small distribution companies under German ownership were ultimately unable to compete with better-financed, American-controlled distributors. By the end of the 1970s four of the six largest distributors were American-controlled: Cinema International Corporation, Twentieth-Century Fox of Germany, United Artists Corporation, and Warner-Columbia. The other two German firms are Tobis-Filmkunst, founded in the early 1970s, and Neue Constantin, formed in the late 1970s from the remnants of the original Constantin company (the oldest German distributor, founded in 1950, which had finally gone bankrupt in 1977).

Film production was similarly overshadowed by the Americans. Immediately after the war and throughout the 1950s the American studios and distributors were able to undercut German competition by "dumping" on the German market films made during the war but which, unscreened in Nazi Germany, were new to and popular with German audiences. These American films could be sold at inexpensive yet profitable rates. Moreover, although in the mid-1950s over 100 production companies were registered in West Germany, over two-thirds of these were extremely small companies without the financial means to survive the catastrophic decline in audience numbers that began in the late 1950s. German film production became centered in a few powerful, monopolistic companies that in the mid-1950s made West Germany into the fifth-largest feature-film producer. Nevertheless these monopolies also hindered rather than promoted the cinematic inventiveness necessary to fight in the long run the dominance of Hollywood studio films. Having achieved a few box-office successes, the German film establishment stuck to its formulas—pouring out a succession of imitative films shortsightedly created only for an increasingly misjudged German audience. The

German companies—CCC, Constantin, Gloria—produced countless variations on a limited number of hackneyed themes: detective films based on the novels of Edgar Wallace; adventure films from the novels of Karl May; *Sissi* films starring Romy Schneider as a teen-aged Austrian aristocrat and glorifying the imperial past; *Heimat* films, romantic adventures and comedies filmed in picturesque tourist areas; and, later, pseudoeducational sex films (the Oswalt Kolle films) and soft-porn sex comedies; and other, similar cinematic trivia.

Thus the West German film industry has witnessed in the last quarter-century disastrous declines in the number of cinemas and in the number of viewers attracted to those cinemas. Equally devastating have been the reductions in the number of films produced and in the percentage of box-office grosses that German films took in within West Germany. From over 7000 film theaters in the Federal Republic at the end of the 1950s there remained only 3140 in 1977. The peak audience of 817.5 million in 1956 dwindled to 115.1 million. The number of West German films produced fell from 122 in 1955 to 51 in 1977. Most significantly the West Germans' share of their own domestic market decreased dramatically; the percentage of total distributor's fees paid for the rental of West German films fell during this period (1955–1977) from 47.3 percent to 11.4 percent.[12]

This then is the atmosphere in which the young filmmakers at Oberhausen in 1962 wrote their manifesto declaring the birth of the New German Cinema. Even if the "old" cinema was not quite "dead," by 1962 the signs of its imminent demise were unmistakable. The Oberhausen Manifesto was not, was never intended to be, a declaration of things accomplished; it was rather an optimistic blue-print of things that might be. And to that extent it is considered the turning point, the moment at which younger West German filmmakers turned their backs on the German film establishment. The young filmmakers disavowed (in theory, though not always in practice) all intentions and ambitions to work within that establishment. They set out on their own road toward a form of filmmaking with totally new and demanding standards of artistic quality and, as it has turned out, with new methods of financing, production, and distribution. For example, a group of the New filmmakers established in the early 1970s Filmverlag der Autoren, modeled on a German writers' publishing cooperative, Verlag der Autoren. Founded as an alternative to the production and distribution monopolies, the Filmverlag has been a noble experiment lacking the resources to fulfill all its goals. The Filmverlag had to be rescued from near-bankruptcy in the mid-1970s by the liberal patronage of *Der Spiegel*'s publisher, Rudolf Augstein. Inevitably and unfortunately, the limits of the Filmverlag's capacity for financing and distributing its films have thus far precluded any large-scale commercial success.

The French New Wave of the preceding decade had been an alliance of friends who turned for inspiration to the most creative representatives of the commercial Hollywood film, to Alfred Hitchcock, for example, and to John Ford. The young Germans, on the other hand, united in 1962 only by their opposition to the commercial establishment, embarked upon a different path of conscious noncommercialism, which, in the 1960s and early 1970s, also contributed to the West German cinematic ill-health. The young Germans turned to a form of *auteurist* filmmaking that was innovative and craftsmanlike but also conspicuously aestheticized and intellectual. The very qualities that delighted thoughtful critics and serious filmviewers simultaneously disappointed mass film audiences who were looking for entertainment. The greatest strength of the young filmmakers also became their greatest weakness. The popularity of German films within West Germany continued to decline until the late 1970s. An elaborate system of government film subsidies that has been the backbone of the New German film also contributed, ironically, to the development of an "ivory tower" approach to filmmaking that for a time threatened to extinguish the German film.

Financing the New Film

The signing of the Oberhausen declaration occurred at a festival of short films. Short film production, funded by the West German government or West German industry, had provided the greatest amount of experience to the young filmmakers before 1962. Without film academies (a cultural gap since filled by the film and television academies of West Berlin and Munich) and without admittance to the closed film establishment, the new directors learned to film by making shorts. Acutely aware of the need for adequate financial backing, the young directors, led by Alexander Kluge (trained as a lawyer and thus possessing necessary knowledge of legal–political channels and procedures), lobbied throughout the 1960s and 1970s for a system of film subsidies from federal and state governments and from television. As a result West Germany now possesses one of the most complex—if, as most filmmakers claim, still insufficient—subsidy systems in the world, a system which has proved to be a mixed blessing for the new filmmakers.

West German television is noncommercial and nonprofit, more on the order of England's BBC or America's Public Broadcasting System than of American commercial networks. This is probably most responsible for the contribution of West German television to the financing and production of West German films. Hollywood films are often shown on American television, although made-for-TV movies are almost never shown in film theaters. Broadcasting fees are American television's only contribution to the financing of theatrical films, a contribution made after the fact of—and dependent upon—a film's proven box-office appeal. West Germany's two networks, ARD and ZDF, also purchase finished films for television broadcast but still more money is spent on the prefinancing of film projects. Television functions as a primary, if not always exemplary, backer of the New (and also of the old) German Cinema.[13] Under the provisions of the Film/Television Agreement, first enacted in 1974 and revised in 1979, television provided (through 1978) more than DM34 million for film/television coproductions. Under the terms of this agreement, film production companies must provide at least 25 percent of production costs and television broadcast of a film is delayed for two years after completion in order to permit the film a run in commercial cinemas.

In addition to coproduction funding from television, financial subsidies have also been available through several government agencies. The oldest of these is the *Kuratorium junger deutscher Film*, originally established in 1964 by a decree of the Federal Minister of the Interior. The Kuratorium concentrated on the promotion of first and second works by new filmmakers. For this reason and because it had as its primary objective the implementation of the proposals of the Oberhausen manifesto, the Kuratorium has had an immense impact on the development of New German Cinema. During the first three years of its existence the Kuratorium awarded DM5 million for the full or partial financing of twenty feature films, which included the first films of Kluge (*Yesterday Girl*) and Herzog (*Signs of Life*). The grants of the Kuratorium, usually amounting to DM300,000 per film, were in the form of interest-free loans which were to be repaid for reinvestment in other, newer films. In fact, little of this money was ever repaid. Because of opposition to the Oberhausen principles governing the Kuratorium, the commercial film industry lobbied for the implementation of a new, different film subsidy system which came into being in 1968. As one consequence of the new law, the Kuratorium came under the governance of the individual West German states with a smaller budget (DM1.1 million in 1978) and thus smaller awards to new filmmakers (DM100,000 on the average).

At the federal level film subsidization after 1968 came under the control of the *Filmförderungsanstalt* or Film Subsidies Board. Revised in 1971, in 1974, and again in 1979, the statutes of the Film Subsidies Board provide for film subsidy funds amassed through a tax on cinema tickets—originally a flat rate of DM0.10 and now a percentage rate varying between 2.75 – 3.75 percent of the price of each ticket sold. From such funds (approximately DM19 million in 1977) the FSB provides interest-free loans up to DM350,000 (exceptionally up to DM700,000) and grants up to DM200,000. Grants are awarded to films that attract a certain audience total within a given period of time: usually 250,000 within two years, or 130,000 within two years for films judged to be "valuable" or "extremely valuable," or 150,000 within five years for children's films. Obviously less responsive than the Kuratorium to film quality and more attuned to box-office success, the Film Subsidies Board resulted from a compromise between the lobbies of the New German Cinema and the traditional, commercial entertainment industry. Since Film Subsidies Board funds are given to producers, they encouraged the young directors to establish their own production companies and to produce their own films.

Funding for the new filmmakers has also been provided through the Federal Ministry of the Interior which each year awards the German Film Prizes, awards for short and feature films ranging from DM30,000 to a grand prize of DM500,000, for the best German films of the year. (The determination of "best" films is, of course, as arbitrary in Bonn and Berlin as it is in Hollywood.) Grants are also available for new film projects, and the total amount distributed through the Ministry has been approximately DM6 million per year during the past few years.

The New German Cinema clearly has benefited from resources and subsidies that might well be envied by young independent filmmakers elsewhere. West German television, the Kuratorium, the Interior Ministry, and even the controversial Film Subsidies Board have all played an important role in the rebirth of quality filmmaking in Germany. While counting their blessings, the New German filmmakers still feel that much more could be done. They frequently are constricted by the necessity of financing, not through just one of the major funding sources but through a combining of dribs from this source and drabs from that. Above all, they consider West German expenditures on film sparse when compared to the more than DM1 billion granted annually to subsidize music, opera, and theater in the Federal Republic. Schlöndorff, for example, in his diary of the filming of *The Tin Drum* specifically refers to the resources available to

West German theaters and wishes similar resources were available to filmmakers: "No matter how good *The Tin Drum* is, I imagine what could have been made of it if a homogeneous ensemble had worked on it for six months or a year. . . . Just when the crew had finally come together, it was dissolved. For the next film everything will have to be begun again from the beginning."[14]

Not only the subsidy amounts but also the methods by which these amounts are divided and distributed have caused controversy. The criteria of "quality films" and "good entertainment films" often invoked in justifying loans and grants are obviously subjective. The easing of financial conditions for films earning government certification as "valuable" or "extremely valuable" has been politicizing. Who determines "value" in a film? Jean-Marie Straub and Danièle Huillet have been the most notorious victims of the West German Film Evaluation Office; their *Chronicle of Anna Magdalena Bach* was given a certificate only after appeal, and their *History Lessons* was denied a certificate even after appeal. A more recent but equally publicized victim has been Hellmuth Costard, a Hamburg filmmaker, whose 1978 film *The Little Godard* is a protest against the prevailing film subsidization system. Costard's film poses, among other questions, the question of how and why a filmmaker, who works with an audial/visual medium, should have to submit a written scenario as part of any subsidy application.

Even more serious are the thematic compromises necessitated by such a subsidy system. Whenever film projects must compete with each other for limited funds, questionable subjectivity will enter into the awarding of funds. Films based on literary classics have, for example, had an easier time obtaining funding than films based on original scenarios. Politically and socially critical films, on the other hand, are far less likely to receive subsidies than noncontroversial works. Most strikingly, the two best-known German films dealing with political terrorism in the 1970s, the collective film *Germany in Autumn* (1978) and Fassbinder's *The Third Generation* (1979), were both made without subsidies.

Clearly, even though the West German subsidy system is better than others, it too is plagued by inconsistencies and inequities and tainted by politics. It is a wise, an experienced, and perhaps—as some critical observers say—a compromised filmmaker/director/producer who is able to find his or her way through the complexities of financing a film. In fact the subsidy regulations that have encouraged directors to produce their own films have been accused of altering for the worse the very nature of New German filmmaking.

Directors who produced their own films in the 1960s have gradually
been replaced in the 1970s by producers who direct their own films;
the ingeniously crafted films of the 1960s and early 1970s are being
replaced by larger, safer, and more compromised film "productions."[15]

The ablest filmmakers—Fassbinder may be the best example—
nourish their creative habit by learning to combine their own limited
resources with cash awards, subsidy grants and loans, coproduction
money from television, funds donated by private companies in order
to gain a tax advantage, and the more traditional funding arrange-
ments of the established commercial cinema. Finally, in spite of all
reforms and funding innovations, it remains difficult in the Federal
Republic of Germany for a newcomer to fund a film. Apparently the
only thing harder than financing a first film is financing a second film,
even when the first film was a success. For example, Helke Sander,
regarded as one of the most promising feminist directors, released
her first long film in 1977. The *All-Around Reduced Personality* was
regarded as one of the best German films of that year, both by
German and foreign critics. It was, however, not awarded a German
Film Prize that year nor, when Sanders applied for support for her
next film, was she awarded any grant or loan. Although financing has
become easier for the "new establishment" of New German Cinema,
including Fassbinder, Herzog, Schlöndorff, and a few others, financial backing remains elusive for the newer or slightly less accomplished or slightly more radical filmmakers of the late 1970s and early
1980s.

Oberhausen and Its Successors

West German film historians differentiate between the "young"
German filmmakers—that is, the Oberhausen group and their immediate successors in the 1960s—and the "new" German filmmakers
of the 1970s. For Americans such a division may seem an unnecessary
confusing of issues. Whatever it is to be called, the "young" German
or the "new" German cinema has now existed long enough that one
can distinguish between its early representatives and its later ones.
What may seem to Americans to be a unified West German "new
wave" has in reality been more a series of ripples following one after
the other since 1962 at Oberhausen. The coming of the New German
Cinema has been a series of fits and false starts with relatively little
continuity between the group from 1962 and the best-known names of

1980. Of the signers of the Oberhausen manifesto only Alexander Kluge has gained a truly international reputation. Other Oberhausen names—Rob Houwer, Vlado Kristl, Edgar Reitz, Christian Rischert, Peter Schamoni, Haro Senft, Franz Joseph Spieker, Hans Rolf Strobel, Herbert Vesely, Bernhard Wicki—may sound familiar, vaguely familiar, or totally unknown to Americans. Some of the Oberhausen group went on making films; some continued to work on films, although not as directors; some now work in television; some gave up filmmaking, driven out by the precariousness of film financing; some became part of the establishment they denounced at Oberhausen.

The filmmakers who signed the Oberhausen document and thus initiated the development within West Germany of a strikingly new alternative cinema have not, by and large, been the true beneficiaries of that development. Straub, Schlöndorff, Fassbinder, Herzog, Wenders, and Syberberg represent a post-Oberhausen second generation who were able to take advantage of the film environment created by the Oberhausen group and who have in turn provided an impulse to still younger directors. In 1979 Alexander Kluge described the development of the New Cinema in this way: "The so-called New German film comprises four generations in the last seventeen years. First the Oberhausen and pre-Oberhausen group, . . . then the later New directors (Schlöndorff, Syberberg, Fassbinder, Kückelmann,[16] Herzog, Wenders, etc.), then the third generation (Schroeter, Costard, Praunheim, Hörmann, Lemke, Kahn, Stöckl, etc.). Today we have again a numerous and obviously creative new generation that is clearly taking a different path than those who have already arrived. Compared to the original 'young German film,' who as a rule are now forty-year-olds, they are the truly young film."[17]

New Films with a New Consciousness

Many of the early works of the New filmmakers from the late 1960s (it took five years for Oberhausen to have a visible effect) were earnest, if stylistically inadequate, attempts to practice the good intentions of the Oberhausen manifesto. For these directors the New Cinema meant a turning away from the old genres and from the conservative and opportunistic attitudes of the old industry. This retreat from the policies of the film industry of the Adenauer era brought with it the selection of "relevant" social topics (hardly surprising, given the social context of the late 1960s). It also brought with it an enduring disregard for making films that would "entertain" in the conventional, commercial film sense. Thus German films of the late 1960s and the 1970s were very frequently "serious" and unrelentingly demanding of the viewer. One of the primary developments in West German cinema of the last few years has been a rediscovery of the principle that films can be entertaining and serious. This development was perhaps initiated and surely stimulated by Fassbinder's rejection in the early 1970s of Straub's "minimalist" austerity. Fassbinder's subsequent move into work on television films for the sake of finding a truly mass audience also signaled a move away from cinematic elitism.

In the 1960s, however, entertainment was the least of the concerns of German filmmaking. While seldom as severe as the films of Straub and Huillet, many of the debut films of young German directors in the late 1960s were afflicted by a woeful seriousness unalleviated by the stylistic innovations that distinguished the Straubs' films. Often heavyhanded and unremittingly pessimistic, these films, however, deserve credit for their attempts to treat socially relevant themes. Ulrich Schamoni's *It* (1965), for example, reflected the relatively new and delicate question of abortion and women's rights in its portrayal of a young woman who has an abortion rather than let a child interfere with her relationship with her husband. Edgar Reitz's *Mahlzeiten* (1966) documented the failure of a modern marriage in which the husband ultimately commits suicide and the wife marries an American Mormon and moves to Utah (Mormon evangelism was itself a timely theme in West Germany in the 1960s). Johannes Schaaf's *Tattooing* (1967) attempted to explore the consequences of the "generation gap."

It is undoubtedly significant that four of the major West German directors—Herzog, Kluge, Schlöndorff, and Straub—also made their first films in 1966 and 1967, but each avoided such single-issue films about contemporary society. Herzog's *Signs of Life* and Schlöndorff's *Young Törless* had historical settings. Straub's *Not Reconciled* was set in the Adenauer era but had as its main theme the causes and consequences of the Nazi period. Kluge's *Yesterday Girl* had a contemporary setting but its concern with the effects of "yesterday," its wit, and above all the complexity of its narrative and its style set it clearly apart from the films of Schamoni, Reitz, or Schaaf.

Despite the example of Herzog, Kluge, Schlöndorff, and Straub, one-issue films have continued to be made throughout the 1970s, although directorial approaches have matured along with the issues themselves. Generational conflicts seen in *Tattooing* are still apparent in more recent films such as Rüdiger Nüchtern's *Schluchtenflit-*

zen (1978), Christel Buschmann's *Gibbi West Germany* (1980), or Adolf Winkelmann's *On the Move* (1978). By and large the conflicts presented in such films seem as unresolvable in 1979 or 1980 as in 1967.

Marital failure has been a recurrent but evolving theme in West German films. For the wife in Reitz's *Mahlzeiten*, remarriage appears to be the only alternative, especially for a woman with five children, and the second marriage seems a relatively optimistic resolution of the film. In Volker Schlöndorff's later *A Free Woman* (1972) an unhappy first marriage ends not in suicide but, more conventionally, in divorce, and the wife's brief attempt at emancipated independence ends, too, with a second marriage. In Schlöndorff's film, however, the second marriage is a decidedly mixed blessing, a rather happy compromise for the wife but a compromise nevertheless. Christian Rischert's *Lena Rais* (1979) also documents the failure of a marriage, but here a proletarian marriage fails because of the husband's brutality and utter insensitivity. Neither suicide nor divorce ends the marriage or the brutality, but somehow Rischert's film manages a more optimistic conclusion than either of the two earlier films. Rischert's unresolved and open-ended conclusion focuses attention on the gradual self-assertion and determined self-liberation of the abused wife.

Pregnancy, abortion, and their effects on male-female relationships have undergone an even greater evolution in film since the mid-1960s. Schamoni's *It* had seemed daring because its female protagonist had an abortion. Heide Genée's *1 + 1= 3* (1979) seems daring because its unmarried protagonist chooses *not* to have an abortion. In Genée's comedy, as in the earlier film, pregnancy catalyzes a crisis in a relationship. In *1 + 1= 3*, however, the modern, liberated, unmarried, but long-lasting relationship clearly *needs* a crisis. The main character uses her pregnancy to end one relationship, begin another, and yet in the end to remain happily free of both.

The New Comedy: Where Is It?

It and *1 + 1= 3* also differ significantly in that the latter is, in the context of the New German cinema, a surprisingly successful comedy. Its good humor stands in contrast with the almost total lack of comedies by other German directors. The earnestness of the Oberhausen impetus and the turn away from "entertainment" in the 1960s seems to have banned comic sensibility from the West German cinema. There have, of course, been a few exceptions to this general rule, even in the late 1960s. Franz Josef Spieker attained box–office success with his first feature film, a satire called *Wild Rider, Inc.* (1966). Beginning with *Get to the Point, Darling* in 1967, May Spils made a series of funny films that were hardly highpoints of cinematic comedy but managed to be sophisticatedly amusing without resorting to the cloying cuteness of the romantic comedies of the 1950s. Other good comedies have also appeared, but infrequently. In 1975 two serio-comic films were well received in Germany, one by the critics and the other, surprisingly, by film audiences. They were Alexander Kluge's *Strongman Ferdinand* and Bernhard Sinkel's *Lina Braake,* the story of an old woman who, forced from her apartment and into a nursing home, learns the financial tricks necessary for taking her revenge on the bank that had forced her move. Finally, the absurdist, anarchic comedies of Herbert Achternbusch, such as *Bye-Bye Bavaria* (1978) or *The Comanche* (1979), have brought him the reputation, within Germany at least, of being the only true comic genius in Germany since the silent film comedian, Karl Valentin.

The German comedies that have been shown in the United States are those made by the best-known German directors, all of whom are essentially noncomedic filmmakers. Even those films that have sometimes been billed as comedies—Fassbinder's *Satan's Brew* (1976) or Schlöndorff's *A Free Woman,* for example, are at heart quite serious films by serious filmmakers. The comic effects of Fassbinder's *Despair,* one of his funniest films, surely derive more from Nabokov's novel and Stoppard's screenplay than from Fassbinder's handling of this material. The grotesque comedy of Schlöndorff's *Tin Drum* can already be found in Grass's novel.

Belly laughs are few in the New German Cinema, although smiles are sometimes produced by Kluge's intellectual wit, Fassbinder's sometimes slyly outrageous juxtapositions (for example, of pop music and emotional narrative in *Bitter Tears of Petra von Kant*) and melodramatic exaggerations, Wenders's gentle and sardonic humor arising from meetings between his skeptical characters, or Herzog's frequently grotesque characters and images (the mechanic who pulls his own tooth, the polyester American banker, the emblematic frozen turkey carried by Bruno S., or the dancing chicken in *Stroszek*). Humor in New German films is often wry and ironic, frequently bitter, and usually evidence of cosmic jokes played on humanity.

Expressions of the New Consciousness:
Worker Films, Women's Films

The world of the New German Cinema is no laughing matter. These films, however, compensate for their lack of humor with an intense sense of social justice. The social conscience of the new directors may derive from, or perhaps only coincides with, early experience as documentarians, either as independent short filmmakers or, more often, as the creators-under-contract of television films. Documentary background is especially evident among two groups of filmmakers almost unknown in the United States: women and the so-called *Berliner Arbeiterfilmer* (Berlin Worker-Filmmakers).[18]

The distinctive latter group grew out of the student protest movement at the end of the 1960s and the beginning of the 1970s when an attempt was made to consolidate student political activism with working-class labor activism. Among the students of the Film and Television Academy in West Berlin this activity first took the form of short documentary films and later of longer feature films treating the problems, especially the working and living conditions, of blue-collar workers. Financed primarily by television, the first short documentaries with titles like *Renter Solidarity* (Max Willutski, 1969) or *Loneliness in the Metropolis* (Christian Ziewer, 1968) gave way to feature films, frequently using lay actors playing their own experience: *Dear Mother, I'm Fine* (Christian Ziewer and Klaus Wiese, 1972), *The Wollands* (Marianne Lüdcke and Ingo Kratisch, 1972), *The Long Misery* (Max Willutski, 1973), or *Wages and Love* (Lüdcke/Kratisch, 1973).

Similarly committed, politically and socially, are several of the recent films made by West German women. Although sexual equality was written into the *Grundgesetz* or Basic Law of the Federal Republic, practical implementation of the law has in fact been slow, and West German women still have less social and economic equality than women in the United States. Women directors have produced a small but increasingly visible and independent body of work. Although these filmmakers belong to the same generation as the male directors of the New Cinema, the majority of them did not manage to make their first feature films until the mid– and late–1970s. May Spils, Erika Runge, and Ula Stöckl nevertheless managed to direct or codirect films in the late 1960s, but most women of this generation were able to make only short films or television films. Although women directors have begun making films only in the last few years, they had already affected the development of New German Cinema as actors (Margarethe von Trotta, Karin Thoma), scenarists (Jutta Brückner), editors (Heidi Genée, Beate Mainka-Jellinghaus), or producers (Karin Thoma, Regina Ziegler) for male directors. The most prominent women filmmakers presently at work in Germany include Jutta Brückner, the maker of a "photofilm" (a montage of documentary photographs plus voice-over narrative commentary) *Do Right and Fear No One* (1975) and of a narrative film *A Totally Neglected Girl* (1976); Heide Genée, the director of *1 + 1= 3* (1979) and an earlier film of a story by Fontane, *Grete Minde* (1976); Helke Sander, whose *All-Around Reduced Personality–REDUPERS* (1977) was named as Film of the Year in Hanser Publishers' *Film Yearbook 78/79* and who is founder, publisher, and editor of *frauen und film*, an important journal of feminism and film; Helma Sanders-Brahms, director of *Beneath the Pavement is the Beach* (1974), *Shirin's Wedding* (1975), *Heinrich* (1976), and, most recently, *Germany, Pale Mother* (1980); and Ulrike Ottinger, director of the bold feminist satire, *Madame X–An Absolute Ruler* (1977). Margarethe von Trotta, who acted in films for Fassbinder, Schlöndorff, and Achternbusch, wrote the scenario for Schlöndorff's *A Free Woman* (1972), coscripted and codirected *The Lost Honor of Katharina Blum* (1975), and directed *The Second Awakening of Christa Klages* (1977)—one of the most successful first films of the New Cinema—and *Sisters, or The Balance Of Happiness* (1979). Trotta's *Second Awakening of Christa Klages*, a sympathetic portrait of a woman who robs a bank for a political motive, must be regarded as one of the thematically more daring products of the New Cinema, a film whose theme applies to men as well as to women.

Creating the New by Building on the Old: Literature Adaptations

Schlöndorff's *The Tin Drum* is a film adaptation of Günter Grass's famous novel, published in 1959. Schlöndorff has built his career on skillful film revisions of nineteenth– and twentieth–century writers—Heinrich von Kleist, Robert Musil, Bertolt Brecht, Marguerite Yourcenar, Heinrich Böll, and Günter Grass. Filming a famous novel has obvious advantages for a filmmaker. A film project based on such a known and safe subject as a literary classic is more

Angela Winkler in Volker Schlöndorff/Margarethe von Trotta's
The Lost Honor of Katharina Blum.
Courtesy of The Museum of Modern Art/Film Stills Archive

likely to find financial backing. A film adaptation of a novel or play of acknowledged quality brings with it a ready-made audience and even has a chance of recapturing part of the audience alienated by the mindless films of the 1950s.

That such a ready-made audience also brings with it ready-made expectations that most films cannot fulfill has not deterred cinematic borrowings. Thus, many of the best-known recent West German films have been adaptations of dramas by Goethe and Schiller, Gorky and Shakespeare, Ibsen and Brecht, and of novels and stories by nineteenth-century writers such as Kleist, Eichendorff, Hoffmann, Büchner, Storm, Meyer, Anzengruber, and Fontane, early twentieth–century writers such as Thomas Mann and Brecht, and contemporary writers such as Böll, Grass, Peter Handke, Günter Herburger, and Patricia Highsmith, the American writer whose thrillers have been filmed by Hitchcock and Chabrol, and in Germany by Hans Geissendörfer and Wenders.

All of the best-known New German directors have at one time or another adapted literature to the screen. Wenders has filmed texts by

Handke, Hawthorne, and Highsmith and is working in Hollywood on a film of Joe Gorres's *Hammett*. Fassbinder has filmed his own plays, plays by Franz Xaver Kroetz (*Jail Bait*), by Marieluise Fleisser (*Pioneers in Ingolstadt*), by Ibsen (*Nora Helmer*), and by Clare Booth (*Women in New York*), as well as novels by Fontane (*Effi Briest*), Oskar Maria Graf (*Bolwieser*), and Nabokov (*Despair*). Recently Fassbinder has filmed Theodor Döblin's *Berlin Alexanderplatz* as a monumental fifteen-hour television series. Kluge has adapted his own stories as films; *Yesterday Girl*, for example, first appeared as a short story, "Anita G." Straub, even though his completed films often bear little resemblance to their sources, has used texts by Brecht, Böll, Corneille, Schoenberg, Mallarmé, and Franco Fortini. Even Syberberg and Herzog have adapted literary works: Syberberg in his first two feature films *Scarabea* (from a story by Tolstoy) and *San Domingo* (from a story by Kleist), and Herzog in two of his latest films *Woyzeck*, based on the nineteenth-century drama-fragment by Georg Büchner, and *Nosferatu*, based on Bram Stoker's *Dracula* by way of Murnau's 1921 film version.

Despite the good repute lent by the adaptive work of talented directors, there can be no question that most serious German critics and filmmakers regard literary adaptations, in general, as retrogressive. The artistic success of Schlöndorff's version of *The Tin Drum* seems to be the exception proving the rule of mediocrity encountered in most such adaptations. Literary adaptations tend to crowd other, more original film projects out of subsidization funds, especially during politically conservative periods (such as 1976–77) when controversial, socially critical projects are viewed with special alarm.[19] Representative figures published by a member of the Berlin Film Subsidies Board show that the average film project during 1974–78 had a one-in-four chance of being subsidized, while one of every two proposals for adaptations of literary sources received subsidies. The commission member, Alfred Nemeczek, finds responsible not only the conservatism of other commission members but also the trepidations of the filmmakers themselves. Any sensible filmmaker, according to Nemeczek, looking for quality and economic feasibility, "comes by himself to the equation 'Good Book = Quality + a large Readership = Economic Feasibility = Subsidy.'" Moreover, as Nemeczek points out, "the development of good original material costs more time and thus more money than a literary adaptation, and in the year 1978 scarcely a producer is spending money on the development of material."[20]

The subsidy commission's eye for literary "quality" has had a further effect on the New German films. Unlike Hollywood, the gifted directors of the New German Cinema have seldom turned to middle-brow popular novelists for their material. One finds no *Rebecca*, no *Rosemarie's Baby*, no *Carrie*, let alone a *Godfather* made in Germany. Even the "thrillers" of Patricia Highsmith adapted by Wenders and Geissendörfer are in fact bloodlessly cerebral when compared to the spine-tingling pleasures of Du Maurier or Mario Puzo or Stephen King. Characteristically, Wenders's *Hammett* is being made in America with American production money. German popular novelists have been left to the hands of mediocre directors.

Most of the finest works of the New Cinema have been, and continue to be, either creations of the filmmakers themselves or based on original screenplays by others. Rosa von Praunheim (born in 1942 as Holger Mischwitzki) is notable as one of the foremost filmmakers within the Gay Liberation movement. One of Praunheim's early films was characteristically titled *Not the Homosexual Is Perverse, But Rather the Situation In Which He Lives* (1970) and one of his most recent films is *Army of Lovers or Revolt of the Perverts* (1978), a documentary on homosexuals in the United States. More acclaimed as a gay filmmaker is Frank Ripploh whose graphic, honest, and autobiographical *Taxi zum Klo* has been enthusiastically received by the American press, including reviewers for such resolutely straight publications as *Newsweek* and the *New York Times*.

Since 1971 Niklaus Schilling (a Swiss now working in the more liberal environment of West Germany) has directed four exceptionally inventive, satirical, and romantic films: *Nightshadows* (1971), *Expulsion from Paradise* (1976), *Rheingold* (1977), and *The Willi Busch Report* (1980). Peter Lilienthal, born in 1929, is one of the oldest New filmmakers and has been making films since 1955. Lilienthal has gained international attention only in the last ten years, however, with his films dealing with tyranny and political resistance, such as *La Victoria* (made in Chile in 1973), *Calm Rules the Land* (1975), and *David* (1979), the story of a Jewish boy in Nazi Germany. (Lilienthal's own family had fled to Argentina during the Nazi period.)

Reinhard Hauff, too, has attracted attention recently with his last four socially concerned feature films: *The Brutalization of Franz Blum* (1973), a record of the effects of a young man's imprisonment; *Paule Pauländer* (1975), the story of a farmboy and his brutal father; *The Main Actor* (1977), an uncomfortable film in which are examined the unforeseen and unfortunate consequences of using a young amateur as the main actor in a film (as Hauff had done in *Paule Pauländer*); and *Knife in the Head* (1978), in which an innocent man becomes caught between the police and the urban terrorists of the 1970s.

Werner Schroeter, with his eerie operatic constructions such as *Eika Katappa* (1969), *The Death of Maria Malibran* (1971), and *Willow Springs* (1973), has long had an enthusiastic following in Germany. With his last two films *The Kingdom of Naples* (1978) and *Palermo or Wolfsburg* (1980) Schroeter has turned to a more traditional narrative style and to more "relevant" themes and may thus gain international recognition.

Politicizing the Genres of the Old Cinema

Whatever the sources of the narrative material in recent West German films, the themes frequently reflect a concern for social issues and political questions. The best New German films seldom establish a historical setting without simultaneously commenting upon contemporary West Germany or the recent German past. Even the least explicitly political films, like those of Herzog or Wenders, strive for a universality that comments upon the present. Schlöndorff's *The Sudden Wealth of the Poor People of Kombach*, set in the 1830s and ostensibly far removed from modern concerns, draws attention to its implications for the present with a litany of modern American place names at the end of the film. Even adaptations by these filmmakers of classical literary works can be relevant to modern political concerns. Wenders has said, for example, that he found in Hawthorne's *The Scarlet Letter* the same issues that are central to his films with modern settings. Syberberg modernized Kleist's *San Domingo* by relocating the action in Bavaria at the end of the 1960s, thereby using Kleist's narrative as a commentary upon the contemporary West German counterculture. Other filmmakers modernize historical narratives by stylistic procedures. Fassbinder, for example, in *Fontane Effi Briest* continually undermines viewer involvement in the Wilhelminian narrative, drawing the viewer back to the present by a series of alienating devices such as an ironic narrative voice, printed quotations, and white footage. Such intrusions into the fictional narrative draw the viewers back to their present.

Bruno S. in Werner Herzog's Every Man for Himself and God
Against All. *Courtesy of The Museum of Modern Art/Film Stills
Archive*

Film adaptations of literary works were also a mainstay of the "old" German cinema, but these adaptations were, for the most part, reverent, sentimental, and studiously apolitical. Some of the more conservative New German Cinema adaptations—especially during the mid-1970s—have taken the same approach to their literary sources. Other, more courageous directors have adapted, but with an awareness of the political significance of any work of literature or any film. Similarly the New Cinema has taken another favored genre of the old industry, the *Heimatfilm* or romance played out against idyllic landscapes, and employed it for socio-political commentary. The truest representative of this generic subversion is probably Peter Fleischmann's *Hunting Scenes from Lower Bavaria* (1968), adapted from a play by Martin Sperr, in which the scenic forests, bucolic villages, and rococo churches of rural Bavaria became the facade not of spiritual grandeur or romantic sentimentality but rather of rural bigotry and ignorance. Abram, almost the only character portrayed sympathetically, has been jailed for a homosexual act and becomes the victim of a vicious manhunt. A related film, set in the not–too–distant future, is Uwe Brandner's *I Love You, I Kill You* (1971), in which the often romanticized provincial hunting party is transformed into a futuristic game that turns lovers into hunter and hunted. Still other films, like Geissendörfer's *Sternsteinhof* (1976), de-sentimentalized the "romantic" German past simply by a realistic presentation of its unhappy narrative.

Productive Poverty: Style in the New German Film

The early New German Cinema reflected its lack of production money. The first book of interviews with the post-Oberhausen filmmakers, Bronnen and Brocher's *Die Filmemacher* (Munich, 1973), emphasizes the consequences of insufficient funding. Jean-Marie Straub, who has always been a most controversial filmmaker and has therefore suffered even more than others from funding difficulties, maintains stoically that he would never have made any of his films differently even if he had had more money. This, however, is distinctly a minority opinion. Although the best of the new filmmakers were able to make a virtue of necessity and to turn financial weakness into aesthetic strength, a lack of money is clearly visible in many New German films.

Hitler. A Film from Germany.
Courtesy of Zoetrope

The typical New Film of the late 1960s would have been a low-budget chamber film shot in black and white during a period of several days with a very limited number of takes. Directors often served as their own scriptwriters and editors. Location shooting was minimal, unless the location was the director's home city. Soundtrack music was found rather than created. Stories were more-or-less contemporary (no expensive costuming) and limited to a few characters played by a small cast of unknown, low–paid professionals and even some amateur actors.

Abetted by the absence of the unions that sometimes plague Hollywood productions, the ablest, most inventive directors were capable of such creative manipulation of sparse materials that their films demonstrate primarily their ingenuity and only secondarily their minimal resources. For example, Fassbinder, early in his career, and

Straub/Huillet made minimalist artworks of their movies by further
stripping already spare sets, narratives, dialogue, and camera movement, thus establishing in *Not Reconciled* and *Chronicle of Anna
Magdalena Bach* or *Katzelmacher, Why Does Herr R. Run Amuck?*,
and *Merchant of Four Seasons* cinematic illustrations of the principle
"less is more." Kluge made art in *Yesterday Girl* or *Artists Under the
Big Top: Perplexed* by clever directorial and editorial manipulation of
actors and nonactors, of fictional fantasies and quasi-documentary
episodes, of ideas and facts. Herzog transcended budgetary restric-
tions, he has said, by stealing—whether actually or metaphorically—his first camera and by finding (rather than constructing) real
landscapes and people that force us to reexamine what we take for
granted. The most recent exercise in making much out of little is
Syberberg's monumental seven-hour *Hitler. A Film from Germany,*
shot in four weeks at one studio on a budget of DM1 million.

Germany in Autumn: the Exemplary New German Film

Lotte Eisner, the great authority on the German films of the
Weimar period and a living link with Germany's cinematic past, said
in a recent filmed interview: "With *Germany in Autumn* I understood that New German Cinema was born."[21]

Germany in Autumn is representative of the New German Cinema
both thematically, having been made in response to a specific political
situation, and stylistically, since it is a collection of several short
documentary and fictional works written and/or directed by Alf Brustellin, Bernhard Sinkel, Rainer Werner Fassbinder, Alexander
Kluge, Maximiliane Mainka, Edgar Reitz, Katja Rupé, Hans Peter
Cloos and Volker Schlöndorff and bound together by Alexander
Kluge's narrative soundtrack.

In 1966 a group of French filmmakers including Godard, Lelouch,
Marker, Resnais, and Varda made a collective film, *Far from
Vietnam,* in response to one major political event, the Vietnam war.
In three weeks in autumn 1977, in response to violence and political
terrorism in West Germany, but even more in response to the West
German government's reaction to terrorism, the collective of Ger-
man filmmakers made *Germany in Autumn.*

The idyllic landscapes evoked by the film's title do appear, but only
as an ironic counterpoint to the film's real theme. One poster used to
advertise the film in West Germany shows an autumn forest scene of
white birches, the ground covered with wet autumn leaves. In the

midst of this scene are two German policemen on horseback. The photograph was taken during the funeral of three West German terrorists, Andreas Baader, Gudrun Ensslin, and Jan-Carl Raspe, members of the now-extinct Red Army Faction. Nearly 1,000 young mourners, guarded by nearly 1,000 police and photographed by what seem to be nearly 1,000 reporters, attended the funeral.

Germany in Autumn was an independently funded and rapidly organized attempt to portray the mood of the Federal Republic as it experienced its own vulnerability to political terrorism, as it reacted—and overreacted—to a small group of terrorists and, in so doing, jeopardized the personal liberties of all its citizens. Like many of the films of Fassbinder, Kluge, Schlöndorff and others, *Germany in Autumn* tears away what the filmmakers believed to be the romanticized mask of modern West Germany, strips away the facade of a supposedly liberal, peaceful, and prosperous capitalist democracy to reveal a dangerously resurgent fascism.

The flaws of *Germany in Autumn* are as representative of the New Cinema as are its strengths. It gives its audience no smooth, singleminded narrative; it is rather an episodic film, part fiction, part documentary, with as many themes and styles as there are names in the *Germany in Autumn* collective. The film is disjointed, despite the skillful editing of Beate Mainke-Jellinghaus, who has worked on nearly all of Herzog's films and several of Kluge's and Fassbinder's and is probably the most accomplished West German film editor, and despite Kluge's voice-over narrative, which attempts to unite disparate sequences. The filmmakers have acknowledged that the film has shortcomings but point out in defense of its unevenness that *Germany in Autumn* was intended to be a spontaneous and fragmentary experiment that remains unfinished, in spite of cutting and reediting done after initial screenings at the 1978 Berlin Film Festival. Alexander Kluge has described the film as, "in spite of its considerable length, a fragment—and the project is to be continued. For example, I intend to produce a continuation of my segment, in the form of another film, with the title *The Patriot*. Others of the filmmakers want to continue in the same way."[22] (Kluge *has* since released *The Patriot* and has collaborated with Schlöndorff and two other directors in a second collective film *The Candidate*, a filmed polemic against the candidacy of Franz-Josef Strauss, the Bavarian conservative, for the West German chancellorship in the fall 1980 elections.)

Like many Germany films of the 1960s and 1970s *Germany in Autumn* is demanding of its audience, even a politically informed audience. For a viewer with little knowledge of West German politics and political terrorism, the film is not only demanding but frustratingly uninformative and sometimes mystifying. While *Germany in Autumn* is a response to specific events in September and October 1977, many unexplained allusions in the film refer to the failed student revolution of a decade before. The film implies, moreover, that the *true* roots of German terrorism, and of the government's response to it, probably lie even farther back: the waving Daimler-Benz banners shown at one point, for example, are unmistakably reminiscent of the Nazi banners in Riefenstahl's *Triumph of the Will*. As in many of their individual works, the filmmakers suggest either that Nazism remains an unresolved issue in modern German life or that fascism is itself part of the fabric of German society, German traditions, and German life.

The terrorism of the Red Army Faction or Baader–Meinhof Gang, as it was called by the right-wing German press, originated in the late 1960s but intensified through the early– and mid–1970s with a long series of bombings, bank robberies, extortionary or retributive kidnappings, and shootings which culminated in the events of autumn 1977 and produced the atmosphere of social paranoia and near–hysteria portrayed in *Germany in Autumn*. On 5 September 1977, the Red Army Faction kidnapped Hanns Martin Schleyer, chairman of the board of Daimler-Benz, head of the Federation of German Industries, and—as the RAF pointed out—a former Nazi SS officer. In return for Schleyer the terrorists demanded the release of eleven imprisoned terrorists and a large ransom, demands which the government refused. On October 13, a Lufthansa jet was hijacked by terrorists. After a series of landings around the Mediterranean, the plane eventually landed in Mogadishu, Somalia, where during the night a group of German commandos retook the plane, killing three hijackers and freeing all their hostages. This resulted early the next morning in the inexplicable deaths in a Stuttgart prison of three imprisoned RAF leaders, Baader, Ensslin, and Raspe, dead by suicide according to the government, by murder according to the radical left. On October 19 the body of the industrialist Schleyer was found.

By the autumn of 1977 West Germans, goaded by the right-wing press, had become obsessed with terrorism. Throughout the mid-1970s there had been scarcely a week without some terrorist incident. And each week some aspect of West Germany's democracy and its basic law had been called into question as being incapable of dealing with terrorism. Poll after poll demonstrated that a majority of West

Germans believed that civil order was more important than civil liberty, that terrorism must be stopped even at the cost of abridging personal freedom. Such willingness to trade liberty for security was viewed by the makers of *Germany in Autumn* as symptomatic of a latent and frightening neofascism among the Germans. The terrorists, besides destroying themselves and a few very visible victims, also destroyed any illusions among German leftists that the authoritarian tradition had been forever eradicated at the end of the Hitler period.

New government decrees limited defendants to three attorneys and forbade defense lawyers to speak to their prisoner clients if the lawyers were *suspected* of participating in their clients' criminal acts. After the Schleyer kidnapping many homes were raided without a search warrant, frequently on the pretext of "present danger." An old law providing for mandatory loyalty screenings for prospective government employees was reaffirmed. Since over 13 percent of all West German employees, including all teachers, are civil employees, by the autumn of 1977 over half a million people, many of them young and politically leftist, had been screened. Such measures produced in West Germany what the head of the German section of Amnesty International described as "a political atmosphere . . . which has reached, and perhaps already gone beyond, the borders of what should be permitted in a democracy."[23]

In this atmosphere *Germany in Autumn* was created as a spontaneous response, hastily financed by a coalition of independent production companies, hastily written and filmed, hastily edited. The episodes of *Germany in Autumn* portray a society caught up in fear, fear of terrorism but also fear of the government's antiterrorist measures. Although much of *Germany in Autumn* is fiction, the viewer senses that all the scenes *could* have happened. In the context of autumn 1977 none of the sequences was unthinkable. Although terrorism has since abated, in 1977 West Germany was quickly becoming a society immobilized by its anxieties. It had already become a society in which the police, by setting up anonymous terrorist hotlines in major cities, encouraged average Germans to accuse and denounce one another. It had become a society in which Heinrich Böll, the Nobel Prize–winning writer, could be branded a terrorist "sympathizer" for having published his attempt to comprehend and to explain the terrorists' motivations.

Böll wrote the satirical episode which is perhaps the most successful section of *Germany in Autumn*. A West German television commission considers for broadcast and ultimately rejects, "at this time,"

a production of Sophocles' *Antigone*. The commission, after long
deliberations, refuses the play on the grounds that Antigone's assertion of family demands instead of civil loyalty might be misunderstood by television viewers. Antigone might be seen as a sympathetic model for female terrorists. Böll's satire, like his story *The
Lost Honor of Katharina Blum*, was filmed by Schlöndorff, who in his
Tin Drum diary referred to Germany as "the poisoned heart of
Europe, even now."[24] Schlöndorff also had been labelled a "terrorist
sympathizer" by the press because of his involvement with a legal
defense fund for the terrorists.

The longest, most personal and yet most far-reaching sequence in
Germany in Autumn is Fassbinder's. In a series of alienating, frequently repelling, and irritatingly underlit shots Fassbinder inter-
laces conversations with his mother, bullying interchanges with his
lover, and his own frightened, even paranoid reaction to the events of
October 1977. Limiting his locale to the claustrophobic confines of his
own apartment, tied to the news and to friends in the outside world
only by the radio and the telephone (like Petra von Kant), Fassbinder
describes a microcosm of West German opinion through his lover's
statements about the hijacking at Mogadishu: "I'd blow up the whole
plane. The others in prison should be shot or hung up. If they don't
obey the law, then the state needn't either." In Fassbinder's conversations with his mother we hear her more sympathetic but equally
frightening assertion that "in such a situation you simply can't get by
with democracy. . . . The best thing would be an authoritarian ruler
who is good and kind and well-meaning."

Fassbinder himself—annoying, abusive, self-indulgent, nearly
hysterical—is superficially the least attractive and least sympathetic
of characters but also in the last analysis the truest embodiment of
democracy. Democracy cannot always be pretty, and his film implies
the necessity of accepting the unpleasant in a democratic society.
Typically, Fassbinder also examines his own vulnerability as an artist
to the social trauma that the film describes. As he defines it at the
beginning of his segment, film functions to improve society by fostering critical discussion. Fear of speaking is the end of democracy and
the end of art. In the atmosphere of October 1977 free discussion had
ended, and fear had paralyzed art: Fassbinder's dictation of a film
script is halted by the sound of police sirens.

While Fassbinder's segment of *Germany in Autumn* is one of the
most remarkable and most discussed, the film's binding voice is
appropriately Alexander Kluge's. Kluge treats the immediate problems of West German society by taking an ironically witty and broad

view of the events Fassbinder had taken so earnestly and personally. Kluge filmed the story of Gabi Teichert, a fictional German history teacher who no longer knows what to teach and who sets out in search of "the bases of German history." Armed with a shovel, Gabi is seen marching through a late autumn landscape, "either digging a shelter for World War III or looking for prehistoric remains." Since his first film Kluge has been concerned with the effects of the past upon the present and—more ominously in *Germany in Autumn*—upon the future. Integrity, for an individual or for a society, can be gained only by coming to terms with the past. That the past has not yet been assimilated is demonstrated in Kluge's soundtrack music of "Deutschland, Deutschland über alles," the historical footage of General Rommel's state funeral in 1944, and the references to Imperial Germany. The first individual to appear in the film is the Christian Democrat ex-Chancellor and ex-Nazi Kiesinger; the last face in the first sequence bears a scar reminiscent of the fraternity duelling scars of Germany's elitist and autocratic past. Thematically, stylistically, and structurally Kluge's film-within-a-film sets the tone for all of *Germany in Autumn*: the eclectic juxtaposing of documentary footage with fictional narratives, the ironic commentary of the music, the use of neo-Brechtian intertitles intended to awaken critical awareness in the viewer.

Germany in Autumn likewise represents much that was right and wrong in the New German Cinema of the 1970s. Freed by independent financing from the normal constraints of West German films, *Germany in Autumn* has made explicit the sociopolitical issues implicit in much of the New Cinema. A concern with the issues of autumn 1977 is only a particular manifestation of the New Cinema's general concern with the conflict between the individual and society. Even in its refusal to please and entertain its audience, *Germany in Autumn* exemplifies the New Cinema's attitudes. In place of entertainment the viewer is offered a challenge and an earnest consideration of the causes and consequences of contemporary issues.

The new New German Film and the Hamburg Declaration

Since its inception New German filmmaking has been more a cottage craft than an industry, a craft created by a relatively small crew of friends. Familiar names—not only of directors but of actors, editors, scenarists, and cinematographers—constantly recur in the credits of the New Film. Most directors have worked on many occasions with their crews. Thus in the past few years a star system has begun to develop in the German film cottage; we recognize not only Fassbinder's name but also that of Hanna Schygulla, his recurrent leading lady, or Irm Hermann or Brigitta Mira or even his cameraman, Michael Ballhaus. We begin to know not only Herzog but also Bruno S. or Klaus Kinski and his cameraman Jörg Schmidt-Reitwein and the music of Popol Vuh. We begin to know the names of actors Angela Winkler, Edith Clever, Peter Kern, and Bruno Ganz as well as we know the names of their directors. Wim Wenders, who left Germany for California, was followed by his cameraman, Robby Müller, whose name appears among the credits for the Willie Nelson film *Honeysuckle Rose* and Peter Bogdanovich's *Saint Jack*.

Times surely have changed for some of the New Filmmakers and for some of those who have worked with them. Herzog, Fassbinder, Wenders, Schlöndorff and a few others seldom face a lack of funding, as long as their films are not too politically explicit, too critical. But there is also a newer New Cinema in West Germany with names still unknown in the United States. It is this third or fourth generation of directors who may lead West German filmmaking in the 1980s. Frank Ripploh, Herbert Achternbusch, Alf Brustellin and Bernhard Sinkel, Hellmuth Costard, Hans Geissendörfer, Reinhard Hauff, Peter Lilienthal, Rosa von Praunheim, Helke Sander, Niklaus Schilling, Werner Schroeter, Margarethe von Trotta are only the most promising among the new names of the New German Cinema.

West Germany is no longer a "cinematic wasteland," as it was once called in the early 1960s by *Sight and Sound*, the best-known British film journal. There now exists in the Federal Republic a tradition, however short, of reputable and occasionally brilliant filmmaking. More importantly there has arisen an apparatus for the continued production of quality films through the establishment of film academies to train new filmmakers, through the enactment of new laws for film funding, and above all through a new awareness that West Germans can, in fact, create film masterpieces.

Despite the accomplishments of the last decade and despite their firm foothold in the establishment, West German filmmakers still feel there is much to be accomplished. Funding has increased but is still inadequate. Problems of alternative distribution and film exhibition remain almost overwhelming. Thus, in September 1979 the West German filmmakers gathered in Hamburg. This meeting was originally planned for Munich, a major center of West German film production during the 1960s and 1970s, but was moved to Hamburg to protest what was seen as interference and politicizing by Munich's

(top) Klaus Kinski in Werner Herzog's Aguirre, The Wrath of God; *(bottom) Bruno Ganz in Wim Wenders's* The American Friend. *Courtesy of New Yorker Films.*

conservative government. At the Hamburg Film Festival nearly 100 West German filmmakers issued a Hamburg Declaration:

Our Strength is Diversity
On the occasion of the 1979 Hamburg Film Festival we German filmmakers have met. Seventeen years after Oberhausen we have drawn up a balance sheet:
— The strength of the German film is its diversity. In three months the 1980s will begin.
— Fantasy cannot be administered. Commissioners cannot determine what a productive film should do. The German film of the eighties can no longer be diverted by commissions, institutions, and interest groups as it has been until now.
— Above all: we will not let ourselves be divided
    — neither feature films from documentaries,
    — nor filmmakers who have already made films from the new generation,
    — nor films that reflect the medium (and do it practically by experimenting) from the narrative film and the commercial film.
— We have proven our professionalism. We can therefore no longer consider ourselves apprentices. We have learned that only the audience can be our ally: Those are the people who work, who have wishes, dreams, and interests; those are people who go to the movies and people who do not go to the movies and even people who can imagine a totally different kind of film.
— We have to keep moving.

Manifestoes, including those of Oberhausen and Hamburg, may amuse us or amaze us with their hyperbole. Theory usually outstrips practice. Such declarations do, however, provide us with convenient, illuminating self-portraits and reveal significant changes that have occurred in the years between 1962 and 1979. The Hamburg filmmakers reveal their self-assurance, their confidence, their sense of their own accomplishments. The Oberhausen manifesto had been a statement of things to come; the Hamburg declaration is more a statement of things that are.

A book on New German Cinema is already a book devoted to the things of the past. Heralded as the new wave of the 1970s, the New German Cinema is already being superseded by a newer wave, the films of Australia. The West German Cinema may be last year's fashion, but it is more vigorous than it has ever been before. The New German Cinema is not dead; it has merely gotten older. At the beginning of the 1980s it has been transformed from a potential into a resurgent and productive reality.

2

Alexander Kluge

Chronology

1932   Alexander Kluge born on February 14 in Halberstadt.

1960   *Brutalität in Stein/Die Ewigkeit von Gestern* [Brutality in Stone/The Eternity of Yesterday], codirected with Peter Schamoni, 12 min.

1961   *Rennen* [Race], codirected with Paul Kruntorad, 9 min.

1963   *Lehrer im Wandel* [Teachers in Transition], codirected with Karen Kluge, 11 min.

1964   *Porträt einer Bewährung* [Portrait of an Accomplishment], 13 min.

1966   *Abschied von Gestern* [Yesterday Girl], 88 min.

1967   *Frau Blackburn, geb. 5 Jan. 1872, wird gefilmt* [Frau Blackburn, Born on Jan. 5, 1872, Is Filmed], 14 min. *Die Artisten in der Zirkuskuppel: ratlos* [The Artists under the Big Top: Perplexed], 103 min.

1968   *Feuerlöscher E.A. Winterstein* [E.A. Winterstein, Fireman], 11 min.

1969   *Die unbezähmbare Leni Peickert* [The Inimitable Leni Peickert], 60 min.

1970   *Der grosse Verhau* [The Big Mess], 86 min.
        Ein Arzt aus Halberstadt [A Doctor from Halberstadt], 29 min.

1971   *Wir verbauen 3 X 27 Milla. Dollar in einen Angriffsschlachter/Der Angriffsschlachter* [We Sink 3 X 27 Billion Dollars in an Attack Ship/The Attack Ship], 18 min.
        Willi Tobler und der Untergang der 6. Flotte [Willi Tobler and the Decline of the Sixth Fleet], 96 min.

1973   *Besitzbürgerin, Jahrgang 1908* [A Woman of Property,
            Born in 1908], 11 min.
            Gelegenheitsarbeit einer Sklavin [Occasional Work of a
            Female Slave], 91 min.
1974   *In Gefahr und grösster Not bringt der Mittelweg den Tod*
            [In Times of Danger and Great Need the Middle Way
            Brings Death], 89 min.
1976   *Der starke Ferdinand* [Strongman Ferdinand], 90 min.
1977   *Die Menschen, die das Staufer-Jahr vorbereiten* [The
            People Who Are Preparing the Staufer Jubilee],
            codirected with Maximiliane Mainka, 42 min.
            Nachrichten von den Staufern [News of the Staufer],
            codirected with Maximiliane Mainka, in two parts, 10 and
            12 min.
1977   *"Zu böser Schlacht schleich' ich heut nacht so bang"*
            [Tonight So Full of Fear I Steal Away to the Bloody
            Battle], revised version of *Willi Tobler und der Untergang
            der 6. Flotte*, 82 min.
1978   Contributes to *Deutschland im Herbst* [Germany in
            Autumn], codirected, 124 min.
1979   *Die Patriotin* [The Patriot], 121 min.
1980   *Der Kandidat* [The Candidate], codirected, 129 min.

*Film is not a matter of auteurs but rather a dialogue between the
viewers and the author.*

IN A SATIRICAL SEQUENCE of Alexander Kluge's *Yesterday Girl*
(1966) a young mother is approached by two government officials who
tell her that she must surrender one of her two children so that its
brain can be removed. "The choice is yours," they tell her. Modern
life, Kluge tells us, is filled with choices, many of them false and every
bit as absurd as the choice given to the mother in his film. The power
of cinema, in Kluge's view, is its ability to point out false choices and
to make the viewer aware of the possibilities of not having to make
such choices.

Of the major figures of West German cinema in the 1960s and
1970s, Alexander Kluge is one of the oldest (he was born in 1932) and
one of the earliest practitioners of the New Cinema. Although his
films have not received acclaim from the American public and critics
to the same extent as those of Fassbinder, Herzog, Wenders, or
Schlöndorff, Alexander Kluge remains one of the most significant

figures in West German cinema. One of the originators and signers of the 1962 Oberhausen Manifesto, Kluge was an initiator of the young filmmakers' rebellion against the cinematic establishment in the 1960s. As the head of the Institut für Filmgestaltung in Ulm and as the author of works on film theory, aesthetics, and economics, he has been an influential and representative voice of the New German Cinema. As a lawyer and as a prose writer who was a member of the famous West German literary group, Gruppe 47, Kluge brought a measure of authority, veracity, and respectability to an art form long neglected in West Germany. Finally, not unlike Lessing, whose eighteenth-century dramas were practical applications of his literary theories, Kluge has created films that demonstrate his cinematic/ aesthetic theories. His work first drew international attention to the "new" films of West Germany: Kluge's *Yesterday Girl* was hailed by one respected German film critic as the best German film since 1933, and it more importantly won eight prizes at the 1966 Venice film festival, thus becoming the first postwar German film to win an important international film award.

Kluge shares with Straub the reputation of being the most intellec-tual of the young German filmmakers. This is a designation that Kluge himself disputes, insisting that his films appeal equally to the viewer's intellect and senses. Indisputable, however, are the intelligence, the subtlety, the complexity, and above all the wit of Kluge's films. In a national cinema frequently characterized by and criticized for its lack of humor, Kluge's films are notable exceptions. The sparse comic elements in German film tend toward either the sophomoric, as in Herzog's *Aguirre* (in which a severed head continues to count), or the outrageous and grotesque, as in Fassbinder's *Satan's Brew.* Kluge's films, on the other hand, often present a very sophisticated, dryly ironic comedy.

Kluge's humor, however, elicits smiles or chuckles rather than guffaws. His humor is sometimes so subtle that his viewers miss his point entirely. Especially for Americans, uninformed of the philosophical traditions, political situations, and social forms that Kluge satirizes, the humor of films like *Yesterday Girl* or *Strongman Ferdinand* (1975) is for the most part lost. This, above all else, seems to be responsible for Kluge's failure to find a significant audience in the United States. Americans, raised on a comic diet of broad and sexual humor or the situational, conversational comedy of films like *Bringing Up Baby*, *Adam's Rib*, and Neil Simon's *Plaza Suite*, and lacking a context for Kluge's extremely allusive style, are as often confused as amused by Kluge's films. For Kluge humor is one more way of making a thought-provoking, political point. Kluge's films offer their richest rewards to a viewer who sees the wit of the final scene of *Occasional Work of a Female Slave* (1973), for example, in which the female protagonist sells to factory workers sausages wrapped in political flyers as she is spied upon by a factory security officer who speaks the film's final lines: "We think these sausages are an encroachment upon industrial peace. It must have some meaning—but what?"

Almost all the New German filmmakers view West Germany as a morass of soulless materialism. Although it lacks the pervasive sense of alienation of Wenders's films or the all-encompassing pessimism of Fassbinder's, Kluge's work also criticizes West German society by depicting the political issues that continue to plague contemporary West Germany. It comes as no surprise that Kluge was one of the principal organizers of the cooperative film *Germany in Autumn* (1978), a denunciation of West German governmental repression during the 1970s.

While socio–political criticism always appears in Kluge's films, this criticism derives more from attitudes toward a film's content than it does from the content itself. Narrative turning points or climaxes appear to the viewer only after the film has ended—if at all. To say that *Yesterday Girl* is the story of a young woman, a petty thief, who experiences three unhappy love affairs, becomes pregnant, and finally delivers herself to the police in order to have her baby, tells us very little about the film as seen by the viewer. We see only the court proceedings against Anita G. that result from a theft; only the outcome is seen of the affair she has with an employer, as Anita walks away, suitcase in hand, through the streets of Frankfurt.

Kluge's major films can be divided, with few exceptions, into three broad categories: 1) science fiction stories—*The Big Mess* (1970) or *Willi Tobler and the Decline of the Sixth Fleet* (1971), for example; 2) stories of individuals who are in some way representative of contemporary society, such as *Strongman Ferdinand*; and, most frequently, 3) stories of individuals who, as antagonists of contemporary society, delineate the weaknesses and limitations of society—*Yesterday Girl*, *The Artists Under the Big Top: Perplexed* (1967), *Occasional Work of a Female Slave*, or *The Patriot* (1979). For Kluge, story line is less important than the characters he creates and the contexts into which he places them.

Just as his thematic concerns have a basis in the everyday reality of modern West Germany, so too does character often arise out of an encounter with a real person. As the inspiration for Anita G. in *Yesterday Girl*, Kluge has mentioned an inmate of the Preungesheim

Women's Prison in Frankfurt (HKS, 154).[1] He also found the obsessed industrial security officer, Ferdinand Rieche, in a face: "I saw
the face of this security type in front of me. And then I decided to
make a film about it" (HKS, 154). Kluge's point is that his stories
originate not from an idea but from an image, and Kluge considers his
work more sensual than intellectual. The proper image moves directly from the senses to the subconscious, bypassing logic and
rationality, which tend to abstract and thus dilute human experience.
While his characters do not originate as ideas, they do develop in
response to Kluge's ideas and to the medium in which they are
presented. The main character of *Yesterday Girl*, for example, first
appeared in a short story, "Anita G.," in Kluge's first prose collection,
Resumés. Kluge says that, after meeting the model for Anita G., "the
preliminary outline changed a few times. And when I wrote the story
of 'Anita G.' it deviated from what I wrote as a scenario" (HKS, 154).

Whether as characters, images, or ideas, Kluge's protagonists are
shaped by their social context and by their past. In Kluge's film, we
are constantly faced with the interrelatedness of the social and the
personal. Anita G., Leni Peickert of *Artists Under the Big Top:
Perplexed*, Roswitha Bronski of *Occasional Work of a Female Slave*,
even Ferdinand Rieche of *Strongman Ferdinand* are seen not as
immutable figures, but rather as socially determined personalities.
Their idiosyncracies are shaped by a unique German past, and they
react to a unique West German present. Referring specifically to
Anita G., Kluge has said: "Her story would be another one if she lived
in another society. And it would also be another one if the Germans
had another history." Under other circumstances Anita G. "would be
a social being and probably a first-class functionary" (FK, 488).

Society shapes the individual not only historically, through the
formation of character, but also through the personal expectations it
arouses and then fails to fulfill. West German society, for Kluge,
seems to be not so much malignant (as it clearly is in Fassbinder's
films) as arbitrary and whimsically frustrating: "On the one hand,
society does not give human beings what they can demand; but, on
the other hand, it is so nonaggressive that it does not stimulate a
direct struggle" (FK, 488).

Kluge's films are socially critical but not politically revolutionary—a fact that has sometimes brought attacks on his work
by German leftists. *Yesterday Girl* and *Artists Under the Big Top:
Perplexed* were criticized by revolutionary students of the late 1960s
and *Occasional Work of a Female Slave* by feminists (especially in the
feminist film journal *frauen und film*) in the mid-1970s. As a political

liberal, Kluge takes such criticism earnestly but refuses to yield to ideological pressure.

Abortion is a central issue in *Occasional Work*: Roswitha Bronski is an abortionist and an abortion is graphically depicted. By shifting viewer attention from the woman who receives an abortion to the woman who gives one and to the act itself, Kluge short-circuits easy, liberal, proabortion attitudes. Roswitha's motivation for her work is presented ironically: "In order to afford more children of her own, Roswitha works as an abortionist." And the vividness of the abortion sequence testifies to the essential repugnance of such a procedure. Kluge both accepts and rejects abortion. He perceives the social and political necessity of legalized abortion: "In a social situation like ours, you have to ask politically for abortion not to be punished." On the other hand, he insists upon an acknowledgement of its essential inhumanity: "If you think that human life is sacrosanct, then you can't be in favor of abortion" (K, 40).

Kluge's ethic, like his art, is built upon apparent contradictions that are actually part of an ongoing dialectic, between the social and the personal, thought and feeling, the ideal and the real. If on a rational level the content of Kluge's work seems contradictory, on an emotional level one discerns thematic and ethical unity. There is a fundamental optimism in Kluge's work that distinguishes him from many of his contemporary filmmakers. Fassbinder, for example, perceives the necessity for change as acutely as Kluge but, unlike Kluge, seems to find no means of effecting it. The presentation of both sides of social issues to an activist audience will lead eventually to social change, although such change may be decades or centuries in coming and is not to be achieved by violence: "I don't believe you really achieve change by decisions, or by killing the past, or by killing people. . . . A better way to change things is to accept the past and to complete it" (K, 30).

Society's most essential shortcoming, in Kluge's view, is its establishment of institutions that soon assume their own identity and authority and cease to respond to the needs of the individual. The humane values espoused by Kluge are anathema to most social institutions: the court, the police, the medical establishment, capitalist enterprise, government agencies, the schools and the universities, even the family. "In the same way that the entrepreneur accumulates money, the family accumulates warmth, human relationships, for themselves. Happiness for themselves, and neglect for anyone else" (K, 27).

Strongman Ferdinand. *Courtesy of The Liberty Company*

With the exception of Anita G., the main characters in Kluge's films are all individuals who look for (but never find) solutions to the dilemmas of modern existence, who are internally driven to work for change. Kluge's heroines are all marked by their inability to accept things as they are, by their urge to change and to improve. Even Ferdinand Rieche, the unsympathetic and outrageous security officer of *Strongman Ferdinand*, possesses, in a perverted form, a capacity for utopian fantasy. The power that pulls Leni Peickert toward her ideal circus in *Artists* or Roswitha Bronski toward industrial espionage in *Occasional Work* is the same power that leads Ferdinand Rieche toward the violence that concludes *Strongman Ferdinand*. Kluge also shows that at another time this urge led to the construction of the concentration camps: "It is the same power . . . that simply is active in various social locations. . . . It is not to be prevented by mere morality or good will from making—in a wrong social location, in an alienated form—something like a concentration camp" (HKS, 165).

Kluge's most sympathetic characters and almost all his protagonists are women. Significantly like Brecht's dramatic female protagonists, such as Shen Te in *The Good Person of Sezuan,* women are treated sympathetically in Kluge's films because of their noninvolvement in exploitative social processes. Social innocence and personal integrity have not been gained by women but rather have not yet been lost by them. Kluge has said in this respect:

"In a society dominated by men—a society whose mentality and institutions, from school to university to the law courts, are essentially rather masculine—it's not capricious to describe some men as 'character-masks.' They are. And in so far as they belong to institutions and are formed by institutions, they become more like character masks. . . . It's always the suppressed element in society that has to be described: the dominant element describes itself; there's no need to add to it in the cinema." (K, 29)

Society functions through institutions established and operated primarily by men. Most men (Kluge points out the figure of Dr. Bauer, the idealistic Attorney General in *Yesterday Girl,* as an exception) thus bear a stigma, perhaps even a culpability, that most women have avoided by their social passivity.

Above all, among Kluge's heroines, Anita G. seems to embody a social innocence that renders her vulnerable to the institutional forces around her. Fundamentally Kluge has an ironic, Brechtian view of individuals and societies, a view that is simultaneously optimistic and pessimistic. For Kluge goodness is inherent in human nature but human goodness has a hard time surviving in modern society. By the conventional standards of bourgeois morality or institutional legality, Anita G. commits immoral or illegal actions: adultery and petty theft. Beyond the traditional codes of the environment in which Anita G. lives, however, there exists a code shared by filmmaker and viewer that sympathetically judges Anita G. innocent.

Anita G. is misused or misserved by almost all the men and institutions she encounters. Early in the film, during Anita's trial for the theft of a sweater, apparent truth (immorality of the individual) is refuted by ironic truth (immorality of the system) as the camera depicts the inhumanity of the judiciary by photographing the back of the judge's head and shoulders, showing the viewer a circle of short hair, a faceless robed figure who, in a rapid monotone, mumbles "pertinent" sections of the West German legal code. Unmistakably the judge's way of speaking reflects his way of thinking and betrays his inability or unwillingness to respond humanely to Anita's dilemma. A Jewish refugee from East Germany, Anita has made the grievous error of thinking that she can exist in West Germany without money—the ultimate sin in a materialist society. When the judge denies the significance of Anita's past—her existence as a Jew under the Nazis and her upbringing as a capitalist in East Germany—he is echoing what Kluge sees as a hallmark of contemporary West Germany: a refusal to acknowledge the past. "The Federal Republic would certainly not exist without the DDR nor without the Third Reich. And I think someone who has concrete experience of our society's history and who comes into an ahistorical society which is pressured not to notice its past will have conflicts. And these conflicts can't be observed on the level of pure common sense, or on the level on which institutions function" (K, 36).

Clearly Anita G. is one of these "historical" individuals in "an ahistorical society." Her conflicts are initially manifested in the crime for which she is tried, a trivial, unpremeditated, and even ludicrous crime. When the judge asks why she had stolen a sweater in the summertime, Anita replies: "I'm cold even in the summertime." Anita G. is a victim, an exploited innocent who is ultimately driven into imprisonment and a nervous breakdown. Victimization, however, is not in itself heroic. It appears that Kluge was attracted to her story not for Anita's negative qualities but rather for the indomitability that she displays, for the perseverance with which she attempts to construct a stable existence from the shambles of her past. Anita G. too possesses a measure of the same vitality embodied by Kluge's other heroines.

As with Kluge's other heroines, we experience an identification with Anita G. and a sympathy for her, but we also criticize her. Kluge has said, "there should be no total identification" (FK, 489) with his characters. Kluge intends that we should understand his heroines and comprehend their motives rather than admire their actions. In assessing the relative quality of his protagonist's actions, Kluge emphasizes the impossibility of "pure" actions. Referring to the dubious activities of Anita G. and Leni Peickert, Kluge has said: "the more practical a person's activities are, the more faults will emerge. The less practical the activities, . . . the fewer faults" (K, 39). The actions of Roswitha Bronski in *Occasional Work* may seem more absurd because they are less utopian, but "Roswitha, whose path in my opinion is closer to the right one because it's more effective and more practical, has more opportunities for making mistakes. The only possible way to avoid mistakes is to do nothing" (K, 40). The ambivalence of attitude toward Kluge's protagonists and their actions diverts significance in his films away from theme and onto form and style: "The formal level reiterates the contents, in a precise, nonverbal form that cannot be reproduced in words" (HKS, 170).

Kluge's ultimate purpose as a filmmaker is to establish a critical awareness or, as he calls it, "reality" in the mind of the viewer. Presumably this awareness will then lead to change. As an instrument of social change, cinema has possibilities not available to the other arts. Kluge has said that cinema's potential lies in the fact that "it's rather trivial and derives from the fairground. It has more to do with Punch and Judy than with serious art" (K, 37). In making such a statement Kluge refers to the imagistic vitality of film, its ability to jar the mind and to jolt the senses through the power of its images. Where Werner Herzog perceives this power as an antidote to the stagnation of overintellectualism, Kluge views it politically. Film "hasn't been developed from the viewpoint of a small, educated society; it's made for plebeian people, for the proletarian component" (K, 37). Cinema is, in effect, a means of bridging the gulf between the artist/intellectual and the masses, in whom lies the potential for social change.

Kluge is attracted to the universal effectiveness of cinematic imagery, but he is also wary of the passivity that film can induce in the spectator. Film is honest as an art form and as a political instrument only to the extent that the viewer remains aware and active. The dangers of viewer passivity are nowhere more obvious than in German cinema, which produced Riefenstahl's *Triumph of the Will*, an ultimate example of cinema's ability to manipulate its audience. These dangers are inherent not only in Nazi films but also in the "entertainment" films of the Hollywood tradition. "The viewer is simply 'bound.' He doesn't know what to do with his excitement. This 'entertainment' practice [*Unterhaltungspraxis*] is cynical to the extent that it turns the viewer into an object" (FM, 238).

Instead of turning the viewer into a passive object, Kluge would have the film itself be passive, thus inducing activity in the viewer. Again and again Kluge speaks of cinema as merely a means of activating the "real film" that already exists in the mind of the spectator. "The viewer really produces the film when the film shown on the screen activates the viewer's own 'film' in his head. Through this dialogue between viewer and screen film becomes a mass medium" (FM, 234). Or, as Kluge told another interviewer, "film is not a matter of *auteurs* but rather a dialogue between the spectators and the author. . . . For me the film produces itself in the head of the viewer, not on the screen" (HKS, 158).

Surely this insistence on viewer autonomy has cost Kluge some of his potential audience, especially in the United States, but really everywhere that film audiences have been accustomed to the excitement and involvement of "active" narratives, of cinematic entertainments that counteract rather than elicit viewer "activity" or critical awareness. Even when Kluge's films do find a sympathetic audience willing to forego the pleasures of entertainment for the pleasures of critical activity, audience response is not always enthusiastic. That these films have not been as approachable for American audiences as the films of Herzog, Wenders, and Fassbinder can only be due to the inability of American audiences to make the associations that Kluge expects of the viewer. "The film is no more important than that which the viewer brings to it" (HKS, 166).

The associations and connotations that Kluge expects the film to evoke often simply cannot be produced in a viewer ignorant of the peculiarly German cultural icons of Kluge's film: German personality stereotypes, German laws, German linguistic forms, German popular music reminiscent of the Nazi era. "The film is assembled in the viewer's head, and it's not a work of art that exists on the screen for its own sake. Therefore the film has to work with associations" (FK, 489).

For the viewer who is able to make the appropriate connections, however, much of the power and the beauty of a Kluge film lies precisely in its richly allusive style and its witty resonances, in its simultaneous appeal to the mind and to the senses. Kluge himself believes that a film's immediacy derives from its form, as a recapitulation of physical brain functions: "These images correspond precisely to the brain's way of functioning. A brain never only perceives something in the present. When I see something in the present, it reminds me . . . of something in the past, something earlier . . . and thus I perceive that and make a connection with the future" (HKS, 167). The similarity of this formal concern with Kluge's thematic insistence upon the ineradicability of social history is obvious.

Kluge also rejects the auteurist principle that the film director is ultimately the sole creator of film art. Kluge sees himself as an initiator and a mediator of the film's materials, but he does not consider himself sovereign in a final determination of the film product. Kluge views as the task of the filmmaker the selection of an image—a face, a person, a situation—around which a context can "crystallize." After the writing of the script, the director "has a more interpretative function; he is to a certain extent a midwife" (FK, 488). Similarly, in describing his reluctance to fit filmed images to a preconceived directorial notion, "I am not of the opinion that it is the task of the midwife to cut to measure children with too long legs or a crooked nose. And we do exactly that as film *auteurs*" (HKS, 158).

In keeping with this principle Kluge has at times granted great creative latitude to his film crew and his actors, in particular to his sister. A physician, rather than professional actress, Alexandra Kluge has played the main role in both *Yesterday Girl* and *Occasional Work of a Female Slave*. In *Occasional Work* the film narrative took a much different course than that originally envisioned by Kluge. In deference to his sister's opinion of the direction the narrative should take, Kluge made a film he had no intention of making when he began. "I can't say, 'what I want to express is more important than what my sister wants to express. . . .' And I have to admit it is more interesting to document my sister's error" (HKS, 159–60).

In *Yesterday Girl* his sister created another diversion from directorial intention, but in this instance the unexpected result matched perfectly with Kluge's own inclination of letting the film create itself. Anita's lover, Pichota, tells her Brecht's famous story in which Herr Keuner says that if he loved a person he would make a sketch and attempt to make the person more like it. When the story was told by the actor playing Pichota, it was misunderstood by Alexandra Kluge so that a reversal originated with the actress, not from Kluge's scenario but well-suited to the film's general portrayal of Anita G. as having difficulty with the abstractions that underlie social institutions. The "error" moreover reinforces Kluge's thesis that society should in fact adapt to the individual.

Such fortuitous results—Kluge would never call them "accidents" since they seem to originate as subliminal truths—affirm Kluge's belief that a director should only "establish a contact, set in motion a communicative process between the actors, the rest of the crew, and the cameraman" (FK, 488).

Kluge, moreover, counteracts cinematic verisimilitude by using direct sound and by allowing the voices of the film crew occasionally to be heard on the sound track. In *Yesterday Girl* a digressive hotelman inquires whether he is boring his listeners; the unseen crew responds in the negative, reassuring their subject. Some disruptions of seamless narration do not reveal the filmmaking process to the audience but instead draw the viewer deeper into the story. In the penultimate shot of *Yesterday Girl* Anita G./Alexandra Kluge stares into the camera, silently confronting the audience with their own complicity in her fate, a complicity affirmed by the film's final shot, a title: "Everyone is responsible for everything, but/If everyone knew that/We would have paradise on earth." We are left with a challenge, not a conclusion.

Like Straub or Godard, Kluge is convinced that cinematic mimesis has nothing to do with existential reality. Film realism or naturalism is an unacceptable seduction of the viewer into a suspension of disbelief, into an acceptance of a cinematic artifice which counters social progress by pandering to the viewer's regressive desire for entertainment. Of paramount importance to Kluge is the effect attained in the mind of the viewer. A "believing" viewer is not an aware or critical viewer. Kluge seeks to establish through his films "an authentic effect." But authenticity is not reality, at least not in the traditional aesthetic sense, because "the reality that we encounter everyday is not formed. I consider the formative principle, forming by an author, to be a mistake" (HKS, 157). Nevertheless, the realism that Kluge seeks "has to be produced. . . . I am realistic for an anti-realistic reason. And this dialectic leads to the fact that I sometimes shatter all realistic methods while trying to be realistic" (HKS, 158).

Kluge's manner of making films was praised by one German critic as "this 'impure,' provocatively fragmentary anti-method."[2] The consistency of Kluge's cinematic practice helps to clarify what, stated as theory, seems only confusing or abstract. Deviations from conventional narration are for Kluge a means of moving beyond conceits, deceits, artificiality, and the repressed and repressive realm of logic. Logic, Kluge knows, provided rationalizations for Nazism. Similarly, as Kluge has pointed out in regard to the question of abortion, one could reasonably conclude that, if abortion is permissible, then mass euthanasia of the elderly, the ill, the handicapped might also be logical. Kluge looks for a means to bypass logic, to touch the spectator's fantasy without fostering cinematic illusions. "We must seek to overcome realism so that the illusion that here is a likeness of society won't occur at all. This illusion is correct neither in documentary films nor in feature films" (FK, 491).

Kluge's film style is thus directed toward the disintegration or destruction of illusion: direct sound; printed titles—sometimes ironic, sometimes not—to separate and comment upon narrative sequences; nonprofessional actors; improvised dialogues; unexpected shifts in narrator perspective; time rearrangement; literary, philosophical, or political quotations; pious aphorisms and bourgeois

Occasional Work of a Female Slave. *Courtesy of the Film Center of the Art Institute of Chicago*

homilies; visual quotations of old drawings, prints, and films; old photographs of his own family; nursery rhymes and children's stories; popular and trivial music used as commentary; a mixing of factual and fictive, of "real" and surreal material. These stylistic elements—distributed among visual imagery, printed texts, texts spoken on the soundtrack, and music—intertwine to form a complex matrix of associations, allusions, and indications, which, rather than disseminating supposedly objective authorial truths, tease the mind of the viewer into activity.

The clearest thematic and formal influences on Kluge's work are the films of Godard and the dramas of Bertolt Brecht. In addition, however, Kluge has also acknowledged the influence of silent film form on his work: "Film must give fantasy a space in which it can move and must nevertheless communicate something pictorially. In silent films I always liked the titles. . . . I like to see that, because at that moment my mind begins to work and has a moment's time to develop fantasies independently" (FK, 490).

It is not only titles inserted between shots that the silent film has lent to Kluge's work. Kluge has written, "I would make no films if the film history of the 1920s did not exist. Since I have been making films, I have made them with reference to this classical tradition."[3] He has referred to Soviet silent film, particularly *October* and *Arsenal*, as a "formal canon, the freest and most direct that I know of in the cinema. . . . If there is a point from which I proceed, it is precisely these films" (HKS, 169). Since Kluge in *Occasional Work of a Female Slave* quotes from, and elsewhere cites as a model, an early Soviet sound film, *Chapayev*, we can assume that Kluge perceives other virtues in these early Soviet films, especially political engagement, ideological commitment, and the effectiveness of editing and montage, the most essential elements in Kluge's elliptical, associative style.

Clearly it is Kluge's manner of cutting and assembling his film material that makes his films unique. While early Soviet editing in, for example, the films of Eisenstein experimented with the communication of authorial ideas through shot-to-shot juxtapositions, editing or montage in Kluge's films is intended to arouse not just one but many possible concepts in the mind of the viewer. "The cuts make it possible that the viewer can see all my films many times; in every case he sees another film" (HKS, 166).

This, then, is the crux of what Alexander Kluge, the lawyer-author-filmmaker, hopes to achieve: a combining of actuality and thought in the mind of the viewer. Kluge looks for images that do more than entertain; he seeks images that provoke reflection, images that go beyond rationality and logic to the realm of fantasy and feeling. The viewer "should use his senses and his feelings of protests, his feelings in general. . . . He should use the characteristics that he otherwise doesn't like to use, that he has become unaccustomed to, through parents, schools, and the mass media. . . . There, where repression is sharpest, it is typically especially barren and unenjoyable for the senses" (HKS, 176). The senses, the feelings and fantasy—these are for Kluge the guarantors of individual freedom and social progress; they are the source of the sure knowledge that false choices such as the one faced by the young mother in *Yesterday Girl* can be met with more than passivity. Our brains can be removed only if we allow them to be. Our thoughts are our own and can make us free but only if our minds stay active. And the true power of cinema is its ability to activate our minds. As the first title in *Occasional Work* tells us: "Roswitha feels a great power within her, and she knows from films that this power actually exists."

3

Jean-Marie Straub/Danièle Huillet

Chronology

1933	Jean-Marie Straub born on January 8.
1936	Danièle Huillet born on May 1.
1962	*Machorka-Muff*, 18 min.
1965	*Nicht versöhnt oder Es hilft nur Gewalt, wo Gewalt herrscht* [Not Reconciled or Only Violence Helps Where Violence Reigns], 55 min.
1967	*Chronik der Anna Magdalena Bach* [Chronicle of Anna Magdalena Bach], 94 min.
1968	*Der Bräutigam, die Komödiantin und der Zuhälter* [The Bridegroom, the Comedienne, and the Pimp], 23 min.
1969	*Les yeux ne veulent pas en tout temps se fermer ou Peut-être qu'un jour Rome se permettra de choisir à son tour/Othon* [The Eyes Do Not Always Want to Close or Perhaps One Day Rome Will Permit Itself to Choose in Its Turn/Othon], 82 min.
1972	*Geschichtsunterricht* [History Lessons], 88 min.
	Einleitung zu Arnold Schoenbergs Begleitmusik zu einer Lichtspielscene [Introduction to Arnold Schoenberg's "Accompaniment to a Cinematographic Scene"], 16 min.
1974	*Moses und Aron* [Moses and Aron], 110 min.
1976	*Fortini Cani* [The Dogs of Sinai], 83 min.
1977	*Toute Révolution est un Coup de Dés* [Every Revolution is a Throw of the Dice], 11 min.
1979	*Dalla nube alla resistenza* [From the Cloud to the Resistance], 103 min.

You can never make your films intelligent enough,
because people have enough stupidity to put up with in
their lives.

JUST AS THE POLITICAL LEFT has always been plagued by
ideological differences, significant differences of cinematic intention
and aesthetic theory also distinguish West German filmmakers who,
viewed from a broader perspective, appear very similar in political
stance and cinematic approaches. Consider, for example, Alexander
Kluge and Jean-Marie Straub, whose films, at first glance, seem
closely akin politically, thematically, and formally. Linked by their
opposition to the commercial cinema and their advocacy of a Brechtian "counter-cinema," Kluge and Straub are nevertheless (in
Straub's view, at least) totally dissimilar filmmakers: "Kluge always
goes on about the film created in the minds of the spectators. I don't
believe it" (E, 12).[1] According to Straub, at a film gathering in
Mannheim some years ago Kluge "climbed onto the stage and said,
'What we are doing is new. We make films which are going to be
created in the minds of the spectators. That is completely new and
nobody has done it before. My films are like . . . those of Straub, for
instance.' Then I was furious and stood up and said, 'The things I do
are not new at all, they are traditional. Anyone who makes films
progresses a tiny step forward on his road, in one direction, and . . .
only tiny steps'" (E, 12).

Straub's assessment is correct, at least to the extent that he is more
extreme than Kluge cinematically, politically, and, one assumes, in
his view of life. Straub's work has been labelled, at various times,
Minimalist, Reductionist, Deconstructionist, or Counter-cinema.
He and his wife, Danièle Huillet, his cowriter and coeditor since the
first film in 1962 and his codirector since 1974, are indeed the fun-
damentalists of modern German film. The Straubs are radical
filmmakers and, as is implicit in the preceding quote with its insistence on "tradition," radical even in the most literal meaning of the
word: of or pertaining to the root or origin. The Straubs believe they
can circumvent the hackneyed conventions of commercial filmmaking and in some sense recover the movies' original capability and
power, as manifest in the early films of Renoir and Griffith and, later,
in the films of Dreyer and Bresson. Extreme in the noncommerciality
of their films, in their political commitment, and in their insistence
upon utter aesthetic purity, the Straubs stood alone at one far end of
the West German cinematic spectrum during the 1960s and early
1970s.

The inclusion of the Straubs in any list of West German filmmakers might well be questioned, since they both are French by birth. They moved to Germany only in 1958 and since 1969 have lived in Rome. Seven of their eleven films were made in German, however, and their influence on the development of West German film in the late 1960s and early 1970s (the earliest films of Fassbinder, to give only the most obvious example) was very significant if short-lived. Because of the singlemindedness of their film theory and practice the Straubs have come to be "filmmakers' filmmakers." Of all the West German filmmakers before Fassbinder, they were the most interviewed and reviewed in Europe's leading theoretical/critical film journals: in West Germany's *Filmkritik*, of course, but also in England's *Screen* and *Enthusiasm*, in Italy's *Bianco e Nero* and *Filmcritica*, and in France's *Positif* and *Cahiers du Cinéma*. The Straubs became in effect the touchstones by which other, alternative feature filmmakers tested their own works, either in emulation of or in reaction to such works as *Not Reconciled* (1965), *Chronicle of Anna Magdalena Bach* (1967), *History Lessons* (1972), and *Moses and Aron* (1974).

The Straubs' films are exercises in austerity. They are so elliptical that a story emerges, if at all, only after the film is over. They are usually slow–paced, with sparse camera movement and attenuated shots that frequently linger on settings before and after the characters arrive or leave, thus drawing our attention to the soundtrack and to the world beyond the camera's frame. The actors are deliberately nonprofessional, nonemotive, and sometimes incomprehensible, speaking their often unilluminating dialogue in deliberate monotones. The rhythms of language mean as much or more than the words themselves. The Straubs have eschewed the postproduction dubbing that has been characteristic of (and, so say the Straubs, nearly the death of) recent West German and Italian commercial filmmaking; thus, their films always have "original" or "live" or "natural" sound, in which speech is sometimes muted or lost through the sound of the wind, through actor movement, or through noises intruding from off the set.

Film narrative that might deceptively lead the viewer into a mis-guided "suspension of disbelief" is avoided, thus "story" or narrative action is minimal. In their reconstruction (one hesitates to say "adap-tation") of literary works the Straubs sometimes delete and revise until the original work is nearly unrecognizable. Continuity, even from shot to shot, is frequently avoided. The viewer of a Straub film is not a passive spectator but rather an active participant in the de-velopment of the film's sense.

Because of the frequent unintelligibility of their films, because of their refusal to compromise or to make concessions to conventional viewer expectations, Straub and Huillet have been as often vilified as praised, not only by the public and by the popular press, but also by reviewers who, because of their experience with noncommercial cinema might have been expected to be less close-minded. Straub himself related to one interviewer "the things they wrote about *Not Reconciled* in Berlin [at the Film Festival in 1965]. . . . One wrote: 'One would do well to spread the cloak of merciless silence over this piece of filmic superfluity.' Or: 'As ugly as a film can be ugly,' that was *Die Zeit* [an influential, and usually liberal, weekly newspaper]. Or another newspaper: 'The worst film since 1895.'" About the Straubs' Bach film one German reviewer reportedly wrote: "unfilmic, terrible, Bach was no wooden puppet!" (FM, 34).

In a similar vein a *New York Times* writer in 1969 reviewed three early Straub films: "Mr. Straub, an introspective, often mystic movie-maker, leaves a viewer more often perplexed than convinced, more often only vaguely aware of his philosophy or of his plots and their convolutions. . . . [He] weaves a spider's web of intrigues, short but most often disjointed vignettes, full of angst and turgid with talk. His cast, dispassionate but serious, are merely colorless people expounding on the past and the present with about as much fervor as a lecture on semantics."[2]

As might be expected, the Straubs have also always faced a continual struggle to find financial backing for their commercially unprofitable films. They received scant support from the various government agencies that have subsidized the development of much of the New German Film. The making of each film, even of their short films, has been a nearly endless search for the money needed for production. Because of the unprofitability of their films the personal life of the Straubs has been as austere as their cinematic style. Moreover, because of their absolute unwillingness to compromise or to surrender any control over their work, the Straubs have, more than any other West German filmmakers, exposed the power structures and financial dependencies that underlie nearly all filmmaking.

While their refusal to make concessions has won them immense respect among some filmmaking colleagues, they have sometimes angered other filmmakers by their willingness to make their films with so little financial backing. One of their most important films, *History Lessons,* was made, for example, for only 30,000 West German marks (at that time approximately $15,000), a minuscule sum for a full-length film. Offers of money have sometimes been refused, too,

Straub/Huillet's Moses and Aaron. *Courtesy of The Museum of Modern Art/Film Stills Archive*

for the sake of artistic integrity. Straub says that he could have made his Bach film much earlier if he had been willing to accept a "name" actor in the main role. "I even found one idiot . . . who would have fully guaranteed the film if I had accepted Curt Jürgens as Bach" (FM, 31). Another potential backer suggested Herbert von Karajan. Without such a guarantee of commercial appeal financial support was much more difficult to find.

Such negative responses from press and public and such discouragement from film producers distress but do not defeat the Straubs. And sometimes they have found ardent supporters, notable among them Jean-Luc Godard, who called *Not Reconciled* "a marvelous film" and who became one of Straub's financial backers for the filming of *Chronicle of Anna Magdalena Bach*, and Richard Roud, the influential director of the New York Film Festival and author of a monograph in 1972 on Straub, making him the first post-World War II German filmmaker to be taken so seriously in the United States.

What the Straubs' admirers find in their work is, above all, innovation. Straub and Huillet try again and again in their films to clear away the accretions and debris of over half a century of filmmaking. The cinema, in Straub's view, has in a sense become a victim of its own popularity. Even before entering the theater, a film audience has, because of its own cinematic experience, a good idea of what a film will say, how it will be said, and what it will mean. Cinema can be renewed and renewing only through a reduction, an elimination, a destruction of film conventions and conventional film meaning: "I think we should make films that have absolutely no signification because if not we're making trash. . . . A film . . . that signifies something . . . can only be trash, since it confirms people in their clichés. A film must destroy, every minute, every second, what it has said the minute before, I believe, because we are suffocating in clichés" (CC, 49). Or, as Straub has also said, "My films will become more and more unfilmic because the films one gets to see are becoming more and more filmic" (FM, 42). Or, yet again, in response to an interviewer's question of whether there is a cinematic syntax in Straub's films: "Yes, certainly. . . . But a syntax that tries again and again to stop being one, that one tries somehow to destroy in each new film" (HKS, 206).

What the Straubs strive for is a stripping away of all that we have come to expect from conventional movies. Beneath the veneer of convention there still lies a capacity to move the viewer and to handle important themes; but the filmmaker, in Straub's view, must be constantly on guard against all the elements of traditional cinema that have been rendered impotent through repetition, against all clichés of action and acting, of image and sound, of cinematic construction, of point-of-view and language.

Consider first of all the Straubs' view of film narrative, of the action found in commercial films. A story that entertains must be, in their view, essentially dishonest and even in an aesthetic sense pornographic: "Commercial films are becoming more and more filmic, that is, they are becoming more and more pornographic. Film is like a snake that bites its own tail" (FM, 42). Of American films in the early 1970s—for Straub the epitome of commercial movie-making—he says they "are becoming ever more brutal and try to distance people ever more from reality; the chasm between life and what is delivered on the screen is becoming bigger and bigger" (FM, 42). "Story" diverts the viewer from reality, tricks the viewer into an acceptance of a fiction as fact. For Straub the viewer's "willing suspension of disbelief" when viewing a commercial movie can only be wrong, in an aesthetic, a political, even an existential sense, because the viewer relinquishes autonomy, loses his or her critical faculty, becomes a passive object in the cinematic project:

Straub: When a film is running that relies on deception, then nothing at all is really happening. What happens can only happen in the viewer and can only happen through combinations of images and sounds . . .

Huillet: of forms . . .

Straub: of forms that then pass through the ears and the eyes and through the brain of the viewer and through the consciousness (HKS, 209).

One concludes that the essential difference between the film aesthetics of Kluge and Straub is that Kluge emphasizes the importance of the viewer while Straub emphasizes the importance of the work of art, the film itself. Straub is, for example, more insistently Brechtian in what he sees to be the "correct" manner of presenting the material of the film. *Not Reconciled*, in fact, bears as a subtitle a quote from Brecht's *St. Joan of the Stockyard*, "Only violence helps where violence rules," and as an epigraph Brecht's statement of dramatic *praxis*: "Instead of wanting to create the impression that he is improvising, the actor should rather show what the truth is: he is quoting." Such a dialectic of the actor and the material also exists in Kluge's films but exists much more intensely in the Straubs'. In Kluge's films the actors may even, through improvisation, create their material; in the Straubs' films they do not.

Actors who "act," in the conventional sense, obscure the material of the film. Instead of an objective and critical presentation, we are thus given a subjective rendering of the character portrayed, which is again a deception of the viewer. What we then see is the actor's idea of what the character is about; what we should see is the material, the actor presenting the material, and the actor's "own work" (HKS, 210). Thus one finds in the Straubs' films a frequent employment of nonactors, or of actors who are coached to speak nonprofessionally. The best-known example is Johanna Fähmel in *Not Reconciled*, played by a woman who lived in the Straubs' apartment building in Munich. Given her lines only at the beginning of each day's shooting, without the context in which they were to be spoken, she realized only at film's end that her character was supposed to be slightly mad.

The use of nonactors in no way implies an attitude of carelessness toward the text, however. Straub tells the story of an old man in *History Lessons* who had to be endlessly coached until the seemingly insignificant coloring word "ja" was eliminated from one of his lines. What the Straubs seek is an absolute elimination of all subjective emphasis, all sense of an actor "emoting," which colors and alters a text. Rather Straub and Huillet strive to awaken in the viewer an awareness of the "actor's work" and of the fact that the actor "confronts the text with his own experience" (FK, 71).

To say that the Straubs have a reverence for their texts is somehow a paradox. Attempts were made to prevent the screening and distribution of *Not Reconciled* and *History Lessons*, by the publishers of Heinrich Böll's *Billiards at Nine-Thirty* and of Brecht's *The Affairs of Mr. Julius Caesar*—the literary sources for the two films—on the grounds that the Straubs had unconscionably butchered the originals. On the other hand, the Straubs' films of Corneille's *Othon* or of Schoenberg's *Moses and Aron* or their short–film reading—in both the figurative and literal senses—of a Mallarmé poem in *Every Revolution is a Throw of the Dice* (1977) are faithful in the extreme to their dramatic, operatic, poetic sources. Of the deletions made in Böll's novel, Straub has said, "We . . . cut the anecdotes and psychology out of Böll. They might be very funny when you read them but I do not believe there is any point to put them again on the screen" (E, 16). Similarly, in writing the scenario for *History Lessons* the Straubs selected out of Brecht's novel fragment "everything which was an economic reflection of the way a bourgeois democracy or a capitalist society functions. That is, leaving out everything that was anecdotal" (FK, 70).

What seems most meaningful to the Straubs is their cinematic reconsideration of an existing work of art, whether it is by Böll, Brecht, Schoenberg, Mallarmé, Corneille, or Franco Fortini and Cesare Pavese in the Straubs' later Italian films, *Fortini Cani/The Dogs of Sinai* (1976) and *From the Cloud to the Revolution* (1979). Each literary source is a reflection of the author's attitude toward historical events: Böll's attitude toward the Nazi era in *Billiards at Nine-Thirty*, for example, or Corneille's attitude toward Roman history. Straub describes *Othon* as "a series of mirrors, the mirror of Tacitus reflecting history that he knew directly or indirectly, then the mirror of Corneille reflecting Tacitus, my mirror reflecting Corneille, the mirror of contemporary reality" (CC, 49). Each Straub film is then a further reflection of the source material, part of a dialectical process in which the Straubs see themselves as intermediaries: "There's more to it than just the little thoughts that we could have. We want to show something already formed by the past, something that affected us, and give it to people so that they can take a stand regarding it just as we did when we made the film" (HKS, 211). Thus, filmmaking is, and film-viewing should be, a coming to terms with important historical issues and political questions.

Even *Chronicle of Anna Magdalena Bach*, which, despite being the best-known of the Straubs' films, is somewhat of an anomaly in that it is not based on a preexisting literary or musical text, has at its core a perspective on what Straub calls "historical moments in which a crisis begins, or will begin. The Bach film, for example, that's really the last moment before this Christian—what should we call it?— construction collapses" (HKS, 208). The "chronicle" of the title is itself a fiction constructed by Straub from historical materials, and the figure of Bach's second wife provides the perspective or point-of-view that Straub considers necessary. As Böll or Brecht provide a viewpoint on their material so too does Anna Magdalena Bach: "this external point is precisely the consciousness of Anna Magdalena" (F, 607).

Clearly the figure of Anna Magdalena Bach should be regarded not as an instrument of verisimilitude or as a figure who should make us believe that we are seeing Bach as he really was. She is rather a constant reminder (more often audial than visual) that the Bach we see on the screen is a modern rendering of an actually unrecapturable historical figure. Thus, the title of the film: we are viewing not the life of Bach but rather a twofold fictional filtering—through the "chronicle" and through the film—of historical "fact." Huillet views such a combining of "fiction" and "fact" as the key to a film's effectiveness: "For us fiction is important because, when it is mixed with documentary footage or a documentary situation, there arises a contradiction and sparks can fly" (HKS, 210).

It is possibly this mixing of factual and fictional modes, along with the Straubs' radical restructuring of existing literary works, that is most responsible for audience discontent and publisher dissatisfaction. The viewer is accustomed to films that "faithfully" re-create a literary work or that sentimentally fictionalize and emotionalize the life of a composer. Such artifice is dishonest and deceitful—dishonest in its misrepresentation and deceitful in its presentation of its dishonesty as truth or "reality." Thus in *Not Reconciled* Straub saw his goal to be not a film version of Böll's novel but rather a "cinematographic, moral, and political reflection on the last fifty years of German life." Instead of historical accuracy in costuming and an explicit time progression Straub sought "to eliminate as much as possible any histori-

cal aura in both costumes and sets, thus giving the images a kind of
atonal character. And by putting the past (1910, 1914, 1934) on the
same level as the present, I have made a film which is a reflection on
the continuity of Nazism both with what preceded it (first anticom-
munism, then anti-Semitism) and what followed it."[3]

The most significant theme of Böll's novel was, for Straub, the
inescapable presence of the past, and this theme guided Straub's
shaping of and ellisions within the film's underlying structure. Content has become form in *Not Reconciled*; thus the avoidance of
"historical aura in both costumes and sets"; thus also the thorough
and unannounced and therefore confusing intermingling of the present and various points of the past.

Content determines form also in *Every Revolution is a Throw of
the Dice*, in which the end of each line in Mallarmé's text is marked by
a cut to a different speaker, and in *Chronicle of Anna Magdalena
Bach*. Straub's intention was less to make a film about an admittedly
great composer ("It isn't really a cultural film about Bach." E, 1) than
to make a film showing that "there is no division between politics and
life, art and politics. . . . Bach was oppressed" (E, 9). This subordina-
tion of Bach the man to the circumstances of his life and work is
evoked by a deliberate avoidance of camera shots that would cen-
tralize and thereby emphasize the actor playing Bach. Almost all
shots are, instead, off-center or slightly too high or too low. The
viewer identifies neither with Bach nor with the narrative voice of the
actress "quoting" his wife, nor does the viewer psychologize or invent
an unintended emotional attitude. What the viewers should perceive
is not a deceptive and subjective opinion of Bach's existence or of his
music but rather "what goes on with the musician or musicians,
nothing more. The point of what is shown during a piece of music is,
in each case, how the music is made" (F, 607).

As camera location removes Bach from the center of focus, so too
the infrequency of camera movements or cuts formally underscores
the laboriousness of making the music and emphasizes the actual time
needed for its performance. Instead of misrepresentative musical
highpoints, we see and hear each piece, selected for its representativeness, without ellipsis or emphasis. Evident also is an unwillingness to subordinate the soundtrack, and therefore the music itself, to
the visual image. Straub has said, "Starting point for our *Chronicle of
Anna Magdalena Bach* was the idea of attempting a film in which
music is used not as accompaniment, nor as commentary, but rather
as aesthetic material" (F, 607).

Neither Bach nor the conditions of his life can be accurately reconstructed, so Bach's music becomes the film's dominant focus and assumes paramount significance both aurally and visually. All other considerations in making the film—structure, narrative, visual composition, sets, costuming—were subordinated to the music. The music determined the selection of an accomplished Bach musician, Gustav Leonhardt, to portray Bach even though Leonhardt bears little resemblance to what is known of Bach's physical appearance.

The integrity of *Chronicle of Anna Magdalena Bach* lies in its insistence upon accuracy regarding those details that could be verified and its total disregard for details that could not be verified as historically correct. Bach and his wife, in the Straubs' film, do not age, since the viewer should be aware that these people are only representing Bach and his wife. Make-up was not used, since there was no attempt to create the illusion that Bach had returned to life. Historically verifiable facts were, on the other hand, observed to the smallest detail: wigs and costumes, musical instruments, methods of playing the instruments, even the unexpected sparseness of the sets which Straub insists to be representative of early eighteenth-century furnishings. Bach's appearance, his thoughts, his emotions cannot be known, so any film pretending to show these things is a deceptive film. The Straubs' *Chronicle* is honest in the foundation of its text on those things that do remain: Bach's music, his manuscripts, and his letters. "If one is making films that stand on their own feet, . . . they must have documentary roots" (E, 9).

Nevertheless, for the Straubs, film does not consist only of its documentary aspect. A film gains life only in its juxtaposing of data to some human element: for example, the alternating speakers of *Every Revolution is a Throw of the Dice*, the voice of Franco Fortini in *The Dogs of Sinai*, or, in *Chronicle of Anna Magdalena Bach*, the figure of Gustav Leonhardt. Of *Chronicle* Straub has said, "the film consists of bringing [Leonhardt] together with these three realities: writings, texts, and music. Only when an ignition occurs among these four elements, does something come of it" (F, 610).

The concept of an "ignition" or the "spark" of which Straub often speaks sounds surprisingly mystical for such an objective filmmaker, but such references to a spiritual dimension do occasionally occur in Straub's films—in isolated shots of waves or clouds or treetops moving in the wind—and in his remarks: "A film does not consist of images, that is something optical, but of ideas, and this is what moves these wigs, these hands. . . . What makes them move, that is the

wind. It is a film about the wind. And the wind is precisely the work of
Bach. And the period and these texts. And let's say, rather preten-
tiously, the spirit" (E, 10).

In *Chronicle of Anna Magdalena Bach* music is the unifying element. Music is not used as merely an accompaniment to or a commentary upon the visual image, but neither is the visual image
employed only as an accentuation or illustration of the music. Consider, by way of contrast, the visual images that accompany the
performance of music in a conventional Hollywood treatment of a
composer or musician's life. In the Straubs' Bach film neither sound
nor visual image dominates; neither is dependent on the other.
Rather, film—all film, not just *Chronicle*—must be "a complex of
image and sound, and not an illustration of one by the other" (G, 3).

The Straubs' insistence on the equality of the soundtrack has
resulted in the seemingly "empty" visuals that draw attention to the
soundtrack and has also resulted in an insistence upon soundtrack
integrity as represented by original sound. What is heard in a Straub
film is almost always what was heard at the time of filming. Live
synchronous sound has, of course, an immediacy that cannot be
achieved by postproduction dubbing; even the most painstaking
dubbing betrays itself with unavoidable mismatchings of sound and
image. Direct sound, on the other hand, is seldom as clean as dubbed
sound; unexpected noises may intrude upon the planned sound,
sometimes with jarring effect. The Straubs, however, see such noises
as a merit, as an event that may enrich the film. Direct sound, Straub
says, allows a film "to have surprises. To have surprises and to
discover a reality. To experiment with combinations that are a great
deal richer than one might be able to find oneself, with one's petty
intentions" (CC, 53).

Straub denies any intention of using extraneous noise as a constant
reminder that a movie is, after all, a movie. This he considers to be a
foolish overintellectualization of the film. "But if it is there and comes
in by itself, then one shouldn't hide it" (C, 27). Uncalculated sound
can add "sense" (not, Straub insists, "signification") to the interrela-
tionships of actor and text, of sound and image, of fiction and documentary, upon which the film is constructed. During the making of
Othon in Rome "between the lines 'Neither liberty nor servitude'
and 'She wants a master' there's this motor-bike that goes by—
vroom-vroom. We didn't use many types of noises in the film, but we
kept that one. . . . The sound of the bike is a sort of comment, a
raspberry at the words being spoken" (E, 31).

Such intrusions of the external real world into the constructed world of the film are merely a distracting annoyance to those who would uphold the conventional view of the film frame as a hermetic universe. Ultimately for Straub and Huillet, on the other hand, such noises are less intrusions than additions to the truth of the film. The duty of the filmmaker is not to conceal the greater world beyond the frame of the film but to reveal it, "not to falsify reality, but to open the eyes and the ears . . . with reality. . . . And also you're not fooling people who see the film, because if there is someone who is speaking in the wind, with the noises, and has difficulty speaking, that's heard, and that's seen. Giving the opposite impression is a lie. If a film doesn't open the eyes and the ears of people, of what good is it?" (CC, 53).

Implicit in the Straubs' dedication to utter honesty in art is a related dedication to political honesty. What Jean-Marie Straub said of Bach—"there is no division between politics and life or art and politics"—is equally evident in the Straubs' own work and in their motivations. Aesthetic honesty leads to viewer awareness, which leads to political change. For the most part politics is present only implicitly in the Straub's statement that *Chronicle of Anna Magdalena Bach* was dedicated to the Vietcong or the explicit written dedication of *Moses and Aron* "for Holger Meins"—a friend of the Straubs, a photographer and anarchist who died in a West German prison after a prolonged hunger strike—a dedication that West German television deleted before broadcasting the film. Despite such gestures, the Straubs make neither political documentaries nor do they construct fictions with specifically political significance. While their films always have, at least implicitly, political content and intent, the Straubs nevertheless do not usually make films about specific contemporary political issues. They see themselves as social, and therefore political, outsiders who "don't have the right to speak in the name of the working class or the peasant class" (HKS, 208). With their customary forthrightness the Straubs acknowledge their own privileged status as educated artists; thus preexistent art by other artists—Böll, Brecht, Schoenberg, Mallarmé, Fortini, Pavese—seems the most appropriate basis for their meditation upon society and its history. Even those films that deal with relatively contemporary issues—*Machorka-Muff* and the rearmament of West Germany or *Fortini/Cani* and the Arab-Israeli conflict—were made after the fact of the events that inspired them: *Machorka-Muff* five years after rearmament and *Fortini/Cani* ten years after the Six Day War. The real political issue in most Straub films is a meditation upon and contemplation of historical events; it is, in the last analysis, always a question of historical memory. The past must be remembered for the sake of the future.

The Straubs are leftist filmmakers, but even though they have referred to *History Lessons* as "an application of *Das Kapital* to the Roman world" (FK, 76) and have described *Chronicle of Anna Magdalena Bach* as a "Marxist" film, such statements seem to apply as much in an intellectual and aesthetic sense as politically. "I know that I have made a Marxist film, but I don't know if I am a Marxist. I don't know because there are so many ways of being Marxist. I've not read all of Marx. Marxism is a method, not an ideology" (CC, 56–57).

In any event it is surely aesthetic severity, not political extremism, that has cost the Straubs a wider audience. Straub and Huillet profess to want a mass audience and see television as the only way to reach such an audience. For the most part, however, their work is appreciated only by a relatively small group of intellectuals, artists, and fellow filmmakers most concerned with the aesthetic questions explored in their films. Clearly the films of Straub and Huillet remain unapproachable for many viewers who are unable or, more likely, unwilling to have their eyes and ears opened. Still what the Straubs aspire to and may someday achieve is an aesthetically pure and ethically honest mediation between important ideas and an audience willing to confront these ideas, "to make films which radically eliminate art, so that there is no equivocation. This may lose us some people, but it is essential to bring people face to face with the ideas in their naked state" (E, 31).

One may well conclude that the importance of Straub and Huillet for the development of West German film in the 1960s and 1970s lies less in the direct impact of their own films (what positive impact can a film have if viewers refuse to watch it?) than in an indirect impact through the films of other, relatively more popular filmmakers like Fassbinder. If nothing else, Straub and Huillet have caused their West German contemporaries to reconsider many conventional notions of content and form, have led them to reinspect the force and form of the visual image; the limits of the frame; the placement and movement of the camera; the significance of music, language, and soundtrack noise; the interdependence of visual image and soundtrack; and finally the interrelationship of economics and film art. If the films of Straub and Huillet are found to be unappealing, they are also in many respects irrefutable in their logic, their intelligence, and, above all, their integrity.

4

Volker Schlöndorff

Chronology

1939   Volker Schlöndorff born on March 31 in Wiesbaden.
1960   *Wen kümmert's* . . . [Who Cares . . .].
1966   *Der junge Törless* [Young Törless], 87 min.
1967   *Mord und Totschlag* [Murder and Manslaughter], 87 min.
        Ein unheimlicher Moment [An Eerie Moment], 13 min.
1969   *Michael Kohlhaas—Der Rebell* [Michael Kohlhaas, The Rebel], 100 min.
        Baal, 87 min.
1970   *Der plötzliche Reichtum der armen Leute von Kombach* [The Sudden Wealth of the Poor People of Kombach], 102 min.
1971   *Die Moral der Ruth Halbfass* [The Morality of Ruth Halbfass], 94 min.
1972   *Strohfeuer* [A Free Woman], 101 min.
1973   *Übernachtung in Tirol* [Overnight in the Tirol], 78 min.
1974   *Georginas Gründe* [Georgina's Reasons], 65 min.
1975   *Die verlorene Ehre der Katharina Blum* [The Lost Honor of Katharina Blum], codirected with Margarethe von Trotta, 106 min.
1976   *Der Fangschuss* [Coup de Grâce], 95 min.
1977   *Nur zum Spass—nur zum Spiel. Kaleidoskop Valeska Gert* [Just for Fun, Just as a Game. Kaleidoscope Valeska Gert], 60 min.
1978   *Deutschland in Herbst* [Germany in Autumn], codirected, 124 min.

Volker Schlöndorff. Courtesy of New Yorker Films

1979   *Die Blechtrommel* [The Tin Drum], 145 min.
1981   *Die Fälschung* [Circle of Deceit], 110 min.

*The ideal would be for the viewer to have in seeing a film the same
pleasure, the same joy that I have in making a film.*

THE WEST GERMAN FILM has frequently been criticized, even
by its admirers, for its excessiveness: Kluge and Straub, they say, are
too cerebral, Wenders too cold, Herzog too mystical, Fassbinder too
mannered, Syberberg too pretentious. West German film, it is said,
is generally too egocentric and humorless, too unconcerned with the
pleasure of its audience. Despite enduring acclaim for the New
German Cinema from the New York art-film avant-garde and despite
Hollywood's recent willingness to finance films by Fassbinder, Herzog, and Wenders, only Schlöndorff has received an Oscar, the
ultimate symbol of Hollywood esteem.

Schlöndorff has proven himself to be a director not merely willing
but eager to bridge the gap between art and commercial success.
Although elitist film critics obviously prefer the imaginative visions of
Herzog or the lucid intellectualism of Fassbinder, Schlöndorff's films
are a deliberate attempt to reconcile the contrasting demands of
aesthetic quality and commercial appeal. Schlöndorff is, in the best
sense of the phrase, a smart director: clever in his selection of
material, skillful in his adapting and filming of his material, and truly
ingenious in his ability to costume his political commitment in commercially acceptable attire. Schlöndorff's contributions to the New
German Cinema have been an unflagging political engagement and a
long-lasting involvement with the legislation and administration of
government film subsidization. Furthermore, to a cinema without a
tradition and without skilled technicians, Schlöndorff has brought
skill, sophistication, polish, and pragmatism.

While gaining recognition from the Hollywood Establishment,
Schlöndorff and his films have often been received on the East Coast
more with politeness than with enthusiasm. Schlöndorff's films have
seemed to hold few eye-opening surprises of style and form. Schlöndorff presents a consummate craftsmanship in his films and a technical sophistication that consistently pleases and satisfies but seldom
shocks us with unexpected and illuminating images. That Schlöndorff's best-known films have been adaptations from literature surely
has also contributed to the recurrent perception of him as a skilled but
unexciting filmmaker.

Adaptive work does not always preclude critical esteem. Wenders and Straub/Huillet have also worked from literary sources but, in so doing, have stamped their material with their own personalities and have thus so altered the material that it becomes indisputably their own. Huillet and Straub's films of stories by Heinrich Böll—*Machorka–Muff* from Böll's "Bonn Diary" or *Not Reconciled* from *Billiards at 9:30*—bear little resemblance to the original stories. Schlöndorff's *Lost Honor of Katharina Blum*, on the other hand, not only retains the title of Böll's short novel but also attempts to reestablish on film Böll's feelings for his protagonist and his criticism of contemporary West Germany. Alterations do occur in Schlöndorff's adaptations, to be sure, and these alterations have come to dominate much of the critical dialogue concerning Schlöndorff's work, while the sophistication and skill of Schlöndorff's retellings have sometimes gone unnoticed and too frequently unappreciated.

Many of Schlöndorff's adaptive changes are really no more than attempts to simplify (in the positive sense) his material, to untangle and distill otherwise unfilmable narratives. Where the other West German directors have given us exuberant new visions and often clumsy ardor, Schlöndorff has given us a different sort of creative genius, a technical creativity and fidelity to his sources. The best of his films are not just "dramatized literature" (to use Schlöndorff's phrase for what he does *not* want his films to be) but rather finely reconstructed and intelligent adaptations. His films are intended as renewals of their literary sources, intended to evoke responses such as Günter Grass's after seeing *The Tin Drum*: "I forgot the book and saw a film" (T, 121).[1]

Schlöndorff, born in 1939, was not one of the signers of the Oberhausen manifesto, but he began making films in the immediate wake of the earliest Oberhausen group. Educated at boarding schools, Schlöndorff moved to France in his teens and completed high school and his university education in economics in Paris. For a year he attended film school in Paris and then, between 1960 and 1965, he worked as an assistant director on fourteen films in the flourishing French film industry. He assisted, among others, Louis Malle on *Zazie in the Metro*, *Private Life*, *The Fire Within*, and *Viva Maria*, Alain Resnais on *Last Year at Marienbad*, and Jean-Pierre Melville on *Léon Morin, Priest* and *The Informer*.[2] In 1965 Schlöndorff returned to Germany, to Munich, and immediately began making films on his own as a new but experienced director. Schlöndorff's five years as an assistant in France provided him with extensive technical experience that other West German directors in the early 1960s were trying to gain on their own by making short films. His apprenticeship was, however, a mixed blessing: "One loses one's innocence, one's openness regarding the camera, the actors, the script and runs the danger of adopting habits, even the habits of others" (FK, 307).

Schlöndorff's experience with filmmaking in France does seem to have left a mark on his films, in their feeling of control and visual flair, yet Schlöndorff himself denies a direct or conscious influence of Malle, Resnais, or Melville, preferring instead to credit a more general influence of films *seen* in Paris: "Before I even went into a film studio, I had seen 600 or 700 films within two years" (FK, 307). Of these films Schlöndorff credits those of Renoir as an influence on his own formulation of what film should be and should do. Citing Renoir, Schlöndorff speaks of making films that tell "stories and at the same time tell a lot about society" (FC, 28). Like Renoir, Schlöndorff strives for film stories that appeal emotionally as well as intellectually and that derive their emotional appeal from the creation of credible film characters. Also like Renoir, Schlöndorff believes his characters and ultimately his films are credible only to the extent that they retain and reveal a uniquely national character. He cites an exemplary statement made by Renoir in 1938: "I know that I am French and that I must work in this direction, that is, nationally. I also know that in this way and only in this way I can touch and address people of other nations" (FM, 73).

Schlöndorff's insistence on the importance of a national identity is, on the one hand, unexpected, since his film style comes closest, among the major West German filmmakers, to being nonidiosyncratic and internationally accessible. On the other hand, like Renoir, Schlöndorff paradoxically believes that films can achieve international appeal only when they are firmly rooted in very concrete and national experiences: "A film should be as concrete as possible. That is to say that a German film, precisely so that it will be internationally competitive, must be especially German" (FM, 84). In other words, a film that strives to be international must of necessity become so unspecific, so abstract, that it loses contact with any potential audience. Since his own unsuccessful experience with making an "international" film—*Michael Kohlhaas* in 1969—Schlöndorff has deliberately avoided making films with international "stars" and intentionally denationalized narratives. Schlöndorff is convinced that by trying to appeal to everyone, such films ultimately touch no one. In describing his choice of literary sources, Schlöndorff has written, "it is always literature as information about German history" (T, 48).

While one might expect his decade in France to have given him a less specifically German consciousness, Schlöndorff has described this period as precisely the catalyst for his own awareness of himself as a German. In his diary of the filming of *The Tin Drum* he writes, "At that time, when the book appeared, in 1959 . . . I was not interested in German literature. Only during my long stay in France, being addressed again and again with 'you, as a German,' did I become really aware of my Germanness" (T, 37). Schlöndorff thus came to regard himself as conspicuously German, and in 1979 he wrote, "since *Törless* [his first film] I have made consciously German films" (T, 37). Despite his insistent identification of himself and of his films as German, Schlöndorff is never chauvinistic. On the contrary, he pragmatically chooses national themes and characters for his films because these are the themes and characters with which he himself can best identify and, therefore, best communicate to his audience. What Schlöndorff perceives in his narratives is a universal applicability. He has described his most basic theme in this way: "Someone rebels, and fails. His strength and beauty lie in refusing, this is the moment in which he comes alive, and this is more important than the failure" (T, 48).

Lured back to West Germany by the promise of the new government subsidies for novice filmmakers, Schlöndorff made his first film, *Young Törless*, in 1965. While the funds available were insufficient (a government award covered only one-quarter of the costs of *Young Törless*), nevertheless Schlöndorff moved to Munich and began work on the film. Based on an early novel by Robert Musil, *Young Törless* depicts life in a boys' military school in pre-World War I Germany. One student steals, is caught by another, and becomes ensnared in an endless circle of humiliation, degradation, and torture by his discoverer. Törless impassively observes the development and culmination of this enslavement. Neither victim nor victimizer, Törless must acknowledge his capacity to be either; he also must acknowledge the Pilate-like culpability of his nonintervention. Like the protagonist of many another "school" story—Hesse's *Beneath the Wheel* and Leontine Sagan's protofeminist film *Mädchen in Uniform* are two famous examples—Törless is a representative figure caught in a repressively autocratic environment. At a turning point between childhood and maturity, Törless must confront, in his peers, in the world, and within himself, the human potential for evil. He must confront Everyman's capacity to be both Torturer and the Tortured.

Like many of Schlöndorff's protagonists Törless suffers from the irreconcilability of high-minded idealism with a harsher reality.

Brought up in a world of maternal warmth and goodness, Törless encounters at school a world of horrifying yet fascinating reality in which elegance goes hand-in-hand with violence, eroticism with cruelty, and cruelty with inexplicable enjoyment. Cruelty is clearly inherent in the school, a microcosm of one type of human society in which education ultimately leads only to irrational hypotheses. As the mathematics teacher tells Törless in a crucial scene, "Everything is feeling—even mathematics." The basis of human existence is no more explicable than the irrational numbers Törless encounters. How does one comprehend the square root of minus one?

The school is a world of terrifying uncertainties that replace the certain comforts of childhood, and Törless must bear the failure of reason and logic to overcome his fear that "sometimes terrifying chasms seem about to open up." What Törless, the observer, eventually experiences as the loss of innocence is the dismaying acknowledgment of his own similarity to victim as well as victimizer. His final realization is that "very normal people can commit atrocities. . . . It just happens. That's what we have to guard against! That's what I've learned."

The viewer is tempted to see *Törless* as a specifically German parable about Nazism, anti-Semitism, and German guilt. What Schlöndorff perceived in the story was, however, both more personal and more universal. Schlöndorff's selection of Musil's story was motivated by "the exemplary nature of the plot; its incarnation in so 'German' a frame as a military school, which permitted a certain connection with German film traditions—Stroheim and Lang . . . my very vital memories and experiences from my own boarding school days; an interest in power relationships, crisis situations, 'unnatural' behavior" (FK, 309). Schlöndorff views *Törless* not as a historical analysis of the pre-World War I era, nor as a history of the recent German past; it is rather "an attempt to represent an 'atmosphere' and ways of behavior 'in themselves'—without abstractions" (FK, 309).

More than once Schlöndorff has spoken of similarities between the German films of the 1920s and early 1930s and his own works, not only his first films but also his later ones. He has referred to the style of *The Tin Drum* for example, as "very realistic representations in strangely stylized sets" (T, 116). As Schlöndorff's earlier mention of Lang and Stroheim implies, *Törless* exhibits an even greater similarity to early films, especially to Lang's *M*. The face of the torturer Reiting, like Beckert the child-killer in *M*, is first seen in a mirror. The scenes of torment and humiliation in a dormitory attic are very reminiscent, in

Young Törless. *Courtesy of New Yorker Films.*

lighting and in camera angles as well as in theme, of Lang's treatment of Beckert trapped in an office-building storage locker. Like *M*, *Törless* includes a mock trial scene, and the very ambiguity or duality of victim and victimizers evokes the helpless monster played by Peter Lorre in *M*. More generally the black-and-white starkness of *Törless* is an unmistakable homage to the effective chiaroscuro lighting of many early German films.

While *Törless* looks, at times, like a rediscovered film from the Weimar Republic, Schlöndorff's avowed intention was simply to make a film that looked good. In a frank statement made during the filming of *Törless*, Schlöndorff in effect disassociated himself from the more aesthetically minded practitioners of the New German film in the 1960s: "I don't want to make art but rather a good film. It can look as if it were filmed in 1930 but it should look good" (KR).

The austerely beautiful black-and-white images of Schlöndorff's *Törless* create an effect of carefully constructed realism, rather than expressionist exaggeration. This gripping realism, although deliberately undermined at times by Hans-Werner Henze's haunting electronic musical score, is reinforced by Schlöndorff's use of relatively untrained young actors playing the film's main characters. Schlöndorff's narrative method in *Törless* is representative of most of his films in its establishment of an interplay of realism and contrivance. Although Schlöndorff's films frequently look realistic or naturalistic, closer inspection reveals a studied, almost classical simplifying or streamlining of reality. Questioned about the "literariness" of the dialogue spoken by the boys in *Törless*, for example, Schlöndorff responded: "A literary dialogue is, in contrast to that spoken in reality, on the one hand more compact, more spare, and more precise, and, on the other hand, clearer and more considered. It expresses what is usually only felt or thought. . . . Thus I accept the reproach of being 'unnatural' and strive for clarity of expression" (FK, 309).

Clarity is not the only reward to be gained from placing literary dialogues in a realistic setting. There also arises, so Schlöndorff says, a constructive and enlightening dialectic of "real" situations and "unreal" words. "By the dialectic that unfolds between word and reality is revealed the sense or nonsense of that which is said" (FK, 309). Such a theoretical formulation of the processes involved in making— and viewing—his films is reminiscent of Kluge or the Straubs, and therefore in a way misleading. Schlöndorff's films are neither so complex and intellectual as those of Kluge, nor are they so austere and unemotional as those of Straub/Huillet. The stylistic clarity and structural simplicity for which Schlöndorff strives detach us only infrequently from his stories and his characters. Detachment can provide understanding, but only when an emotional sympathy is firmly established. "Cinema, after all, appeals through the emotions as much as any intellectual understanding. To share emotions we need to see people and believe them. This is the lesson to be taken from Renoir" (FC, 34).

The stylized beauty of *Young Törless* made it one of the early successes of the New German Cinema. Along with Ulrich Schamoni's *It* and Kluge's *Yesterday Girl*, *Young Törless* was shown at several international film festivals in 1966 and was positively received, if not a resounding success. Schlöndorff was given a federal German film prize for direction, and his initial success with *Törless* helped him finance his second film, a thriller titled *Murder and Manslaughter* (1967), and his third, *Michael Kohlhaas – The Rebel* (1969).

Schlöndorff was one of the first West German directors to investigate and to exploit the possibilities of international cofinancing. *Young Törless* had been cofinanced by a French production company and initiated what for a very short time seemed to be a potential "French-German new wave." *Murder and Manslaughter*, although a box-office failure, made a profit for its producers through astute sale of foreign distribution rights.[3] When Schlöndorff looked for financing for *Michael Kohlhaas* in 1968, he was therefore prepared to accept foreign investment in what he had originally conceived as another "German film." Schlöndorff found American production money for his film but, in return, was persuaded to make of *Michael Kohlhaas* an international film, with an English scriptwriter (Edward Bond), English and French leading actors (David Warner and Anna Karina), and location shooting in Czechoslovakia. As Schlöndorff admits, the film became an international disaster: "Since I was the only one who, to some extent, spoke all these languages, I functioned primarily as a translator. My own work and concentration on the film became impossible" (FM, 84).

Resolved never to make a film again under such conditions, Schlöndorff returned to "German films" and became more cautious in matters of financing. He became, in the early 1970s, one of the major beneficiaries of the newly developing possibilities of cofinancing through German television, and his next four films, *Baal* (1969), *The Sudden Wealth of the Poor People of Kombach* (1970), *The Morality of Ruth Halbfass* (1971), and *A Free Woman* (1972) were coproductions between Schlöndorff's Hallelujah Films and the Hessian television network, Hessischer Rundfunk. Schlöndorff of course perceived the limitations of working on films for television: "Television is prepared to pay for a certain amount of quality, but it is not prepared to honor quality exceeding the usual television norm. This usual television norm lies somewhere beneath what one could call an international cinema norm" (FM, 80). Schlöndorff, however, like Fassbinder, also sees television as a means to a new mass audience, a way to retrieve the audience lost to filmmakers in the 1950s. To have a film shown on television during early evening hours means "that we are no longer pushed into the art-ghetto where we were before, where viewers are numbered in the hundred thousands. Rather the same people who would refuse to go to the cinema to see our films very probably do see them on television" (FM, 79).

Two important Schlöndorff films of this period—*The Sudden Wealth of the Poor People of Kombach* and *A Free Woman*—are superficially quite dissimilar. *A Free Woman* takes place in modern urban West Germany, while *Sudden Wealth* is set in the 1820s in rural Hesse. Despite this chronological diversity, each film charts the course of a rebellion and its failure: in *A Free Woman* there is an attempt at independence and emancipation by a woman trapped in an autocratic marriage; in *Sudden Wealth* an attempt at wealth and freedom by a group of peasants trapped in an autocratic society. Schlöndorff has said, "among my films, those, strangely enough, are the two that have the most resemblance. Both keep with narrative cinema and at the same time give a lot of information from outside— almost like documentary—combining both information and emotion in each film" (FC, 30).

Despite Schlöndorff's accurate assessment of resemblances between the two films, there are also notable differences, especially in the degree of emotional attachment between viewer and character. In *A Free Woman* we identify and sympathize with the main character. In *Sudden Wealth*, on the other hand, structural and stylistic detachment from the characters precludes emotional involvement by the viewer. *Sudden Wealth*, however, compensates for its lack of emotion with the ironic, objective clarity of its point-of-view.

Sudden Wealth, based on a true story, depicts seven peasants' clumsy robbery of a tax collector's coach in 1822. As clumsy in enjoying their new wealth as they were in obtaining it, the peasants quickly give themselves away, are caught, convicted, and executed. Set in a potentially romantic rural area, the film avoids all sentimentality through the use of stark black-and-white photography, and the camera observes the action and the characters with a stationary, mid-shot objectivity. The film's unrelenting distance from its characters is emphasized structurally by a voice-over reading of a contemporary chronicle. The chronicle is a subjective focus of the peasants' actions and their executions, but its subjectivity is made evident only by off-hand comments of the narrative voice such as "the court record notes contentedly. . . ."

Despite the detachment rigidly enforced by its style and structure, *Sudden Wealth* is ultimately effective because of the utter consistency and comprehensiveness of its viewpoint. The central narrative point—that the peasants were totally, utterly trapped by their society—needs no comment; objective illustration of their enslavement suffices. The peasants' banditry is unmistakably a rebellion, perhaps the only rebellion their ignorance could conceive, but it is doomed to fail. Freed by law from serfdom and bondage to the land, the peasants are still bound by ties that go deeper than any edict. They are trapped by ignorance, by superstition, and by all the institutions with which they have contact: by conscription into the military, by the social upper classes, and by the Christian religion that teaches

The Sudden Wealth of the Poor People of Kombach. *Courtesy of New Yorker Films*

them to serve and to stay in their place. Schlöndorff's film is most effective in its observation of the small daily abuses and indoctrinations that weave an inescapable web of servitude: a child at a wedding recites a poem by Gellert, "Contentment with One's Condition"; and over an image of the peasants plowing a rocky field are heard the voices of a teacher and his students memorizing a medieval verse extolling the acceptance of one's lot.

One of the story's ironies is its assertion that poverty is itself the peasant's strongest oppressor. The peasants quickly give themselves away by conspicuously squandering their new wealth. The only robber who benefits from his stolen wealth is the ambiguous and stereotyped figure of a Jew, who, unbound by the cultural and social snares that trap the others, is able to flee to a new life in America. The film's cruelest irony, perhaps, is the narrator's assertion that each of the robbers, save one, repents of his crime before his execution, for the sake of salvation.

Sudden Wealth and Schlöndorff's other films from the early 1970s mark a significant change in his career. He began a collaboration, variously manifested, with his wife, Margarethe von Trotta, who shares responsibility for most of the Schlöndorff films in the first half of the 1970s. She first appeared as an actress in *Baal*, then as actress and cowriter for *Sudden Wealth*, as cowriter and lead actress for the semiautobiographical *A Free Woman*, and finally, in 1975, as cowriter and codirector for *The Lost Honor of Katharina Blum*.

The Lost Honor of Katharina Blum became one of the landmark successes of the New German Cinema, proving that a politically conscious film could also please an audience. Like Trotta's own later film, *The Second Awakening of Christa Klages*, *Katharina Blum* is, despite its female protagonist, not a film only about women. Trotta has said, "This is not particularly a film about women's problems; it's a portrait of a particular group in Germany and, more specifically, of a person who was defiled by that group."[4]

The group to which Trotta refers is the very popular and influential right-wing press of West Germany. Katharina Blum is a young and idealistic woman who, by falling in love and spending one night with an army deserter, becomes enmeshed in a nightmarish manhunt by the police and press for all "terrorists" and "terrorist sympathizers." With her reputation and consequently her life destroyed by the attacks of the press, Katharina Blum ultimately attempts to redeem herself and her "lost honor" by shooting the journalist most responsible for her public vilification.

The omnipresent daily illustrated tabloids of the reactionary Springer Press were the immediate target of both Heinrich Böll's short novel and the Schlöndorff/Trotta film of the novel. (Not coincidentally, both Böll and Schlöndorff had been labelled "terrorist sympathizers" by the Springer newspapers.) The *Zeitung* of the film is a very thin disguise for Springer's *Bild Zeitung*, the most sensationalistic and popular West German newspaper. The *Bild Zeitung* and its West Berlin equivalent, the *Berliner Zeitung*, have a combined circulation of over 4.5 million in a country with a population of approximately 60 million. Victimized by the *Zeitung's* scandal-mongering, the film's protagonist is told not to worry because "no one reads those newspapers." "Everyone I know does," she replies.

The right-wing press is only the most immediate target of *Lost Honor*, however. Clearly the yellow journalism of the *Zeitung* is but one manifestation of a more universal social threat in which are implicated the police and parts of the West German government. Böll was concerned not only with the origins of Katharina Blum's act of violence but also with the causes of most social violence. Böll's story bears the subtitle, "How Violence Arises and Where It Can Lead," and Katharina Blum's act of violence is seen as only one instance of a more general social rage against a political and economic system that mouths democratic principles but frequently and repressively betrays those principles.

The Lost Honor of Katharina Blum was a crucial film, not only for Schlöndorff's career but also for West German filmmaking generally. In 1975 the New German Cinema had reached a turning point at which the New Films were deemed an aesthetic success but a popular failure. West German movie houses continued to close and filmmakers like Fassbinder and Herzog were acclaimed abroad but ignored at home. Schlöndorff and Trotta's *Katharina Blum* most shrewdly and skillfully managed to combine quality and popularity.

The Lost Honor of Katharina Blum also awakened old controversies over *how* a literary work should be filmed. In one respect at least, there is a discernible change in Schlöndorff's attitudes toward a literary source in the decade between *Törless* and *Katharina Blum*. In a 1966 interview Schlöndorff had said of *Törless*: "I never had a 'faithful literary filming' in mind. For all I care, authors can turn over in their graves" (FK, 309). In 1975, faced with a living author who had won the Nobel Prize, Schlöndorff said, "Böll and his people stand right at the center of our film; we are not making an *auteur*–film. The important thing is to tell the author's story the way he intended it: the author must be respected" (FR).

Böll *has* been respected. As in *Törless* and later in *The Tin Drum*, the complex, interwoven narrative structure of *Katharina Blum* was simplified for the film with Böll's blessing. "Together with Böll, Margarethe von Trotta and I decided upon a straightforward, direct narrative" (FR). Schlöndorff makes no apologies for his alterations either of narrative method or of the material itself: "A book is one thing, a film another. With the transition into another medium comes a change in the material. . . . For me film is a realistic medium. . . . To film realistically means to make dense, to abstract, and even to manufacture a certain artificiality—a film reality" (FR).

The most essential change in the transition from story to film is surely the alteration in the protagonist. In Böll's story Katharina Blum is a sympathetic but somewhat enigmatic figure whose motives lie buried within a thicket of subjective flashbacks, anecdotal hypotheses by other characters, newspaper reports, and official police statements. In the film, in the "realistic medium," very little is told at second-hand, and an intense sympathy for Katharina Blum (powerfully portrayed by Angela Winkler—a Böll suggestion) arises in the viewer. Böll's story was a political statement; Schlöndorff and Trotta's film is a less political examination of a very credible social victim. The film's foremost concern is its protagonist: "Someone about whom we know nothing becomes involved in an occurrence that could happen to any of us" (FR).

The film style of *Katharina Blum* is subservient to narrative development. Through camera angle and distance, through shifting points of view, through the use of an alienating electronic musical score, and through editing, Schlöndorff and Trotta deftly move the viewer back and forth between sympathy and objectivity. Black-and-white footage interrupts the color narrative at times, reproducing the point of view of the fugitive deserter's police observers and evoking in the viewers the feelings of justified paranoia experienced by Katharina Blum. Jump-cuts move the viewer from empathetic close-ups to more objective medium shots. *Katharina Blum,* having elucidated the internal psychological development leading to Katharina's murder of the reporter, ends with a pessimistic "documentary" of the reporter's funeral. An elaborately staged media event, the funeral makes clear that one reporter may die, but the *Zeitung* lives on forever.

The filmmaking assurance evident in *Lost Honor of Katharina Blum* was succeeded a year later by *Coup de Grâce,* a confused and complex psychological study of a group of Baltic Germans caught up in 1919 in the fighting between the Red and White Russian armies. Similar in intention to *A Free Woman, Coup de Grâce* attempts to explore the emotional and political development of one woman from a simple girl to an adult who, having joined the Red revolutionaries, demands her execution at the hand of a German soldier she had once loved. The complexities of the narrative offer intriguing possibilities, but complexity turns to confusion despite the richly evoked atmosphere captured by Schlöndorff. Returning to a more traditional form of collaboration, Schlöndorff cowrote the script with Margarethe von Trotta, who also played the main role.

In 1977 Schlöndorff again collaborated with Heinrich Böll in a segment of *Germany in Autumn,* a witty satire of a television commission considering whether to broadcast a production of *Antigone.* And in 1978 Schlöndorff began work on *The Tin Drum,* both his own greatest success and surely the most acclaimed New German film yet produced.

Shortly after *The Tin Drum* was released, Schlöndorff published a diary he had written during the preparation, filming, and editing of *The Tin Drum* between April 1977 and February 1979. Working notebooks have also been published by Herzog and Fassbinder, but these books were written by outside observers. Alan Greenberg enthusiastically testifies to Herzog's messianic approach to filmmaking in *Heart of Glass*, and Hans G. Pflaum more objectively reports Fassbinder's ensemble filmmaking in *Chinese Roulette* and *Satan's Brew*. Schlöndorff's diary, on the other hand, records his own thoughts regarding the difficulties and rewards of assembling the materials for and filming one of the most expensive, most complex, and most skeptically awaited West German films.

Schlöndorff's *The Tin Drum. Diary of a Filming* richly reveals his general working methods and his methods of literary adaptation. *The Tin Drum*, first published in 1959, is the most famous postwar German novel, and its adaptation as a film exaggerated the usual benefits and perils of literary filmings. Production financing was eased by the novel's fame but complicated by its historical setting and structural complexity, which necessitated an extraordinary production budget by German standards. The diary describes the intricacies of combining funds from government and private, German and foreign sources and the pressures brought to bear on the maker of such a film. A French producer describes as "artistic masochism" (T, 41) Schlöndorff's intention to film *The Tin Drum* in German with German actors. Foreign money was needed, but foreign investors requested the type of casting that Schlöndorff held responsible for the failure of *Michael Kohlhaas* a decade earlier. "Minimum costs of the film, as projected, DM6–7 million. A German film of this scale seems neither financeable nor profitable. Of the American distributors United Artists is showing interest. Discussions in Paris and London: Can *The Tin Drum*, with a suitable cast, be made into an international film? Roman Polanski or Dustin Hoffman as Oskar [the undersized child-protagonist] perhaps, Isabelle Adjani and Keith Carradine as his parents? We soon agree: the star of the film is the story. The more authentically we present it, the more exciting the film will be" (T, 46).

Diary of a Filming takes up the difficult problem of casting the central role of Oskar: should he be played by a dwarf? a child? The solution was found in an actor's son whose physical growth has been stunted, a twelve-year-old who, placed among other children, "is the smallest but gives the effect of being the oldest" (T, 43). Schlöndorff frankly records his reactions to his cast: the child actor, David Bennent, is extraordinarily affecting; Angela Winkler and Mario Adorf as

Oskar's parents are very professional; however, another actor playing the mother's lover is continually troubling and ultimately inadequate for his role.

The diary reveals Schlöndorff's difficulty in adapting the work of Günter Grass, a novelist as famous as and perhaps more formidable than Heinrich Böll. Schlöndorff found Grass's novel to be more intimidating than Böll's because its more personal nature made it harder for Schlöndorff to assimilate. Schlöndorff considers *The Tin Drum* to be an exaggerated autobiography, while Böll's stories were less intensely personal and thus easier to adapt.

Schlöndorff's account is most intriguing in its description of his mental process in adapting a literary work, in his search for an "autonomous narrative structure" (T, 50). As always in Schlöndorff's films, this autonomous structure is created by simplifying the literary narrative. Schlöndorff, with Grass's consent, eliminated the novel's framework and flashback narrative, restructuring the story chronologically. More importantly (he felt), he used the central figure of Oskar as the key to his—and the viewer's—emotional connection to the film's narrative. Schlöndorff concluded that Oskar had to be played by a child, not a dwarf, and had to be presented as an empathetic focus for the film narrative: "My films are only good when I can identify with one person in such a way that I am given a foothold" (T, 39). A dwarf might be perceived as a grotesquerie, but everyone can identify with a child: "Everyone has a childhood that he misses and would gladly have extended, at least in retrospect—and one can identify with a child" (T, 24). Schlöndorff also perceived in Oskar a figure closely related to his other film protagonists, all victims of failed rebellions. Oskar's rebellion is his refusal to grow physiologically, and his glass-shattering voice is the vehicle of his protest.

As he had done in *Lost Honor of Katharina Blum* Schlöndorff employed in *The Tin Drum* an alternately subjective and objective point of view: "It will not always work to stay in Oskar's skin. Just as he speaks sometimes in the first person and sometimes, alienatingly child-like, in the third, so must the film narrative at times be quite subjective and at times show his shock from outside" (T, 44). Schlöndorff's emphasis upon Oskar as the film's narrative focus also influences other decisions and other narrative functions; for example, "the film will be more a description of the relationship of a child to the adults than a milieu-description of the petit bourgeoisie of the 1930s with whom I had nothing to do directly" (T, 94).

Finally the diary reveals what Schlöndorff considers to be the "art" or "creativity" in his work. Decisions regarding casting, narrative structure, or narrative point of view require intelligence, but the truly creative act occurs only at the time of filming, the least perceptible and describable element of the filmmaking process. In a surprising reflection of the spontaneity that has characterized so much of new German filmmaking, Schlöndorff wrote:

Each image should come out of the moment. Shoot what our eyes see rather than re-create what we have thought out. About this really creative aspect of our work I think very seldom, and that's why it appears so seldom here in the diary. I hope it will be so much the more visible in the film. The same is true for the actors: I'm not only making a film with them, but also about them. Our work is always also documentary work. (T, 72)

Schlöndorff's diary is, as he himself realizes, ultimately less revealing of his creativity and work than the film itself: "The real diary is written not in this notebook but in the film" (T, 103). Nevertheless, the diary gives valuable insights not only into the why and how of Schlöndorff's film, *The Tin Drum*, but also, sometimes explicitly, more often implicitly, into his entire career as a director.

Schlöndorff's films are undeniably successful, both with film critics and with film audiences. Schlöndorff has managed an almost unique combining of political commitment and artistic quality within the most commercial, most expensive, and, therefore, most censorable of the arts. Still, Schlöndorff has not yet been accorded the critical respect granted to several other West German directors. No one has called *The Tin Drum* "the film of the century." There has not appeared, in German or in English, a career article or even a truly extensive career interview. Obviously the fact that Schlöndorff's greatest successes have been film adaptations of others' stories has left the impression that Schlöndorff is a smart, skillful, even subtle craftsman but not a true film artist. Schlöndorff's own words, usually modest in the extreme, provide the most convincing affirmation of his creativity:

What does direction in my case actually consist of? Listen, watch, radiate confidence, preserve continuity, hear out and incorporate suggestions, hold together what has once been put together through long selection and preparation: actors, scenes, locations. Little that is creative, really only ordering and preserving. No charismatic personality—but what would someone like that make of *The Tin Drum*? (T, 107)

5

Werner Herzog

Chronology

	Herz aus Glas [Heart of Glass], 94 min.
	La Soufrière, 31 min.
1977	*Stroszek*, 108 min.
1978	*Nosferatu—Phantom der Nacht* [Nosferatu, the Vampyre], 107 min.
	Woyzeck, 81 min.
1982	*Fitzcarraldo*

The real power of films lies in the fact that they operate with the reality of dreams.

IN HIS FILMS Werner Herzog attempts sometimes to create and sometimes to re-create secular mythologies of individual experience and universal mystery. In films such as *Signs of Life* (1967), *Aguirre, The Wrath of God* (1972), *Every Man for Himself and God Against All* (1974), *Stroszek* (1977), *Woyzeck* (1978), and *Nosferatu* (1978), Herzog examines individuals who, so to speak, "fall to earth," who are born full-grown into alien societies. And in films such as *Land of Silence and Darkness* (1971), *Even Dwarfs Started Small* (1970), *Heart of Glass* (1976), and, most especially, *Fata Morgana* (1970), Herzog moves beyond the individual to an almost surrealistic exploration of knowledge and existence and of the impossibility of objective perception.

Werner Herzog sees himself—and would have others see him—as a mystic, a visionary, a dreamer of new dreams, a teller of new truths, and above all a seeker of new images. Herzog deplores our lack of images capable of assimilating the demands of the present and the brutal realities of the past. He has made it his goal to create in his films a wealth of imagery adequate to contemporary human experience. As Herzog has said, more than once, "if we do not find adequate images and an adequate language for our civilization with which to express them, we will die out like the dinosaurs. It's as simple as that."[1] Herzog's films abound with Kafkaesque images that are paradoxically simple and complex, obvious and obscure, rational in form and mystical in meaning, particular and universal.

Herzog's work deals, as a rule, with individuals who are in some respect set apart from the human mainstream: dwarfs, the physically handicapped, athletes, musicians, social outcasts, and even a curiously sympathetic vampire. These isolated beings, by the fact of their separateness, experience life and reality in exceptional and unexpected ways, and Herzog transforms their experiences into intimations of realities and universes that transcend the ordinary and the normal. His stories of insurrectionist dwarfs, of the "wild child" Kaspar Hauser, of the Spanish conquistador Aguirre, and even of Walter Steiner, the Swiss ski-jumper in *The Great Ecstasy of the Sculptor Steiner* (1974), tell us as much or more about ourselves and our existence as they do about their unique main characters who remain mysterious and unrevealed.

For Werner Herzog the everyday world is an existence of restriction, mediocrity, overrationality, and banal evil, an existence so deadening that average "normal" human beings are not aware of their own embedded insensitivity, not even when this deadened existence is counterpointed by the presence of one of Herzog's truer, purer outsiders. Desensitized humanity remains cut off from its own finer "humanness," even when encountering a Kaspar, a Fini Straubinger, a Woyzeck, or a Stroszek. For Herzog's audience, however, this juxtaposition of society and outsider ironically provides illumination, a revelation of Herzog's quasi-mystical insights. The human societies of Herzog's films are usually marked by their inhumanity, yet Herzog discloses a rare and refined humanism in the close identification of the isolated social outsider, the filmmaker, and his sympathetic audience.

Herzog has repeatedly described himself as a late medieval personality, both in his sensibility and in his sense of film as a craft. In actuality—and this is probably most responsible for the fervor of Herzog's many admirers—Herzog seems to be truly a man of the 1970s and 1980s, a secular guru who points the way for his followers toward *true* experience, away from the spiritless, jaded nonexperience of most of humanity. In the films of Werner Herzog the reality of dreams supplants the deceptive reality of the everyday world.

Herzog's films are demonstrably and fashionably antiintellectual and antirational, and Herzog has also acknowledged that he "cannot bear psychological films at all; that's what I can't stand about Bergman" (HKS, 121). Herzog has said, "I am not a theoretical person. I know that I have the ability to articulate images that sit deeply inside us, that I can make them visible. It is an athletic endeavor, like life itself. . . . There is always a key image; everything emerges from that, physically, not by analysis" (FQ, 7–8). Herzog's work is also unselfconscious: "People become unbearable when they are too occupied with themselves" (HKS, 121).

For Herzog feeling is all. He believes in the confirming act, an unthinking or irrational action that Herzog "knows" has the power to alter reality. Nearly legendary already is the often repeated story of Herzog walking from Munich to Paris with a print of *Every Man For*

Isabelle Adjani and Klaus Kinski in Werner Herzog's Nosferatu, The Vampire. *Courtesy of The Museum of Modern Art/Film Stills Archive*

Himself and God Against All after hearing of the serious illness in Paris of Lotte Eisner, the film historian to whom this film is dedicated.[2] Herzog was convinced that he would find Eisner recovered upon his arrival in Paris, and so he did. Herzog also tells of being the goalie confronted by a penalty kicker in a soccer game: "I looked at the guy, and determined that somehow he would kick it into the right corner. . . . I said, 'Go right—go right—don't even look—go right.' I told myself, 'To the right!,' and he kicked—I flew to the left and there was the ball. . . . Sometimes, all I have in my mind is a flash that says, 'Explode.' And so I explode, with shadow-like figures all around" (HG, 13). Elsewhere Herzog has acknowledged that athletes, after music, have been the strongest influence on his films (I, 30).

Herzog takes a physical, nonanalytical approach to filmmaking. In a now-famous statement he noted that "Film is not the art of scholars but of illiterates. And film culture is not analysis, it is agitation of the mind. Movies come from the country fair and circus, not from art and academicism" (HG, 174). Herzog's films—or so he would have us believe—spring full-blown into existence as a set structure of images with a life of their own, as evocative pictures that arise prerationally, if not irrationally.

The production history of a Herzog film frequently rivals the film itself in exoticism and human interest. Here, too, Herzog adds to his own myth. He reports, for example, that his first films were made with a stolen camera; he describes his arrest by African authorities during the filming of *Fata Morgana;* he embellishes his description of an incident during the filming of *Aguirre, the Wrath of God* that actually may never have happened at all; for his documentary *La Soufrière,* he flies to an evacuated Caribbean island, which is threatened by the imminent eruption of a volcano, in order to interview a man who has refused to join the evacuation.

During the filming of *Nosferatu* Herzog found himself constantly at odds with the city fathers of Delft, Holland, where he shot much of the film. And during the shooting of his most recent project, *Fitzcarraldo,* Herzog was accused (quite mistakenly, he has assured the world) by Amnesty International of abusing Peruvian Indians. Whether each story is true in every detail is irrelevant; as Herzog has said, "I will gladly go to the edge of untruth in order to expose a more intensive form of truth" (H, 71).

As is also true of Fassbinder or Syberberg and to a lesser degree of Straub/Huillet, the films of Werner Herzog become inextricable from the personality, from the eccentricities and idiosyncracies of the filmmaker himself. Herzog has often asserted that filmmaking is more important to him than his personal life; perhaps one could say that Herzog's filmmaking *is* his personal life. Characteristically, a 1978 film biography of Herzog by Christian Weisenborn and Erwin Keusch has as its title *Was ich bin, sind meine Filme* [I Am My Films]. With Herzog auteurism is carried to its farthest extension, where the work of art and its creator become virtually indistinguishable.

In the messianic world of Werner Herzog rationality and logical planning are characteristic of the societies that stultify and dehumanize in the name of civilization, separating humanity from the dreams that bear power, purity, and spiritual healing. Accordingly, Herzog sees his films not as naturalistic recapturings of external reality but rather as evocations of the internal realm of universal dreams. "Actually none of my films shows reality, but rather the reality of dreams. . . . I believe the real power of films lies in the fact that they operate with the reality of dreams" (HKS, 116–17). Moreover, it is not solely his own dreams that Herzog would reveal to his audience but also the cosmic dreams of contemporary humanity. "My goal is always to find out more about man himself, and film is my means. According to its nature, film doesn't have so much to do with reality as it does with our collective dreams—it chronicles our state of mind" (HG, 23). Thus, we are not surprised to learn that the actors in *Heart of Glass* were hypnotized. Herzog: "It is a key film for me" (H, 77).

Just as dreams have a basis in reality, so too do Herzog's films relate to contemporary human existence. Even those films that have evoked and taken place in the past—*Aguirre, Every Man for Himself, Heart of Glass, Woyzeck*—are implicitly statements about the present. Likewise, even the most unique characters in his films interest Herzog and Herzog's audience not only by their uniqueness but also by their representativeness. We empathize with Kaspar Hauser or Bruno Stroszek because such figures confirm our own individuality and uniqueness and encourage us to distinguish ourselves from the conformity and insensitivity of "all those others." Even those characters who at first glance strike us with their dissimilarity to ourselves are, in Herzog's view, significant for their human representativeness. He would have us see the characters of *Even Dwarfs Started Small*, for example, as images of ourselves rather than as oddities.

Although seldom shown, *Even Dwarfs Started Small* is regarded by Herzog as one of his most important films. "*Even Dwarfs Started Small* is perhaps the best or the strongest, [the film] in which there is the most power of all my films" (H, 76). It is surely one of his most notorious films. It is an existential horror film, a recording of a chaotic insurrection of dwarfs in an anonymous institution on a barren volcanic island. Apparently random episodes compose the narration of revolutionary events to which Herzog subjects the viewer. The film skillfully evokes a gratingly pessimistic picture of a world gone mad, a stifling, claustrophobic environment with no possibility of escape: beyond the walls of the institution itself lies a forbidding landscape of barren lava beds, arid mountains, and cacti.

The creation of grotesque meaning or meaninglessness in *Even Dwarfs Started Small* is intensified by Herzog's manner of presentation, achieved by style as much as by narrative. Narrative continuity is frequently disrupted by wide-angle photography and by moments when the dwarfs look directly into the camera and disconcertingly acknowledge the filmmaking and film-viewing process. The audience is jarred by a continuous process of viewer identification (we cannot avoid seeing the dwarfs as representatively human) and alienation (we also cannot avoid seeing the dwarfs' physical freakishness and the grotesqueness of their actions).

Even Dwarfs Started Small is metaphoric and perhaps even allegorical. The viewer must perceive the dwarfs' world as a reflection of the "larger" human condition and is appalled and repelled by the irrationality and cruelty of that condition. Herzog's film of the dwarfs becomes a perturbing hall of mirrors reflecting a world of mortal funk from which rationality has been totally banished. From this world there is no exit nor any resolution. All that remains at film's end are a camel incessantly forced to kneel and rise, kneel and rise, and the high-pitched and maniacal laughter of a dwarf.

Even the most apparently aberrant figures, such as the dwarfs, the quasi-historical, megalomanic conquistador Aguirre, or Nosferatu in Herzog's remake of Murnau's classic vampire film, must be considered, according to Herzog, not only for what makes them different from other human beings but also for what makes them the same. Referring to a real, psychotic killer who recently terrorized New York City, Herzog said "he . . . has been called a mad *dog*. He is *not* a mad dog—he is a mad *human being*, perhaps only a step removed from the rest of us. One has to acknowledge him as a human being and to respect his dignity even in his madness. Otherwise, there is the danger that people may start to kill each other like mad dogs" (NYT, 30).

Even at its most esoteric, Herzog's work is intended as a revelation of human existence, of what he has called the "signs or symbols of life" (HG, 23). His humanistic intentions, however, are perhaps less captivating than the intensity and intriguing ambiguity of the images he selects for conveying them. Although Herzog derides structuralism as being nothing more than one, very limited, way of viewing a film (HKS, 117), the emphasis on signs, symbols, and new languages in his films lends itself to semiotic analysis. Herzog's early short film, *Last Words*, is especially compelling as an intriguingly enigmatic and "significant" work that Herzog describes as an almost preconscious construction: "It was really very boldly made and with blind assurance; I filmed it in three nights and edited it in one day" (H, 76).

Herzog has also said that *Last Words* "is my best film. Without this film *Fata Morgana* would not be thinkable; narrative forms and stylizations that I have worked with since would be unthinkable. This film is really like a breakthrough" (HKS, 118). It is a semidocumentary account of the solitary existence of an old man, a lyre player who refuses to speak but appears in the evenings to play and sing. Forcibly removed by his family from voluntary exile on an abandoned island once inhabited by lepers, the old man is another of Herzog's possibly insane yet spiritually beautiful protagonists. Herzog's emphasis, however, is not on the old man's history (which is referred to only obliquely) but on his present isolation within the society which refused to permit his self-chosen exile.

This conflict of individual and society is reflected by language. While the old man refuses to speak, others speak in repetitions: two Tweedledum-Tweedledee policemen say again and again "We rescued him. We brought him over." A man who tells a story of the footprint in stone by the last Turk to leave the leper's island repeats his story, word-for-word, three times. These repetitions, like the repetition of an airplane landing in *Fata Morgana*, tell us that we can trust little of what we see and even less of what we hear. The posed figures, words, and stories imply an underlying reality that is never revealed. In *Fata Morgana* we are left only with enigmas: we *hear* the words, ". . . and at noon in full sun human figures cast no shadows," as we *see* human figures that do cast shadows. Thus, at the end of *Last Words* the old man tells us, "I will not say anything, not even 'No.' And those are my last words."

Herzog has always dealt with visual and verbal expressions that at times threaten to overwhelm both character and action. In *Signs of Life* a German paratrooper named Stroszek is isolated during World War II on an arid and threateningly stark Greek island. Stroszek's increasingly disquieted response to his environment, dominated by incessant heat and light, forms the narrative base of this jarringly episodic film. Like a child, Stroszek encounters unsettling new realities: insects that live trapped within a toy; a man who claims to be a king of the gypsies; an autistic child who sings a strange song and then falls silent; a German soldier–pianist who tells Stroszek to listen for the cough of the composer in the piece being played; the hypnosis of a chicken;[3] a story of men on a submarine who drown because they are captivated by the sight of the sun.

The island ultimately drives Stroszek insane; the violence of the landscape forces him to respond with violence. Fighting fire with fire and light with light, Stroszek tries to fight the sun with fireworks and to ignite with rockets the village near the fortress where he has barricaded himself. As the voice-over commentary tells us, he wants "to make the earth move. Then would be seen what really lay beneath things. He wanted to bring that finally to light." With Stroszek's revolt, Herzog's camera moves back and away from Stroszek as an individual figure, photographing him only from afar, concentrating instead on the visible signs of his rebellion. "He gives signals or signs—the same kind of signs of violence and despair that he himself had received all the time" (S, 112–13).

As the camera moves back and the film moves to a more abstract and universal level of observation, Stroszek's revolt seems simultaneously significant and absurd. Shooting at the sun, Stroszek manages only to ignite a chair and the only casualty of his bombardment of the village is a donkey that lies dead in the village square as the inhabitants scurry past. As is often the case in Herzog's work, apparent cosmic significance turns out to be insignificant and foolish. The beauty of Stroszek's revolt lies in the act itself, not in its results. The film's final commentary is a typically teasing mixture of respect and cold-eyed reason: "In his protest against everything he had begun something titantic, for his opponent was hopelessly stronger. And he had failed as miserably and meanly as all his kind." Herzog has said of *Signs of Life*, "symbols and signs are more important than action. . . . At the end of the film Stroszek [the main character] is not important any more; his signs are more important than his actions."[4] Here, Herzog sounds like a semiotician himself. Clearly his skeptical view of the study of structures and signs in his films is based on a conviction that the scholarly, intellectual analysis of images robs them of their purity and power.

Integrally related to this emphasis on the visual sign is the importance of landscapes in Herzog's films. Herzog claims that all of his films arise out of "landschaftlichen Gegebenheiten" (HKS, 34), or physical features of the landscape, which frequently becomes an antagonist and sometimes even a protagonist in his films. Alaska, Wyoming, Ireland's Skellig Island, the Greek islands, the Amazon jungle, the Sahara desert—Herzog has repeatedly sought out geographic locations that remind us of a time when humanity was not totally in charge of the universe. At its most extreme, as in the documentary *Fata Morgana*, the landscape totally overwhelms the human element; the mythical quality of the desert landscape itself becomes the film's subject.

Herzog once said, "I *do* see something at the horizon, and . . . I am still trying to articulate those images that I see" (I, 35). *Fata Morgana* means "mirage." An optical illusion, encountered most often in desert areas, it is produced by a layer of heated air across which can be seen reflections of distant objects. In a sense, *fata morgana* allows the perception of objects *beyond* the horizon. Filmed at the same time and in many of the same places as his television documentary, *The Flying Doctors of East Africa* (1969), Herzog's *Fata Morgana* could be considered a semidocumentary report on the Sahara Desert and drought-stricken areas of sub-Saharan Africa: Niger, Upper Volta, Mali, Ivory Coast, Kenya and Tanzania. Significantly, however, the title *Fata Morgana* points not toward the object of the filming, the desert landscape, but rather toward the human experience of the landscape. It draws attention to the desert as a metaphor of human existence and to the filmmaking process as a purveyor of visual illusions. In a manner quite different from that of most of his films, *Fata Morgana* reiterates Herzog's typical concerns: the illusory nature of reality, the "real" nature of illusion, and the impossibility of truly objective perception. Made at approximately the same time as *Even Dwarfs Started Small, Fata Morgana* is a fitting companion piece.

Fata Morgana has a consciously tripartite, epic structure: "Creation," "Paradise," and "The Golden Age." The opening sequence establishes the tone, method, and significance of much of the rest of the film. A series of airplane landings, photographed through hazy and distorting heat waves and accompanied by the roaring of motors, transforms the objective event (the landing) into a subjectively perceived abstraction. There follows an incessantly gliding tour of desert landscape accompanied by music of Handel, Mozart, the rock group Blind Faith, and more intriguingly, by Lotte Eisner's reading, in an ancient, vaguely unearthly voice, of a sixteenth-century Guatemalan creation myth. Human traces appear so rarely that when an oil refinery, a radar station, or an abandoned truck appears it conveys an aura of futuristic fantasy: "*Fata Morgana* takes place on the planet Uxmal, which is discovered by beings from the fog of Andromeda and about which they are making a film report" (HKS, 94).

Fata Morgana also ends with a mirage-like apparition of a vehicle moving in the distance, raising a duststorm behind it (the effect frequently masking the cause), reiterating the image of the plane landing at the film's beginning. The viewer is left with Herzog's commentary on the desert, on the film, on filmmaking in general, and probably on life itself: the deluding of the senses, the impossibility of objective perception, and the illusoriness of reality.

In a more typical Herzog film one finds an opposition of geography and humanity, perhaps most perfectly realized in *Aguirre, The Wrath of God*, in which the jungle and the conquistador seem to be well matched, equal opponents. *Aguirre* is generally acknowledged as Herzog's most beautiful film. From its breathtaking beginning—a panorama of a sixteenth-century Spanish expedition inching its way across a lush, mist-streaked Andean mountain top—to its intriguing ending with a circling camera shot enclosing the mad Aguirre alone on a raft drifting slowly down the Amazon, *Aguirre, The Wrath of God* is an elaborate display of rich and lustrous color, of jungle greens and gold. As in *Fata Morgana*, landscape is of incalculable significance in *Aguirre*; in *Aguirre*, however, Herzog has consciously emphasized narrative action: "You know, the earlier films had tension in them, to be sure, but that was seldom narrative tension, but rather tensions between an environment and an individual, tensions between the characters. . . . This film *Aguirre* is much more action-packed" (FM, 16).

Despite Herzog's attention to narrative action and surface beauty in *Aguirre*, there still exists a well-developed "tension between an environment and an individual," between the Amazon landscape and Aguirre. Of all Herzog's protagonists, Aguirre is, with the possible exception of the vampire Nosferatu, quite probably the least agreeable: a cold-blooded megalomaniac, driven mad by dreams of gold, power, and the legendary El Dorado. Herzog nevertheless professes sympathy for Aguirre: "I have never made a film about a figure for whom I have not felt compassion—not even Aguirre" (NYT, 30). And indeed the viewer is compelled in a way to admire Aguirre's power of survival and the grandeur of his delusion, which seems nearly a match for the grand power of the Amazon jungle. "We will produce history," he says near the end, "as others produce plays"; and Aguirre evokes memories of the overweening villains of Shakespearean drama. As do Herzog's other protagonists, Aguirre in his madness points the way to other existential realms, to other worlds unsuspected by more normal human beings.

In the encounter between Aguirre's band and the Amazon jungle, unlike most such encounters in the history of civilization, human society is slowly dismantled and overpowered by the forces of nature. The conquistadors are themselves conquered by the jungle, by an environment powerful enough to repel and disarm any intrusion, to assert its own amorality against the dubious values of the intruders. There is never in Herzog's film any integration of the two realms. Aguirre alone survives at film's end, unassimilated by the jungle's intensity and fecund power. He wears his armor and his colonialist motives to the end.

The jungle, by its very nature, is stronger than any human attempts to conquer and to tame it. Aguirre, by his inspired madness, is raised above a normal human susceptibility to the lethal wilderness. Even in films whose action occurs in a social context, landscapes (the romantic German countryside around Dinkelsbühl and Kaspar's dream of the desert in *Every Man for Himself* or the hallucinatory field of poppies in *Woyzeck*) recur to remind the viewer, as well as the characters, of other worlds and other possibilities.

It is not the use of landscape, of stunning photography, however, that is most responsible for the intensely intriguing and evocative quality of Herzog's films. Herzog's most striking images are those which juxtapose the natural landscape with human objects, juxtapositions that fix the eye and jolt the mind and yet remain intriguingly and pleasingly ambiguous. It is not a valley alone that so disturbs the protagonist of *Signs of Life*, but rather a valley filled with windmills. Similarly, the viewer is disturbed by images that only hint at unexplained and possibly inexplicable mysteries of existence: the footprint in stone in *Last Words*; the "mirage" of the airplane that lands—or takes off—again and again and again in *Fata Morgana*; the hooded horse's head with its unblinking eye staring from the Amazon jungle or the raft impossibly caught in the treetop in *Aguirre, The Wrath of God*; the swan and rowboat, slowly moving past the tower, or the trampling footprint upon Kaspar's name spelled out in garden greens in *Every Man for Himself*; or the endlessly circling, driverless trucks in *Even Dwarfs Started Small* and *Stroszek*.

Some of these images are constructed by Herzog, but others are "found" images as in *Fata Morgana* and Herzog's other documentaries. "What people very often overlook and what is at least as important to me as my fiction films, are my documentaries" (H, 76). Like *Fata Morgana, Land of Silence and Darkness* is a documentary that explores not only the documented object (here, the world of the deaf and blind) but also the filmmaking process (using cinema ironically to explore a sightless, soundless world) and, of course, all of human existence. The world of the deaf and blind is distant and lonely, as the central figure—a woman named Fini Straubinger—makes clear: "When you let go of my hand, it is as if we were a thousand miles apart." It may also be, Herzog implies, a better, more intuitive, more natural world. Perhaps the deaf and blind children who have trouble learning abstract concepts like "hope," "happiness," and "ambition" are better off without them. The man near the end of the film who "learns" a tree by tenderly embracing it may have a lovelier and more direct experience of nature that those who view the tree from a distance. As happens so frequently in Herzog's films, the "abnormal" individuals of *Land of Silence and Darkness*, who, at the beginning of the film, seem so totally different from the viewer, appear different only in degree by the end of the film. Are not their descriptions of our "real" world uncannily similar to normal human perceptions of paradise?

(top) Fata Morgana. Courtesy of New Line Cinema; (bottom) The Great Ecstasy of the Sculptor Steiner. *Courtesy of New Yorker Films.*

Yet another Herzog documentary, *The Great Ecstasy of the Sculptor Steiner*, was filmed as part of a West German television series called "On the Border." The Swiss ski jumper, Walter Steiner, exists on a precarious border between the physical and the spiritual, between airborne freedom in flight and earthbound physical self-destruction. Herzog, as the tensely whispering and suspiciously overawed and adoring commentator, points out Steiner's landing point on his first jump and notes that just beyond that point the ground becomes flat, making a landing possibly fatal. Herzog tells us that "here is the point where this film had its inception." Herzog's film concerns Steiner's fragile ability to push to the ultimate limit, where an almost mystical freedom momentarily exists, where ski jumping becomes ski flying, without destroying himself by pushing beyond that limit.

Herzog, like Steiner, seeks that elusive point where the earth is transcended in flight and where the physical passes into the spiritual: "Ski jumping is not only something athletic, rather it is a spiritual form. . . . That matters to the great ski jumpers, that it is a spiritual form" (HKS, 130). Thus, *Great Ecstasy* like all Herzog's films is concerned with the transcendent spiritual experience that lies beyond all the limitations of the human mind and body. For Herzog, the ski jumper Steiner is an individual who shapes his own existence and renders it into pure experience in much the same way that the woodcarver Steiner discerns and sketches an ideal form and then carves and chisels a piece of wood into sculpture.

In a statement manufactured by Herzog, we read at film's end, "I should be all alone in this world, I Steiner, and no other living being. No sun, no culture, I naked on a high rock, no storm, no snow, no streets, no banks, no money, no time and no breath. Then I wouldn't be afraid any more."[5] The end of fear is to be found only in a silent and solitary place not of this world, but it has curious similarities to the island of the lepers in *Last Words*, to the "Land of Silence and Darkness," and to the unknown place from which Kaspar Hauser emerges.

In many ways *Every Man for Himself and God Against All* is the epitome of Herzog's career so far, and Herzog himself has admitted that Kaspar Hauser is an alter ego: "Kaspar, he seems to me like my own existence" (HKS, 127). The story of the "wild child" foundling of the 1820s, Kaspar Hauser, and his portrayal by the much-abused lay actor, Bruno S., provide one of the purest embodiments of Herzog's cinematic concerns.

Kaspar Hauser, in his struggle to walk, to speak, to learn, to understand, to assimilate the contrivances of our civilization, only reflects the limitations of our own awareness and the impossibility of expressing any awareness we do attain. Kaspar Hauser is an uncontriving individual but at a moment of deeply felt experience the only words that even *he* can find are "Mother, I am far away from everything." And it is really not Kaspar's words that touch the viewer, but the look that accompanies and illuminates the words.

Herzog, like Fassbinder, distrusts language in the form of human speech. More often a hindrance than a help to communication, speech is at best seriously defective. As in Fassbinder's films, well-spoken language is usually in Herzog's films the property and tool of oppressive, "cultured" society; for example, the florid language of the pompous minister, of the pedantic logician, of the effete Lord Stanhope in *Every Man for Himself,* or of the officers, of the insanely logical doctor, of the drum major in *Woyzeck.* For Herzog, however, language has a less immediate socio–political implication than it does for Fassbinder, and in fact Herzog is fascinated by language in a way that Fassbinder is not. At its best, speech in Herzog's films can be touchingly effective, as in the halting yet pointed speech of Bruno S. in *Every Man for Himself* and *Stroszek* or of Klaus Kinski in *Woyzeck.* At its worst, however, it can be dully artificial and sophomoric, as in some of the jarring attempts at verbal humor in *Aguirre, The Wrath of God.* It is, however, when language stops that Herzog's films find their truest voice. Near the beginning of *Every Man for Himself,* printed across a beautiful landscape of undulating grain, are the words: "Can you not hear that terrible screaming all around us that men call silence?" Clearly, Herzog's silences, like his visual juxtapositions, invite a reexamination of everyday existence, a reevaluation of the taken-for-granted.

Silence generally draws attention to the visual image and language detracts from it, but the beauty and power of Herzog's images are frequently reinforced and elaborated by means of commentative music. Like Syberberg, for example, Herzog perceives a close relationship between music and film: "I believe that film has much more to do with music than . . . with literature or theater" (H, 60). Neither restrictive nor indiscriminate in his use of evocative music on the film soundtrack, Herzog in some films has employed no music at all. In others he has used music from sources ranging from Mozart to Leonard Cohen to Popol Vuh, an experimental music group led by Herzog's friend, Florian Fricke. Music in a Herzog film is seldom intended as a simple manipulation of the viewer's emotions in the classic Hollywood tradition of program music. It is instead integrated into the film's structural framework.[6] Music often evokes the transcendent realms intimated by Herzog's visual juxtapositions. In *The Great Ecstasy of the Sculptor Steiner,* for example, Herzog manipulates the viewer's perceptions of the airborne ski jumper Steiner visually with slow-motion, low-angle photography (in the tradition of Riefenstahl's *Olympia*) and aurally with Popol Vuh's unearthly synthesizer music. Herzog's manipulation of the image removes its naturalistic foundation, erases the borderline between earthbound stasis and free, unbound flight, and perfectly evokes the mystical and superreal state described verbally by the ski jumper earlier in the film.

Above all, what Herzog finds in music is an aural counterpart of the irrationality and emotionality which should, he believes, lie at the core of all filmmaking: "Film has much more to do with the emotions than with pure reason. . . . The purely rational is suitable for film just as little as it would suit music. It won't do; music cannot be organized purely rationally; when you compare music, it comes from somewhere else. And that is also the nurturer of film" (H, 69).

Perhaps the most significant feature distinguishing the work of Werner Herzog from most contemporary West German filmmakers is the almost total absence of any sense of filmmaking, or of life, as merely an intellectual exercise. Filmmaking has, he realizes, something insidious about it, something that consumes its creators, the actors and directors that make it exist. "This entire profession has something destructive about it that ruins people" (H, 77). He realizes that its illusion-making is, in some essential way, ridiculous: "I thought to myself, what we are doing here is really the ultimate absurdity. It is undignified, ridiculous, and insane" (H, 78). Nevertheless, he describes filmmaking as utterly necessary for his own existence: "I believe I could not go on living if I knew that this work was to be forbidden to me for the rest of my life. That would be the end of me" (H, 83).

Unlike Straub/Huillet, Kluge, or even Fassbinder and Schlöndorff, Herzog seems to have little sense of formalism and political exigencies; in his films one is seldom aware of immediate socio–political situations or intellectually formulated solutions. For Herzog film and life are unified, immediate, physical, intensely personal, and creative. Werner Herzog crafts his films as he claims to craft his life, and this sense of existential self-confidence is surely Herzog's most profound attraction for his audience. Although it may be a deceptive appearance, Herzog appears to offer affirmation and the possibility of positive solutions to universal existential problems.

6

Rainer Werner Fassbinder

Chronology

1946   Rainer Werner Fassbinder born on May 31 in Bad Wörishofen.

1965   *Der Stadtstreicher* [The City Tramp], 10 min.

1966   *Das kleine Chaos* [The Little Chaos], 12 min.

1969   *Liebe ist kälter als der Tod* [Love Is Colder Than Death], 88 min.
        Katzelmacher, 88 min.
        Götter der Pest [Gods of the Plague], 91 min.

1970   *Warum läuft Herr R. Amok?* [Why Does Herr R. Run Amuck?], codirected with Michael Fengler, 88 min.
        Rio das Mortes, 84 min.
        Das Kaffeehaus [The Coffeehouse], 105 min.
        Whity, 95 min.
        Die Niklaushauser Fahrt [The Niklaushaus Trip], codirected with Michael Fengler, 86 min.
        Der amerikanische Soldat [The American Soldier], 80 min.
        Warnung vor einer heiligen Nutte [Beware of a Holy Whore], 103 min.

1971   *Pioniere in Ingolstadt* [Pioneers in Ingolstadt], 84 min.
        Der Händler der vier Jahreszeiten [The Merchant of Four Seasons], 89 min.

1972   *Die bitteren Tränen der Petra von Kant* [The Bitter Tears of Petra von Kant], 124 min.
        Wildwechsel [Jail Bait], 102 min.
        Acht Stunden sind kein Tag [Eight Hours Don't Make a

Day], five-part television series: 101, 100, 92, 88, and 89 min.

Bremer Freiheit [Bremen Freedom], 87 min.

1973   *Welt am Draht* [World on a Wire], two-part television film: 99 and 106 min.

Nora Helmer, 101 min.

Angst Essen Seele Auf [Fear Eats the Soul: Ali], 93 min.

Martha, 112 min.

1974   *Fontane Effi Briest* [Effi Briest], 141 min.

Faustrecht der Freiheit [Fox and His Friends], 123 min.

Wie ein Vogel auf dem Draht [Like a Bird On the Wire], 44 min.

1975   *Mutter Küsters' Fahrt zum Himmel* [Mother Küsters Goes to Heaven], 120 min.

Angst vor der Angst [Fear of Fear], 88 min.

1976   *Ich will doch nur, dass ihr mich liebt* [I Just Want You to Love Me], 104 min.

Satansbraten [Satan's Brew], 112 min.

Chinesisches Roulette [Chinese Roulette], 86 min.

1977   *Bolwieser,* two-part television film: 104 and 96 min.

Frauen in New York [Women in New York], 111 min.

Despair/Eine Reise ins Licht [Despair], 119 min.

1978   *Deutschland im Herbst* [Germany in Autumn], codirected, 124 min.

Die Ehe der Maria Braun [The Marriage of Maria Braun], 120 min.

In einem Jahr mit 13 Monden [In a Year with 13 Moons], 124 min.

1979   *Die dritte Generation* [The Third Generation], 110 min.

1980   *Berlin Alexanderplatz,* 15-hour television film.

1981   *Lili Marlene,* 105 min.

1982   *Lola,* 110 min.

My films are documents of my personality.

ONE OF THE MOST STARTLING images of the collective film *Germany in Autumn* is Rainer Werner Fassbinder sitting naked at his telephone, distraughtly discussing the terrorist deaths of October 1978 as he distractedly scratches and caresses himself. Fassbinder's sequence is the most intensely and revealingly personal of all the film's individual sections. Arguably *Germany in Autumn*'s most effective sequence, Fassbinder's autobiographical contribution exposes not only his pudgy body and his shrill abrasiveness but also the convincing clarity and unnerving intensity of his reaction to the West German crisis of autumn 1978. His nakedness and his paranoia become a metaphor for much of West Germany itself.

Like his episode of *Germany in Autumn*, all of Fassbinder's works bear the unmistakable stamp of his remarkable personality, although not always so boldly. As is also true of Werner Herzog, Fassbinder's films are his life. Responding to an interviewer's query as to what, for Fassbinder, would be a "perfect" film, Fassbinder once said that for him the finest films are the most personal films. "Look at the films of Fellini . . . for me those are the most perfect films that exist. There is not a weak second there, none, and that is the most personal cinema I know" (FR, 3).[1] More recently, in 1980, Fassbinder declared, "I make films because they affect me personally and for no other reason" (K, 29).

Hailed by Vincent Canby of the *New York Times* as "the most original talent since Godard,"[2] and the first West German filmmaker to be named a "Director of the Year" by the widely read *International Film Guide*,[3] Fassbinder was responsible, perhaps *most* responsible, for attracting international attention to West German films in the 1970s. Even were his films not as good as they actually are, Fassbinder might still be a notable director because of the quantity of works he has filmed. In the decade between 1969, the year of his first feature film, *Love is Colder Than Death*, and 1979, Fassbinder made (counting television productions) thirty-five films. In addition he has written the majority of his own scenarios, has directed theater productions, has acted in films by his friends. Like Straub and Huillet and like Herzog, Fassbinder seems obsessed with his work in films, seems in fact to live his life in and through his films. In mid-1980 Fassbinder completed a monumental ten-part, fifteen-hour television series based on the Alfred Döblin novel *Berlin Alexanderplatz*. In writing his 3000-page scenario Fassbinder used, he has said, "insanely little time for it. . . . I worked for four days straight through, then slept for 24 hours, worked again for four days, and so on. And so one naturally gets into a different rhythm" (K, 35).

The intensity and rapidity with which Fassbinder works sometimes leave visible traces in his films. Not every Fassbinder film is a Fassbinder masterpiece. What is astonishing, however, is the mastery evident in so many of his films: in *Why Does Herr R. Run Amuck?* (1970), *The Merchant of Four Seasons* (1971), *The Bitter*

Tears of Petra von Kant (1972), *Jail Bait* (1972), *Fear Eats the Soul: Ali* (1973), *Fontane Effi Briest* (1974), *Fox and His Friends* (1974), *Mother Küsters Goes to Heaven* (1975), *Despair* (1977), or *The Marriage of Maria Braun* (1978). While film historians and critics may ponder the durability of films made with such offhand speed, Fassbinder himself professes indifference to such questions: "For the most part these are films for throwing away; that is to say, films that are made about a certain matter at a certain time and that then afterwards can be forgotten, for all I care" (F, 75).

Strongly influenced by Straub and Huillet, Fassbinder's early films show the same slow rhythms, monotonous dialogue, and intellectual distance from the characters. Fassbinder later, however, repudiated the elitism and cold intellectuality of Straub and Huillet: "Films from the brain are all right, but if they don't reach the audience, it's no good. . . . He [Straub] tried to be revolutionary and human in an inhuman way" (NT, 54). Fassbinder has acknowledged other influences: early Godard, especially *Vivre Sa Vie*; Bunuel's *Viridiana*; Raoul Walsh; John Huston; Howard Hawks; and the expatriate German Hollywood director, Douglas Sirk (F, 68–69). Thus, as Fassbinder has matured, he has tempered the Straubian coldness of his earliest films with increasing sympathy and with sometimes outrageous melodrama.

Fassbinder has brought attention to his films by the melodrama and sometimes absurd or grotesque estericism of his themes, by the sureness and unique look of his cinematic style, by the sheer number of his films, and—just as importantly, perhaps—by his flamboyantly marketable personality: an outspoken, homosexual, leftist critic of modern capitalist society. Fassbinder obviously and correctly perceives himself as a social outsider. Thus, for him, personal films also mean socially critical films, because personal films reflect not only their maker but also a social context: "The more personal that films are, the more they express about the country in which they have come into being" (FR, 3). For experienced Fassbinder viewers, the parade of posters of West German Chancellors at the conclusion of *The Marriage of Maria Braun* is not only unsurprising, it is almost expected. Fassbinder's films constantly explore the social through the individual, and have done so since *Katzelmacher* (1969) and *Why Does Herr R. Run Amuck*? As Fassbinder and his work have matured, social criticism has only become more explicit.

His stories never occur in a vacuum. Even the most apparently hermetic films have both personal and social implications. For example, *The Bitter Tears of Petra von Kant*—a six-woman, one–set "chamber film"—would appear to have little to do with Fassbinder personally or with broader social issues. Ironically, Fassbinder has more than once called this film his most autobiographical, and its central concerns of love, power, and exploitation are common to all. Even more striking than the personal/social themes of most Fassbinder films, however, is their intriguing narrative style.

One of the notable characteristics of Fassbinder's cinematic style has been the presence of a relatively stable, consistent group of actors and actresses who have reappeared time and again in his films. Fassbinder's work is a totality formed by repetition, variation, and permutation; the reappearance of faces from other Fassbinder films gives the viewer the impression that each film is only one facet of a whole Fassbinder cosmos, that each specific story is only one thread in a universal Fassbinder narrative, a German "As The World Turns," in which characters and themes drop from sight only to surface again in a later episode. A story told as a secondary or even tertiary element in one film may become the main plot of another, as a minor anecdote related in *The American Soldier* (1970) became the narrative of *Fear Eats the Soul: Ali.* Themes of isolation, exploitation, alienation, and insanity—underlined by repetitions of actors, visual imagery, dialogue, and even musical motifs from film to film—create a world-view that is always and uniquely Fassbinder's, however many specific changes may take place between films. We find ourselves as fascinated with Fassbinder's work as an ongoing process as we do with any one specific film, and at least part of the interest of any Fassbinder film is seeing what new persona has been assumed by any given player.

Fassbinder's relationship with his actors is problematic. The early theater and film work of Fassbinder's cast and crew was an essentially communal affair in which Fassbinder functioned as a first-among-equals leader, a system shown in *Beware of a Holy Whore* (1970) to be inherently flawed and fundamentally unworkable. *Beware of a Holy Whore* is an autobiographical examination of the filmmaker, but, more importantly, it is an examination of the interaction of a crew of film technicians, actors, and their director. It is also a demythologiz-ing of filmmaking, the "holy whore" of the title. A film crew is filmed as it waits—and waits and waits—for the Director who will come to give meaning to their existence. Like most of Fassbinder's characters, the actors and technicians are imprisoned behind invisible bars, bound together by their common, and obviously metaphorical, foreignness in a hotel on location in Spain. Living an unreal and impotent existence of endless anticipation, the film crew talk, drink, gossip, quarrel, and randomly exploit each other sexually as they wait for filming, and fulfillment to begin. Fassbinder, playing Sascha the producer, says in the film, "the only thing I can accept is despair."

Beware of a Holy Whore, like many Fassbinder films, is an exploration of despair and of the anxiety of indecision inherent in filmmaking—at least as practiced by the Fassbinder crew in the late 1960s. In his early films and theater work Fassbinder had searched for a means of creating collective art. *Beware of a Holy Whore* is a disavowal of that search.

During the 1970s Fassbinder came more and more to think of his filmmaking work as an ability to make decisions. This decisiveness has led him away from the theater and ever more into films. In 1976, describing his decision to quit as the director of a Frankfurt theater, Fassbinder described as a virtue of film what earlier, before 1970, would have been seen as a defect. In films "it is accepted from the start that one person makes the decisions, and since that is clear from the beginning, one has more freedom to interact and to make suggestions than in a theater group where one began with the assumption: we want to develop something cooperatively" (FR, 3). Thus, during the mid-1970s, Fassbinder acquired a reputation as an *enfant-terrible* director functioning by force of his personality, as an imperious genius who in certain instances directed every detail of a player's work. Referring to El Hedi Ben Salem as Ali in *Fear Eats The Soul: Ali*, Fassbinder has said, "I spoke every word with him as he acted; I indicated every pause and told him 'now look to the left' and so on. . . ." On the other hand, Fassbinder also goes on to say, "but I find the other way better and nicer when one tells the actor—at most—what the background is for a line of dialogue" (R, 97). For the most part Fassbinder gives only a minimum of direction to his players; roles are frequently written with a specific actor in mind so that the screen character becomes an undirected mixture of Fassbinder's preproduction conception of the role and the actor's own personality. In some regards Fassbinder seems to have a more than usual amount of respect for his actors; *The Bitter Tears of Petra von Kant*, for example, bears a dedication "To the one who here became Marlene," apparently an act of gratitude to the actress Irm Hermann who was willing, in Fassbinder's view, to debase her own personality by assuming that of the passive, subservient, and mutely masochistic servant, Marlene.

Many of the actors who appear in Fassbinder's films—Irm Hermann, for example, or even more notably Hanna Schygulla of *Fontane Effi Briest* and *The Marriage of Maria Braun*—are stage players who gathered around Fassbinder during his theater work in Munich's *"antitheater"* in the late 1960s. By the late 1970s Fassbinder claimed to have totally lost interest in the theater: "It's dead. The cinema is much more interesting" (C, 21). Nevertheless, it is not only actors that the theater has contributed to Fassbinder's films. One can also find general theatrical influences such as Brecht's theater of alienation, intellectuality, and political relevancy in most of Fassbinder's films and more specific influences in specific films, such as the obvious if unacknowledged influence of Japanese *noh* drama on the setting and structure of *The Bitter Tears of Petra von Kant*. Moreover, Fassbinder's films often look as if they were being performed on a theater stage: characters arrange themselves in tableaux facing the eye of the camera. Fassbinder's world often seems to be a stage in which the back wall is precisely parallel to the plane of the camera lens, a stage which opens itself up to us the audience.

Fassbinder's characters frequently freeze into virtual inanimacy as the camera slowly and deliberately pans the characters or moves to a close-up searching their faces in vain for meaning. The camera in Fassbinder's films does not merely record characters and actions; it also comments upon them. And camera movement not only recaptures character viewpoint but also recapitulates character movement, as in *The Bitter Tears of Petra von Kant*, where languid pans, tilts, and tracking shots alternate with motionlessness in a precise reduplication of the "elegant" languor of Petra herself. Similarly camera angle is sometimes used metaphorically. In *The Marriage of Maria Braun*, for example, an upside-down shot of Maria's husband Hermann recaptures Maria's viewpoint from her position on her bed. It also, however, concisely conveys the climactic overturning of Maria's notions of Hermann and of their relationship at film's end.

Fassbinder's camera both imitates and subverts conventional Hollywood camera codes, producing unconventional effects with, for example, reversals of an establishing shot followed by a point-of-view shot: the audience is made aware of who is viewing what only after the fact. Such reversals, exemplified in *The Bitter Tears of Petra von Kant* or *Despair*, result in a temporary disorientation in the film viewer, a disorientation serving Fassbinder's modernist purpose of critical distance by the spectator.

Fassbinder compounds such ambiguity of viewpoint by frequent shifts of shot angles from subjective viewpoints of characters within the film to the possibly less subjective viewpoint of an all-seeing observer and back again. This shifting perspective creates viewer disorientation and a frustration of viewer expectation, demonstrating

(top) The Bitter Tears of Petra von Kant; (bottom) Brigitte Mira and El Hedi Ben Salem in Rainer Werner Fassbinder's Fear Eats the Soul: Ali. Courtesy of The Museum of Modern Art/Film Stills Archive.

to the viewer that even spaces that seem open and unrestricted are in fact not. In *Fear Eats the Soul: Ali,* for example, the main characters—now lovers—are photographed from street level on the sidewalk before her apartment building. The pair say goodbye cautiously but tenderly, and the scene is optimistic with a promise of a happier, less lonely future. The optimism of the scene is quickly destroyed, however, when Ali and Emmi part. The camera tilts up the side of the building to reveal Frau Karges, a snooping and sexually envious neighbor, leaning out of her window, maliciously observing their togetherness and their departure. The implicit cynicism of this sudden shift in perspective is then compounded by the viewer's awareness that he or she is *also* spying, not only on the lives of Ali and Emmi but on the secret vices of the neighbor.

Such a shift in perspective invites the audience to be aware of itself as viewer. The audience's hostility to the neighbor's values and judgments implies the possibility of hostility to the audience's own values and judgments. A clever visual image transforms a melodramatic stereotype, the snooping neighbor, into a powerful distancing device that permits a transcendence of immediate emotional responses and evokes critical, intellectual reflection. An intriguing, related sequence occurs in *The Bitter Tears of Petra von Kant* during a conversation between Petra and her friend Sidonie. Petra and Sidonie sit in the background, photographed through a louvered window and framed by the servant Marlene's arm in the foreground as she gracefully leans against the window, listening. The audience is thus quietly reminded of *its* status as eavesdropper as well as voyeur.

Like the use of the camera and point of view, music and language in Fassbinder's film are not always as simple as they first seem. Music comments upon, reinforces, and sometimes contradicts the action. And language, rather than being a means of communication—as one would expect—is more often a means of non-communication and repression.

Fassbinder's films are, in many ways, films about language. In Fassbinder's world the most inarticulate characters are usually the most sympathetic. Language—that is, "proper" grammatical language—is shown to be a means of socio-political oppression. Modern society so perverts individuals and their language that verbal communication becomes nearly impossible and language becomes a social weapon, an aggressive instrument employed by the powerful against the weak.[4] Language retains an ironically communicative function on the level of filmmaker-to-audience, but its original purpose of communication on the level of character–to–character *within* the film is, for the most part, lost.

This identification of language and social aggression has always been a characteristic of Fassbinder's films, and Fassbinder has provided world cinema with one of the ultimate formulations of the inarticulate protagonist. If anything in *Why Does Herr R. Run Amuck?* evokes the audience's sympathy, it is the protagonist's total inability to express his frustration, alienation, and rage. Herr R.'s final rampage is his statement to the world, a statement that is expressed by deed rather than by word. Closely related is the gradually increasing inarticulateness and silence of Hans in *The Merchant of Four Seasons*. As Hans's awareness of his wife's and his friend's betrayal grows, so too do his pain, his impotent rage, and his silence; he never seems so hurt, so threatening, and so insightful as when he gazes silently out the window of his apartment kitchen. In *Beware of a Holy Whore* the most sympathetic character is the French actor Eddie Constantine, who speaks only rudimentary German. A possible exception to this correlation of sympathy and inarticulateness is the ambiguous character Marlene, in *The Bitter Tears of Petra von Kant*, who remains totally silent throughout the film. While Marlene apparently *will* not speak, however, Herr R., Hans, and Eddie Constantine *can* not speak.

In a corrupt and alienated society, language becomes corrupting and alienating. In most Fassbinder films, therefore, there is a continual discrepancy between what the speaker says and means, and what the listener hears and understands. Fassbinder's characters hear only what they are predisposed to hear, and sincere, direct, "authentic" language is derided or ignored when it does occur. Moreover, just as language spoken by characters within the film often serves to humiliate other, less articulate characters, it also reflects reality's cruel repudiation of a character's ideals. In *The Marriage of Maria Braun*, during the film's concluding explosion (or subliminal murder-suicide) Fassbinder comments ironically upon Maria's failed dreams. As Maria lights a cigarette, exploding her gas-filled house, a television announcer at the end of the final soccer match during the 1954 World Cup games screams "Tor! Tor! Tor!," a word meaning both "goal" and "fool."

In his early films Fassbinder showed the influence of such aesthetically purist filmmakers as Straub/Huillet, and even in his later films the minimalist influence, although modified by Fassbinder's later use of Hollywood-type melodrama, is still apparent. It is in fact precisely the blending of traditional themes with a modernist aesthetic that has been most responsible for Fassbinder's cinematic success. He has superimposed a minimalist aesthetic upon popular trivial melodrama: "Melodramatic films are correct films. The American method of making them, however, left the audience with emotions and nothing else. I want to give the spectator the emotions along with the possibility of reflecting on and analyzing what he is feeling" (C, 20). Only in the late 1970s has Fassbinder's stylistic unconventionality been matched by an unconventionality of material, as, for example, in *Chinese Roulette* (1976), *Satan's Brew* (1976), *Despair,* or *In A Year With Thirteen Moons* (1978), where a fascination with melodramatic stereotypes has given way to a playing with existential paradox. Although he has taken a path separate from the minimalists, Fassbinder too rejects language and, in so doing, explores two other possibilities of a film soundtrack: music and silence.

An early Fassbinder film like *Why Does Herr R. Run Amuck?* (codirected with Michael Fengler) faithfully records a dreary modern existence in exhaustive and mind-numbing detail, which in fact becomes the film's main subject. The visual style of Fassbinder's films beginning with *The Merchant of Four Seasons* recaptures a more stylized vision of reality. Action takes place within an identifiably realistic but decidedly nonnaturalistic environment. A film's exterior scenes, for example, may be shot on location in Munich or Frankfurt; extraneous objects or persons, however, seldom intrude upon the action or the relationships of the characters. The world becomes a stage for the ever-shifting relationships of Fassbinder's protagonists. Similarly, extraneous background noise has been eliminated on the soundtracks of the later films, sometimes through a careful manipulation of production sound recording and sometimes through postproduction dubbing.[5]

The disturbing silence of the soundtrack reiterates and reinforces the voids that recur in the visual image; just as there is much to be seen in the empty spaces within the visual image, there is much to be heard in the silence of the soundtrack. In many Fassbinder films the "weighting" of words through alternating silences shows the oppressive uses of language in modern society and impresses upon us the psychic force of the meanings behind the words. Silence enforces a confrontation of the audience with what is left after language has ended and with the questions that remain after the easy answers have disappeared. Silence implies the questions that lead to thought and ultimately to social action. Fassbinder's films, like those of Bergman and many other modernist directors, do not conclude with the words "The End" but rather with music or silence. They remain open-ended even as the visual image fades into an unresolved totality of black or white. Above all, silence functions in Fassbinder's films to keep open the processes of nonemotional, critical examination, of the investigative spirit that might lead to social action and ultimately to social change. Language closes off thought, but silence can counteract language.

Fassbinder's pictures attain their fullest impact when language ceases. In the absence of spoken distractions, subliminal suggestion becomes conscious statement; emotional response is transformed into rational inspection and integration. Fassbinder has said, "What I previously put into language I now try to put into the structure of movements and into the structure of images, because I believe that that is more effective . . . than language which is beautiful and precise but yet very alien" (F, 86).

Within the "structure of images" nothing is more striking than character and camera placements which juxtapose characters with backgrounds that provide a commentary on the characters' situations. Fassbinder frames his characters within the horizontal and vertical lines of doorways, stairways, and architectural beams, and his framing sometimes threatens to reduce the characters to little more than replaceable elements within a visual composition. At other times, however, framing gives us a claustrophic sense of the entrapment that the characters experience. Doors, windows, and stairways imply the possibility of escape; for Fassbinder, however, they become visual expressions of social oppression and human confinement.

Such framing is found in all but the earliest Fassbinder films. It occurs, for example, as a minor narrative element in *Beware of a Holy Whore*. Jeff, the director, and a passenger are enclosed by the frame of a convertible's windshield, restricted even in an open convertible. In *Fontane Effi Briest* characters are often photographed through doorways in order to make visible the psychological suffocation experienced within Wilhelminian society. In *Fear Eats the Soul: Ali* this type of framing becomes an integral part of Fassbinder's narrative style, unifying nonsequential shots, contributing ironic commentary to the supposedly objective exposition, and reminding the audience to retain its critical rationality.[6] By the late 1970s, in *Despair* or in *The Marriage of Maria Braun*, such framing has been completely assimilated into Fassbinder's more mature and more complex cinematic style. In these later films claustrophobic framing continues to occur, but less self-consciously and with a decreasing sense of staged artifice, its understated ubiquity only reinforcing the atmospheric oppressiveness.

Fassbinder also communicates with the viewer by means of juxtapositions of characters and symbolic objects. In all of Fassbinder's films, from the earliest to the latest, clothing functions not only as an element of naturalistic setting, i.e., as "costuming," but as a

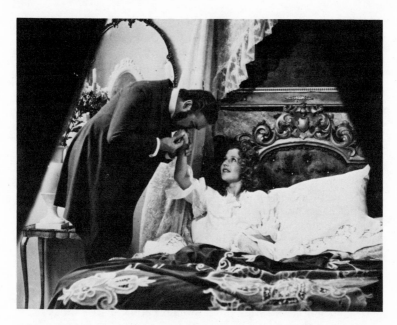

Effi Briest. *Courtesy of The Museum of Modern Art/Film Stills Archive*

metaphor of socio–political restraint and existential constriction. In *Why Does Herr R. Run Amuck?* one of the last shots before R. "runs amuck" is of the strained cloth of the seat of his pants filling the screen as R. bends over to adjust his TV set. This image of fabric pulled almost to the breaking point perfectly captures the reality of Herr R.'s existence. Appropriately, after the murders, we see only R.'s clothing flying past the bedroom door. Similarly the stifling Wilhelminian clothing in *Fontane Effi Briest* is the obvious correlative of suffocating social mores; the most familiar still from this film shows Effi and her lover, dressed in the wool-and-lace clothing of the parlor, picnicking on the beach. In *Fox and his Friends,* too, clothing is the emblem of social caste. When Fox, at his lover's insistence but at his own expense, buys a new wardrobe at an exclusive homosexual salon, we see a specific instance of his general exploitation by his upper-class homosexual lover and friends and of the usurpation of his personality.

In *The Marriage of Maria Braun* clothing as an emblem of a sterile and emotionless socialization process has been perfectly integrated into the film narrative. It is a process initiated by language: Maria boldly and assertively answers a crude remark by an American GI who, out of embarrassment, gives her two packs of cigarettes. Maria trades the cigarettes for her mother's brooch, barters the brooch for a dress, and uses the dress twice to gain a job. The replacement of emotions by clothing and other, related "things" is epitomized in this film by Maria's absent-minded placing of her purse into a vase of red roses (previously established as emblems of Maria's relationship with her absent husband). Most striking of all is the notoriously operatic clothing in *The Bitter Tears of Petra von Kant*, where Petra's seduction of Karin is conducted in ankle-fettering neo-Valkyrian costume—appropriate enough, given Petra's career as *haute-couteur* designer.

Not infrequently, hairstyles perform a similar function. Petra von Kant puts on a wig as she "assembles" herself and her mask-like persona on the morning of the film's first day. Maria Braun combs her hair into a curly, postwar "poodle" style, sighs at its foolishness, but says that "maybe Americans like poodles." The unmistakable implication is that West Germany has become a faithful and clever pet of its American master.

Just as effective and ultimately more enigmatic is the use in *The Bitter Tears of Petra von Kant* of unclothed and hairless mannequins that stand and lie in varied poses around Petra's apartment as silent observers of the plot and frequently as character emblems: rather than seeing Petra and Karin in bed together, the audience sees two of the mannequins with arms and legs entangled in a lifeless embrace in Petra's bed. In *The Bitter Tears of Petra von Kant*, moreover, the juxtaposing of the female characters to the only vaguely female mannequins is reiterated by a juxtaposing of the female characters with the oversized nudes of a voluptuous Baroque mural that forms the backdrop for much of the film's static dialogue. As Karin relates her husband's abuses to Petra, the genitals of one of the mural's male nudes hang threateningly over Karin's head. The visual motif of the mannequin occurs in other films, such as *The Merchant of Four Seasons*, in which the merchant's wife, Irmgard, in pursuit of an adulterous affair, is photographed in ironic juxtaposition with a shop-window mannequin dressed as a virginal bride.

Such vivid visual juxtapositions are further reiterated by the soundtrack. *The Marriage of Maria Braun* begins with sounds of wartime bombing that merge with the sounds of postwar reconstruction, with the sounds of Maria's adding machine and typewriter, and ultimately with the sounds of the film's concluding explosion. A witty, intriguing soundtrack counterpoint between Verdi and the Platters reinforces the operatic costumes and storyline of *The Bitter Tears of*

Petra von Kant. Fassbinder created in *Bitter Tears* a high-camp synthesis of old and new that neatly depicts the refined-to-sterility modern sensibility that is the target of his critical scrutiny. Traceable, one supposes, to Straub/Huillet, Godard, and further back to Brecht, such dialectical syntheses of high- and low-art forms, of character and symbolic objects, of character and shot-framing, of character and set or costuming, of language and silence, of soundtrack and visual image, of drama and melodrama lie at the heart of Fassbinder's cinematic style and stylization. They convey his central thematic antithesis: exploited and innocent (in the Brechtian sense) individuals opposed to alienating and evil modern society.

Fassbinder's description of his reaction to Franz Biberkopf, the protagonist of *Berlin Alexanderplatz*, applies to many of his film characters. Franz Biberkopf is a person who "wants to believe that a human being can be good even within the society in which he lives, that a human being—whom he considers to be good by nature, just as I do—could be good even inside society which I consider to be bad. . . . [This] I do not believe" (K, 30). The difference between Fassbinder and his few sympathetic characters is insight, insight into .the destructive and essentially evil nature of the society in which they live. This insight is what Fassbinder would impart to his audience.

Fassbinder has said, "I don't make any films which aren't political" (FC, 14). Through pragmatic descriptions of social repression his films become political documents calling for social change. Even at their quirkiest, most ambiguous, most enigmatic—as in, for example, *The Bitter Tears of Petra von Kant* or *Chinese Roulette*—Fassbinder's films assert, if only implicitly, that individual happiness and social "propriety" cannot be reconciled, and the impossibility of reconciliation frustrates and defeats every individual. Alienation leads inexorably and invariably to individual acts of violence, directed at society but ultimately only self-destructive. The murderous rampages of Herr R. in *Why Does Herr R. Run Amuck?*, of Karin's father in *The Bitter Tears of Petra von Kant*, or of the deceased husband in *Mother Küster's Journey to Heaven* destroy a few lives, but society at large is impervious to such attacks. Individual rage leads most often only to self-destruction, whether conscious, as in Hans's ritualistic suicide by alcohol in *Merchant of Four Seasons* or Fox's death by drugs in *Fox and his Friends*, or unconscious, as in Ali's suffering from stomach ulcers in *Fear Eats the Soul: Ali*.

We sympathize with the violence of most Fassbinder protagonists, but at his bleakest Fassbinder is also capable of showing us a world which precludes sympathy, as in *The Third Generation* (1979). An examination of the motiveless and mindless "radical chic" political terrorists of the late 1970s, *The Third Generation* represents Fassbinder at his most pessimistic. In this film violence is not only ineffective as a weapon against society; it actually has been coopted by society. As one character, a police commissioner, says, "I recently had a dream . . . in which the capitalists invented terrorism in order to force the state to protect them better."

The only bright spot in Fassbinder's bleakly pessimistic view of modern existence is the possibility of individual human contact. Only love seems to hold out a redemptive potential, but even faith in love is usually a faith misplaced. *Merchant of Four Seasons, Bitter Tears of Petra von Kant, Fox and his Friends, The Marriage of Maria Braun*—each is a story of failed love. Even in Fassbinder's most optimistic film, *Fear Eats the Soul: Ali,* Emmi's love for Ali will probably not be sufficient to cure him. And, as Fassbinder himself has suggested, love itself may be nothing but a refined form of exploitation. As Petra von Kant and Fox are abused and exploited by their homosexual lovers, an awareness grows in the viewer that a yearning for love is the weak point in the otherwise impregnable interpersonal armor that the individual builds around him/herself. Fassbinder has said, "There is no love, only the possibility of love" (F, 47), and, more cynically, "love is the best, most insidious, most effective instrument of social repression" (FC, 10). One *can* survive—Fassbinder's protagonists are, after all, surrounded by social survivors—but apparently only at the expense of integrity, honesty, intimacy, and love. The essence of modern existence as presented in Fassbinder's films is alienation, manipulation, and exploitation. Insight into this harsh truth triggers either impotent rage or the awful, hopeless despair that characterizes Fassbinder's protagonists and, one cannot help but think, all of modern society.

The stylization of Fassbinder's long, static takes in which we are confronted by the cold, silent stares of his characters prevents total emotional involvement with the characters. Fassbinder creates a sterile screen world of almost total artificiality. But artifice is for Fassbinder the means by which to express a truer, internal reality: "The realism I mean and I want is one that takes place in the head of the audience and not the one up on the screen; the latter doesn't interest me at all; people have that every day" (F, 85). Like Brecht, Fassbinder strives for a certain intellectual distance. Fassbinder's characters, like Brecht's, represent not only people but also intellectual concepts. Social change comes with understanding, not with mere feeling. Fassbinder's characters, however, are more than ideas.

In spite of the distancing and alienation, they frequently become people that we care about: "I think I go farther than [Brecht] did in that I let the audience *feel* and *think*" (C, 20).

Despite the amplitude of Fassbinder's work, the thematic core of his films remains the oppressive antagonism between personal emotion and social form, between personal freedom and social restriction, personal honesty and social hypocrisy, personal normality and social perversity, personal happiness and social propriety. At a climactic moment in *Fear Eats the Soul: Ali* a narrow-minded, bigoted woman says, "But happiness . . . what's that? There is, after all, such a thing as decency!" This remark is characteristic of the nigglingly destructive social attitudes and pressures that inexorably destroy all possibilities of individual happiness.

Fassbinder has said "I am a German making German films for a German audience" (SS, 4). Most of his films deal with contemporary German questions and problems: bigotry and racism, xenophobia, social alienation, the isolation of the elderly, the difficulty of making contacts in a depersonalized and depersonalizing society, exploitation, and the selling of the soul. The specifics may be German, but these are problems of all contemporary Western European and American systems. Fassbinder supposedly intends his films to be accessible and meaningful to a specific audience with specific problems; he would have us believe that he is making films not for a cosmopolitan, international elite, but for the average West German who lives with these problems. Fassbinder, however, is really dealing with problems that are both particular and universal. Non-Germans can and do relate to his films, just as Germans have always related to Hollywood westerns. "It would be my dream to make a German film that would be so beautiful and so crazy and so wonderful and that could nevertheless be critical of the system, just as there is a great number of films from Hollywood which are by no means so simplistically affirming as is always superficially maintained" (F, 90).

Author's note: Deaths are surely as important as debuts, but this book was already in press at the time of Fassbinder's death in early summer 1982. I might have evaluated Fassbinder somewhat differently, had I been viewing his work as over-and-done rather than as an on-going process. At the very least, many of my present-tense sentences would have been put into the past. The good, it seems, still die young.

7

Wim Wenders

Chronology

1945   Wim Wenders born on August 14 in Düsseldorf.
1967   *Schauplätze* [Scenes], 10 min.
        Same Player Shoots Again, 12 min.
1968   *Silver City*, 25 min.
        Victor I, 4 min.
1969   *Alabama—2000 Light Years*, 24 min.
        3 Amerikanische LPs [3 American LPs], 15 min.
1970   *Polizeifilm* [Police Film], 12 min.
        Summer in the City, 145 min.
1971   *Die Angst des Tormanns beim Elfmeter* [The Goalie's Anxiety at the Penalty Kick], 100 min.
1972   *Der scharlachrote Buchstabe* [The Scarlet Letter], 90 min.
1973   *Alice in den Städten* [Alice in the Cities], 110 min.
1974   *Aus der Familie der Panzerechsen* and *Die Insel* [From the Family of the Crocodiles and The Island], episodes of the television series "Freizeitheim"/"Ein Haus für uns," each 25 min.
        Falsche Bewegung [Wrong Move], 103 min.
1976   *Im Lauf der Zeit* [Kings of the Road], 176 min.
1977   *Der amerikanische Freund* [The American Friend], 123 min.
1980   *Lightning over Water: Nick's Film*, 89 min.

*Cinema is in a way the art of things, as well as persons,
becoming identical with themselves.*

IN AN ESSAY WITH the intriguing and revealing title "Emotion Pictures (Slowly Rockin' On)," first published in *Filmkritik* in 1970, Wim Wenders enumerated the qualities in the Westerns of John Ford that have since disappeared from American films: "I miss the friendliness, the care, the thoroughness, the confidence, the seriousness, the calmness, the humanity of the films of John Ford; I miss the faces that are never forced into anything, the landscapes that are never simply only backgrounds, the feelings that are never obtrusive or strange, the stories that, even when they are funny, never make fun" (T, 21).[1] The qualities that Wenders admires in Ford's films are also admirably present in Wenders's own films. While John Ford had created in his films the world of the American Old West, Wenders re-creates a modern landscape in which the only frontiers are those of the individual spirit. The aridity of Ford's Western desert has been replaced by the sterility of western urban technology. The landscape has changed but its metaphoric character has not.

Wim Wenders creates films of rootless wanderers. He records lonely and alienated travels through a coolly static world. He depicts solitary transients in an americanized pop culture of television and rock and roll. Wenders's movies capture a world in which intimacy occurs only fleetingly in chance encounters between strangers, and violence sometimes seems to offer the only possibility of physical contact. Wenders, in his low-key and purposefully undramatic film narratives, excels in the creation of chilling mood and anxious atmosphere. Wenders peoples this stark film world, however, with sympathetic characters who convey a promise of individual warmth despite the coldness of their social context, and move us as they move through the indistinguishable and interchangeable cities of the western world. "I always used to like the connection between motion and emotion. Sometimes I think the emotion in my films comes only from the motion: it's not created by the characters" (W, 14).

Wenders's reputation as a director rests on a relatively small body of work consisting of seven films made in the early– and mid–1970s: his seldom-seen first film, *Summer in the City* (1970), *The Goalie's Anxiety at the Penalty Kick* (1971), *The Scarlet Letter* (1972), *Alice in the Cities* (1974), *Wrong Move* (1975), *Kings of the Road* (1976), and *The American Friend* (1977). Fortunately for the German cinema, critical success has hardly diminished the output of Fassbinder,

Herzog, or Schlöndorff. Wenders, on the other hand, lured to Hollywood after *The American Friend*, has now worked for several years on his *Hammett* film, encountering dislocation and a creative impasse, apparently resolved only as filming finally began in 1980. In the meantime, however, Wenders has also moved into producing other directors' films, including Peter Handke's *The Left-Handed Woman* (1977) and, as an assistant producer, Christopher Petit's *Radio On* (1979). Wenders has, in addition, recently made a documentary tribute to, about, and with American director Nicholas Ray, *Lightning Over Water: Nick's Film* (1980).

Wenders, unlike Herzog and Fassbinder, who are for the most part self-trained filmmakers, or Straub and Schlöndorff, who served apprenticeships with various French directors, is a film school product, a Munich Film Academy graduate whose first films were practical exercises for the academy. Like the critic-filmmakers of the early French New Wave, Wenders has written film and music criticism, for *Filmkritik* and for Munich's *Süddeutsche Zeitung*. He was schooled in the various styles of the international cinema, and the influence of an earlier generation of filmmakers is very consciously acknowledged by Wenders, both within his films and in his interviews and writings.[2] In addition to the unquestionable influence of John Ford, Wenders has identified the traces in his work of Robert Bresson and Yasujiro Ozu.

As Wenders has said in comparing the look of his films to that of other recent German filmmakers, "I think it's more the surface of my films that is more American than that of other German directors. But I think that my films are finally more un-American than the others. [My films] certainly use the language of the American cinema" (FC, 45). Any given frame of a Wenders film may *look* American because of its "realistic" lighting, its controlled visual balance, its apparently objective point of view. A Wenders film may begin and end in a conventionally Hollywood manner, moving from some distanced universal viewpoint to the specifics of an individual narrative and back again at the end. *Alice in the Cities*, for example, begins with a subjective distance shot of an airplane aloft before moving to a more "objective" medium shot of one of its protagonists under a New Jersey boardwalk. It ends with an aerial movement away from a medium shot of its two main characters on a train to a shot taken at such a distance that the characters become invisible and the train itself becomes little more than a moving line in an abstract landscape. Such a narrative framework (if not the final movement into an abstraction of the landscape) might be appropriate for a John Ford Western or even for an Alfred Hitchcock thriller. Yet the arrangement of narrative and the juxtaposition of shots and sequences between the beginning and the end distinguish Wenders's films from those of the commercial American film establishment.

Static shots, in which characters move in and out of the frame rather than being followed by the camera, contribute to the understated calmness of Wenders's film style, as do shots that unobtrusively track moving figures to counteract character motion rather than to create a sense of excitement through motion. In a three-shot sequence near the end of *Wrong Move*, for example, the main characters steadily but almost imperceptibly ascend a mountain. Such shots and sequences stylistically reinforce the frequently aimless meanderings that Wenders's characters undertake in his "road films."

Emotional involvement of viewer with character created by close-ups is often cut short by unexpected long shots that remove the viewer to a more neutral plane. Similarly, shots and shot sequences are arranged episodically, without particular emphasis and at times without apparent order, so we are seldom alerted to "significant" scenes. We remain attentive even to ostensibly inconsequential scenes. All shots thus invite our attention, but we can seldom be sure that our attention has been rewarded. What, for example, should we make in *Alice in the Cities* of a close-up of a key from a North Carolina motel that Philip Winter finds when he is back in Germany? Over a shot of the key in the palm of Philip's hand, he tells Alice, simply, "I forgot to turn it in." An apparently unimportant and unelucidated episode, the close-up of the key in Philip's hand invites interpretation but may in fact be insignificant. Is this a "key" to Philip's dilemma, the Key to Life itself, or just a key to a North Carolina motel room? Suggestively isolated incidents lend an intriguing, if arbitrary, quality to Wenders's films.

Color, or the lack of color, in Wender's films is similarly unpredictable. Wenders generally prefers black–and–white film because it is "much more realistic and natural than color. It sounds paradoxical, but that's the way it is" (W, 12). Color, when used (as in *The American Friend*), is unnaturally vivid, thus heightening the viewer's sense of narrative tension and alienation. Referring to *Hammett*, the Hollywood-produced and financed film on which he has been working since *The American Friend*, Wenders has said: "I would like to make the film in black-and-white. The studio in Hollywood is of course horrified by the idea" (FK, 684).

Music, both as an element of style and of narrative, confirms and confounds expectations. Asked once about the importance of music in his films, Wenders noted that "for the first two films [short films made before *The Goalie's Anxiety at the Penalty Kick*], I had the music first and then added the film" (SS, 5). For the inhabitant of the post-World War II "American Age," rock and roll music has a special meaning. Wenders himself discerns an unusual social purity in it: "The only thing I felt secure with from the beginning and felt had nothing to do with fascism was rock music" (W, 12). Even more importantly for the grown-up Wenders, American popular music has recaptured the spirit lost with the passing of John Ford: "Music from America replaces more and more the sensuality that has been lost to the films. . . . This music is above all the music of the American West the conquest of which was dealt with in John Ford's films and the second conquest of which this music deals with" (T, 21–22).

When Philip Winter, at the beginning of *Alice in the Cities*, sings "Under the Boardwalk," it evokes not only Philip's era, his journey toward the United States, and possibly the "American colonization of the subconscious" (as Bruno, in *Kings of the Road*, characterizes popular music), but it is also a wryly literal commentary on Philip's location under an Atlantic beach boardwalk. Later in the film, Chuck Berry singing "Memphis, Tennessee" during a concert in Germany reinforces the naturalism of this documentary sequence and weaves it into the fiction of *Alice*'s narrative. Furthermore, the song's lyrics, which describe a futile long-distance telephone search for an elusive love lost in Memphis, comment upon Philip and Alice's futile search for the girl's grandmother "somewhere in the Ruhr District." Rock lyrics also create an ironic contradiction of visual image and soundtrack, as when we see a small boy sitting motionless next to a jukebox that plays "On the Road Again." In addition to music that seems to have its source within the frame (a visible jukebox, radio, or singer) one also encounters off-screen commentative music (in *Alice* a melancholy eight–note sequence played by the rock group, Can, variations of which recur throughout the film). Such emotionally evocative music is not, however, employed to reinforce visual images of personal or interpersonal crisis but rather to give the entire film a mood of wistful solitude through its occurrence at seemingly arbi-trary. moments.

Whether in the use of music, of color, or of cinematic syntax, Wenders seldom does the expected. Like the writers Peter Handke and Patricia Highsmith, whose works he has adapted to film, Wenders creates thrillers with very few thrills or, in filming his original screenplays, he unemotionally tells emotional stories. Wenders hesitates to show the viewer narrative climaxes. He cuts short, inter-

(top) Wenders's The Goalie's Anxiety at the Penalty Kick; *(bottom)* Alice in the Cities. *Courtesy of The Liberty Company.*

rupts, or elides what would conventionally be considered "significant" scenes. Instead of feeding viewer expectations, Wenders undercuts our usual sense of what *should* come next and of how it should be presented. He confounds us, however, without circumventing our involvement with his characters. Even when he or they confound us, we stay involved with them because of their intelligence, their intensity, and their wit. Schlöndorff's and Fassbinder's characters are intelligent; Herzog's are surely intense. Seldom, however, are they capable of the humane wit that in Wenders's films so immediately engages our interest in the fates of unfamiliar characters.

Wenders's films examine traditional relationships that fail and unconventional relationships that unexpectedly succeed: relationships between strangers, between parents and children, between characters and their environments, even between characters and the filmmaker. Wenders's first important film, *The Goalie's Anxiety at the Penalty Kick,* points to the failure of all conventional relationships. *Alice in the Cities* explores the salutary interdependence of a German reporter in America, Philip Winter, and a young German girl abandoned by her mother in New York City. Together Winter and Alice travel back to West Germany in an attempt to find the girl's grandmother. Externally a narrative of the pair's journey together back to and into West Germany, *Alice in the Cities* really records the development of the relationship between the two. Similarly, in *Kings of the Road,* a circular journey through the small towns of West Germany undertaken by the two protagonists, Bruno and Robert, is less important than the emotional journey that the two companions take toward each other. And even in his film adaptation of Hawthorne's *The Scarlet Letter,* which he acknowledges to be his least successful film, Wenders claims to have been attracted, at least partially, by the relationship between Hester Prynne and Pearl: "Precisely the idea of the mother and the child. And also the idea of the first generation of Americans . . . that is to say, Europeans . . . living over there" (W, 7). This remark reveals the source of his interest in Hawthorne's novel and in the other authors whose work Wenders has adapted to the screen, but also suggests his concern with national or cultural identities and with the sense of isolation experienced by Germans in America, by Americans in Germany, and all too frequently by Germans in Germany.

It is no surprise to us when Philip Winter tells Alice as he sits in his bath, "I'm afraid of being afraid," or when the main character of *Wrong Move* says at film's end: "Every move I've made has been the wrong move." Endless anxiety, fear of action, and avoidance of involvement are major themes of Wenders's films. They are also a dominant focus of the authors whom Wenders adapts to the screen: Hawthorne, Handke, Highsmith. Like the protagonist of Highsmith's *Tremor of Forgery* (a title self-consciously quoted on a theater marquee in *The Goalie's Anxiety*), who takes up residence in the heat and foreignness of Algeria, growing into his own isolation until he and it become an unseparable unit, the main characters of Wenders's films frequently become in some sense adjuncts of their environments. Even at their most interesting, they are dominated by their environment even as they move and keep moving to avoid the capitulations and small deaths that stasis would bring.

A major achievement of Wenders's films is their evocation of the cool destructiveness and impersonality of modern Western society. Wenders's protagonists move through interchangeable, icy cities which impassively threaten to overwhelm their human inhabitants. Wenders's filmic world is a pop culture universe of media overload dominated by unwatched televisions, ubiquitous advertising, and half-heard rock music, by jukeboxes and Coca Cola, by cars, trains, and airplanes. It is a plastic-and-steel world sterilized by American technology and the impersonal values of the "consumer society." Wenders's protagonists engage us, however, by their unwillingness or inability to be assimilated totally into such a world. In mutually indistinguishable cities best suited to anonymous clones and robots, Wenders's heroes—Philip and Alice, Jonathan and Ripley, Wilhelm, Bruno and Robert—seek a meaning for their own existences. Even in the face of evidence that there may in fact *be* no meaning, these characters endure and, in some fine sense, prevail by creating meaning out of their relationships with each other.

Interesting characters and evocations of atmosphere are important in Wenders's films because these films frequently have little of a story to tell. Neither totally narrative nor totally nonnarrative (as, for example, in the tradition of experimental filmmaking), Wenders's films strive for a delicate balance of substance and style. Wenders himself has acknowledged the sense of a "missing story" in his films, especially his earlier ones (SS, 5). He ses an interest in narrative as a relatively new direction in his work: "When I started shooting, I wasn't interested in stories at all. Even in *The Goalie*, I wasn't that interested in the story. I'm getting more and more interested in stories" (W, 10).

Wenders's early short films made in the academy, such as *Alabama* (1969), tend to be descriptive, situational constructs using musical sound tracks—in *Alabama* Bob Dylan, Jimi Hendrix, and the Rolling Stones—and visual juxtapositions both within the frame and frame-to-frame to suggest a bleakly malevolent context with no real narrative center. The move from these early films to Peter Handke's novel, *The Goalie's Anxiety,* and beyond Handke to Highsmith and *Hammett* is indeed a move toward "stories." Even here, however, as in *The American Friend,* made from Highsmith's *Ripley's Game,* the story virtually disappears. Motivation disappears, effect overshadows cause, and plot yields to the film's mood of anxious tension. Questions answered in Highsmith's novel (Who is Ripley? Why does he tempt Jonathan? What are his connections with the New York and Paris underworlds?) are only teasingly hinted at in Wenders's film.

It is in the two later films *not* adapted from preexisting novels—*Alice in the Cities* and *Kings of the Road*—that Wenders has most successfully achieved an equilibrium of mood, narrative, characterization, and film style. In these, Wenders's best films, the characters and narratives seemingly create themselves, the characters out of the personalities of the actors playing them, and the narratives out of the characters and the situations: "I really prefer films that are invented during the shooting, or that don't have so many inventions but rather *trouvailles.* . . . In *Kings of the Road* there was no invention at all when we started. The only invention was the situation: the truck and the itinerary. The rest was *trouvailles.* . . . We were really looking for the story, trying to follow the loose ends" (W, 13). Wenders's style seems truest, least forced, and most fascinating in the films he has written himself. Rather than being pinned down to the requirements of someone else's story, Wenders is able to let the characters and the narrative grow naturally.

Related to Wenders's notion of "found" action is his uncommon attitude toward his characters, a willingness to let them develop in their own way and to treat them somehow as real beings who should be accorded a certain measure of respect. We find this attitude toward character even in the films based on other writers' novels. In explaining a cut away from a main character in *The American Friend,* for example, (after Jonathan has committed a murder in the Paris subway) Wenders has said: "I thought that, after the murder, he had some right to privacy" (SS, 44).

The best-drawn of Wenders's protagonists—the four main characters of *Alice in the Cities* and *Kings of the Road*—are strikingly Americanized Germans, and these films are themselves explanations and inversions of American film genres. As has been often observed, *Kings of the Road* follows a long Hollywood tradition of male-buddy pictures: the Newman-Redford films, *Midnight Cowboy*, and so forth. *Alice in the Cities* is analogous to an American cinema tradition—not only to Bogdanovich's *Paper Moon*, to which *Alice* has been favorably compared, but to a line of films about single-adults saddled with children, stretching back to *The Kid* and Damon Runyan's *Little Miss Marker* and forward to *A Thousand Clowns* and *Paper Moon*.

While the characters of Kluge, Schlöndorff, Fassbinder, and Herzog are identifiably German (even Herzog's *Aguirre* is an unmistakably Germanic conquistador), Alice and Phillip, Bruno and Robert, even Joseph Bloch of *The Goalie* are new Germans, internationalized inhabitants of a global America. Apart from linguistic differences, they seem to be stamped from the American mold: casual, individualistic, street-wise, and "laid back," embodying few of the stereotypes of German tidiness, efficiency, or orderliness. They are bemused wanderers through a capitalist technology that is rapidly engulfing the humanist values of the past (represented in *Alice*, for instance, by a colony of sturdy bourgeois houses about to be torn down to make way for a high-rise apartment complex, or in *Kings* by the obsolescent village movie houses that serve as stopping places and guide posts on the circuitous itinerary traced by Bruno's work as film-projector repairman). The West Germany of these films is in fact a consumer society well on its way to consuming its own citizens. It is a society of destruction masquerading as progress, of spiritual impoverishment in the guise of material affluence. Wenders's protagonists move, for to stop is to die an American–inspired but German-induced death of the spirit. This central kernel of unhappy modern reality is really little different from that found in Kluge's 1965 film, *Yesterday Girl*. In Wenders's films, however, a small saving grace is to be found in unexpected, fortuitous, even random relationships and in the sense of identity that these encounters engender.

The traditional bonds between husband and wife (in *Alice*, *Kings*, *American Friend*) and frequently even the biological ties between parent and child (*Alice* and *Kings of the Road*) are shown to be untenable in our society, although Wenders can be optimistic about adult-child relationships. In *The American Friend* the only stable relationship seems to be that of Jonathan Zimmerman and his young son. In *Alice in the Cities* Philip Winter's personal growth is directly tied to his involvement with Alice. The deeper his commitment to Alice grows, the more liberated he becomes. The more he relinquishes his independence for Alice's sake, the more he loses his anxiety and discovers a sense of identity. In *Kings of the Road* a similar affinity with children is perceived through recurrent encounters of Bruno and Robert with children. Bruno meets a movie–house ticket girl who is not married because she "prefers," she says, to live with her child. The camera lingers on a group of children who play at a river under a bridge. In one of the film's later sequences, Robert barters with a sly little boy whose values seem far more firmly established than Robert's own. The climax of this intermittent involvement with children comes in a movie house where Bruno and Robert perform, for an audience of children, a boisterously athletic, comic pantomime silhouetted against the back of a movie screen.

To Wenders as well as to his characters, children—and the cinema, as the pantomime scene suggests—represent values lost to the adult world. Wenders's protagonists seek to restore playfulness and grace, frankness and honesty, and simplicity to their lives. These values also form a basis for Wenders's film aesthetics. The children in Wenders's films are never sentimentalized Victorian innocents. On the contrary, they are self-reliant, pragmatic, and skeptical. The bartering boy in *Kings of the Road* or Alice, who easily eludes the police and finds Philip (in an ironic reversal of Philip's difficulty in finding Alice's relatives) and who at a crucial point produces a one-hundred dollar bill to pay for train tickets for herself and Philip—these children are less naive and thus socially less victimized than the psychically wounded adults around them. Alice has a resilience that Philip has to admire and ultimately to envy.

Children, moreover, signify an indomitable optimism, even in the sad and inconclusive separations that end Wenders's films. The ability to walk away from the past, he has said, is the "common idea that *Scarlet Letter* shares with the other films. The idea of starting anew at the end . . . the idea of not losing interest in starting anew. Not losing the energy" (W, 4). Of *Kings of the Road* Wenders has said, "I don't see how I could make a more optimistic movie" (W, 7).

On the other hand, Wenders also says in the same interview, "I can't think of any of my characters who really makes a new start. They're all *preparing* a new start" (W, 7). Wenders's films are never neatly resolved by movie's end. We are left with the feeling that resolution may be neither possible nor desirable. To be sure, *The American Friend* ends with Jonathan's death. Ripley himself, however, is last seen sitting on the beach, and the significance (or insignificance) of Jonathan's death is truly enigmatic, given the ambiguity of his illness throughout the film. *Kings of the Road,* too, ends with separation—seemingly the only possible conclusion but hardly a resolution of the protagonists' relationship. Wilhelm, at the end of

Wrong Move, is left acknowledging only the wrongness of his every move, unlike his predecessor in Goethe's novel, *Wilhelm Meister's Apprenticeship,* who moves toward social integration, and the character in Handke's screenplay, who moves toward social isolation but into artistic creativity. Even *Alice in the Cities,* a most affirmative film, has an open ending. We see a newspaper photo accompanying a report of John Ford's death with the caption "Lost World." This shot is followed by a short dialogue between Alice and Philip on the train to Munich. Alice: "What will you do in Munich?" Philip: "I'll write an end to this story. And you?" Alice shrugs. Like so many modernist films *Alice in the Cities* is an unsealed package. The point is in the seeking, not the finding; in the questioning, not in tidy answers.

Such seeking and questioning, such attempts to apprehend and comprehend reality lead in Wenders's films to a recurrent examination of the medium itself as being possibly more significant than the story filmed. Wenders has called *Kings of the Road* a "film about the consciousness of cinema in Germany." Metacinematic or self-reflexive investigation of visual media—not only movies but also photography, television, painting, even newspapers—reflects Wenders's consciously nondramatic and musing approach to his material. "I never wanted to show things that are shown in general. . . . I think it's too dramatic" (SS, 5). Too dramatic and possibly too deceptive. Reality may seem to reside in the exciting but infrequent climaxes of life, but what of the long valleys that lie between the peaks? Reality is not easily captured; ultimate truths exceed the grasp of any medium. Wenders's films become musings upon media processes, especially in *Alice in the Cities* and *Kings of the Road.* Just as the narrative inconclusiveness of these films initiates thought by refusing to tie together all the threads of plot and characterization, so does their self–reflexivity reinforce openness by exploring the potentials and the limitations of film itself.

At the beginning of *Alice in the Cities* we first see Philip Winter on a beach in the Eastern United States taking Polaroid photos of his surroundings in order to capture, for the newspaper story he is supposed to be writing, the "reality" of America. In a line of dialogue that is specifically Philip's explanation to his newspaper editor but can be understood more generally as a comment by Wenders to his viewers, Philip says: "The story has to do with things that one can see . . . with pictures and signs." American society is saturated with pictures and signs, and Wenders excels in capturing the icons of American life: snack bar signs, highway signs, gas station signs, motel signs, and, above all, ubiquitous American advertising signs. Just before Philip reports to his editor we see a three-shot sequence: a "New York City" highway sign, a dollar bill in Philip's hand, a highway toll booth.

Philip's understandable response to this visually overladen environment is to capture it by camera, but, as we—and more gradually he—come to realize, his photographs are as incapable as his written words of distilling the American essence or uncovering American reality. Early in the film Philip mutters in disgust that his photos "never show what you've really seen." Still Philip clings to his faith in his Polaroid. To a girlfriend in New York, he says, "photographing has something to do with proofs." He refuses to acknowledge his own failures, his own egocentricity, and his real reasons for the photographs, even when the woman tells him, "you always act as if you were the only one to experience things and that's why you keep taking these pictures."

That Philip's search for America is really a search for his own identity has been established previously in Philip's remark to his editor that "when you drive through America, then something happens to you . . . through the pictures that you see. And the reason why I took so many pictures . . . that's a part of the story." The inherent insufficiency of his picture-taking and its egocentric motivation are, however, at best subliminally acknowledged by Philip early in the film. What Philip really sought in America was himself, but like Parzival in pursuit of the Grail castle, the harder he looked for it, the more it eluded him. His relinquishing of self-involvement through his involvement with the girl brings him a sense of identity when he least expects it. This unexpected truth is conveyed to us and, we suspect, to Philip near the end of the film by a series of pictures, taken in a photo automat, showing neither landscapes nor signs but rather the faces of Philip and Alice together. Even here we are made aware of the insufficiency of photography. Each picture shows a new expression on both faces, but each is only a partial aspect of larger reality. These photos only obscure Philip and Alice's relationship.

The insufficiency of photographs as a means to insight is parodied, almost grotesquely, in *The American Friend*, when Ripley, lying on his pool table, snaps shot after shot of himself in what seems to be a vain attempt to comprehend his own personality. Beckert, the child murderer in *M*, and Professor Rath, dressed as a cabaret clown in *The Blue Angel*, had studied their own faces—and their existential situations—in mirrors. In Wenders's films the mirror has been supplanted by the Polaroid, and in *The American Friend* Ripley's photos fall unheeded and unrevealing onto the pool table.

While photography is an insufficient medium, television is a corrupted one. Television—the quintessential technological instrument of western consumerism—is the hollow imagemaker and merchandizer of modern non-culture that threatens the more humane values of the past. Television receivers beam a cold vacuity into Ripley's German "White House" and into the New York City apartment of Derwatt, the art forger in *The American Friend*. Wenders's indictment of television's corruption is, however, most vividly portrayed early in *Alice in the Cities*. Philip, turning on the television in an American motel room, finds a broadcast of Ford's *Young Mr. Lincoln*, but the film is quickly interrupted by an ironic commercial for the United Negro College Fund ("A mind is a terrible thing to waste") and subsequently by a bit of typically American, Red Barber hucksterism. Philip kicks over and breaks the set.

Movies, on the other hand, have for Wenders a purity, an innocence, and an apparent utility, which, one assumes, can only derive from cinema's ability to construct idealized environments. As children use fantasy as a means to happiness, so did adults once use the movies. The homages to John Ford in *Alice in the Cities* imply a reverence less for the man than for the films he created. Significantly, just as Wenders looks back to Ford in his films, so too did Ford, as one of the most accomplished creators on film of the Old West as it never really was, look back to an earlier, purer era.

The "Lost World" caption under Ford's newspaper photo thus assumes a doubly epigonic significance: Ford's feeling for and construction of the lost world of the Old West and Wenders's feeling for the lost world of John Ford himself and Hollywood in its "Age of Innocence." In *The American Friend*, Ripley shows what has become of the Great American Cowboy, and pornography has replaced the Western. The world of movies in which Ford worked is a world that no longer exists. Bruno in *Kings of the Road* travels to one small German cinema after another, trying to keep the projectors running in these slowly dying movie houses. These movie houses, if they survive at all, frequently survive through a perversion of function. At one stop Bruno finds an inept projectionist masturbating in the projection booth while an untended projector spills countless meters of a porno film onto the floor. Bruno responds with mocking laughter, but Wenders's point is serious. The movie house in the modern age is associated with financial *and* spiritual impoverishment, with sadness and decay. Bruno has an apparently unhappy affair with the cashier of the same movie house, and, not coincidentally, Joseph Bloch in *The Goalie's Anxiety* murders a movie house cashier. The commercial cinema has lost its idealism and, with it, its powers of psychic rejuvenation.

The last and one of the most touching sequences of *Kings of the Road* is a conversation between Bruno and an aging cinema owner. Reminiscing, the woman evokes for Bruno the happier cinematic past: "Film is the art of seeing, my father told me." Now, as the woman verifies, pornography has become the only viable alternative to commercial extinction: "But I won't let myself be forced into showing films where people . . . have their joy in living destroyed. Where every feeling for themselves and for the world has to die off." Refusing to succumb, the woman has closed her cinema: "The way it is now, it's better that there is no cinema any longer than that there is a cinema the way it is now." While the impotent descent into sexual exploitation must always have been inherent in the commercialism of earlier cinema, Wenders implies that some equilibrium, now lost, did exist between commerce and humanity or idealism.

Despite the degeneration of the commercial movie system, movies still have the potential of showing us, if not life itself, approaches and attitudes to life through a construction of illuminating fictions about life. Through paradoxical formulations, such as an examination of the death of the cinema in a film like *Kings of the Road* or an investigation into the limitations of a life lived through photographs or written words, as in *Alice in the Cities*, Wenders shows us how to question life and also the importance of not mistaking our questioning for life itself.

A film may look like life. A clever stationary shot out the back window of a moving monorail car in *Alice in the Cities* appears at first to be a backward tracking shot, but it shows us that a film may be either more or less than it seems. Such viewer disorientations force us to question other shots, compel an admission that we are watching a film, not life itself. At Philip Winter's protest over the difficulties brought into his life by his involvement with Alice, she tells him: "What else did you have to do? Just scribble in your notebook." The examination of life can be a road leading nowhere if there is no underlying human relationship to be examined. Near the end of *Alice in the Cities* Alice tells Philip, "you haven't taken any photos in a long time." Philip then frames in his viewfinder, but does not photograph, a shot of Alice standing next to a young woman holding a little boy in her arms.

Life experienced through the viewfinder of a camera is not a life lived. Life photographed is life encapsulated, life turned static and dead. It is the present turned past and is not life at all. Thus we sometimes find in Wenders's work a playing with ideas of time. The

German title of *Kings of the Road* is *Im Lauf der Zeit* or "In the Course of Time," a title that links the notions of travel, time, and life. Similarly, in *Alice in the Cities*, a New York cabby tells Philip, "In this city you lose all sense of time." Neither time nor life can, or should, be held up for inspection. Life and time go on and on, and happiness lies in being in and of them. Formulations such as these seem, however, not only trite but even somehow misrepresentative of Wenders's films. These films are not philosophizing statements but rather tantalizing evocations of place, personality, and mood. Important links seem to be missing in each narrative chain; Wenders's films are no more clearly sequential than life itself. Motivations and conclusions are often only hinted, and frequently they are comprehended only subconsciously, just like time and reality.

Wenders does not make political films, at least not in the same sense as Kluge or Schlöndorff or even Fassbinder. Nor does Wenders explore the world of the outsider as does Herzog. Wenders's protagonists are loners, but in the American sense of the lonely searcher who avoids both material and emotional encumbrances in order to keep moving, to keep seeking an identity, to avoid the repetition signifying stasis and death.

For Wenders "cinema is in a way the art of things, as well as persons, becoming identical with themselves" (W, 12). Movement, including the movement of motion pictures, is a metaphor of life itself: "the stability of the characters is something I'm only able to establish by putting them on the road and involving them in a lot of movement. Motion . . . motion pictures" (W, 14). For Wenders's protagonists motion is the key to the process of "becoming identical with themselves." For Wenders's viewers these "emotion pictures" are the key to a process of examining life in order better to live it.

8

Hans-Jürgen Syberberg

Chronology

1935   Hans-Jürgen Syberberg born on December 8 in Nossen-dorf.

1965   *Fritz Kortner probt Kabale und Liebe* [Fritz Kortner Rehearses Kabale und Liebe], 110 min.
        Romy. Anatomie eines Gesichts [Romy, Anatomy of a Face], 90 min., later shortened to 60 min.

1966   *Fritz Kortner spricht Monologe für eine Schallplatte* [Fritz Kortner Reads Monologues for a Recording], 71 min.
        Wilhelm von Kobell, 16 min.

1967   *Die Grafen Pocci—einige Kapitel zur Geschichte einer Familie* [The Counts Pocci—A Few Chapters in the History of a Family], 92 min.

1968   *Scarabea—Wieviel Erde braucht der Mensch?* [Scarabea—How Much Earth Does a Person Need?], 130 min.

1969   *Sex-Business—Made in Pasing,* 100 min.

1970   *Nach meinem letzten Umzug . . .* [After My Last Move . . .], 72 min.
        San Domingo, 38 min.

1972   *Ludwig—Requiem für einen jungfräulichen König* [Ludwig—Requiem for a Virgin King], 134 min.
        Theodor Hierneis oder: Wie man ehem. Hofkoch wird [Theodor Hierneis or: How One Becomes a Retired Royal Cook], 84 min.

1974   *Karl May,* 187 min.

1975   *Winifred Wagner und die Geschichte des Hauses Wahnfried von 1914–1975* [Winifred Wagner and the His-

Hans-Jurgen Syberberg with Winifred Wagner. Courtesy of The Liberty Company

tory of the House Wahnfried from 1914–1975], 303 min.

1977   *Hitler, Ein Film aus Deutschland* [Hitler, A Film from Germany], 407 min.

*Film is the music of the future, and the continuation of life
by other means.*

HANS-JÜRGEN SYBERBERG is not an ingratiating man. In 1978 he assessed his fellow West German filmmakers in this way: "They all look greedily to their Mecca, America, without recognizing how hopelessly lost they have to be there, a movie generation, hooked on America and without an aesthetic concept, searching for an identity" (H, 47).[1] And in an open letter to the West German press in 1977 he said of the German film producers, the German film critics, and West Germany itself: "I have nothing more in common with these people. Why should I, and what use or pleasure is it to anyone? We are living in a dead country" (SS, 227).

Hans-Jürgen Syberberg could be considered the James Joyce of the New German Cinema—innovative, associative, and sometimes offensive. His four-part, seven-hour film, *Hitler, A Film From Germany* (1977), like Joyce's *Finnegans Wake*, is more notorious than known, more spoken about than seen. It has only been through the patronage of Francis Coppola and his Zoetrope Studios that Syberberg's *Hitler* has been shown at all in the United States—in a brief series of epic film evenings arranged for a handful of large American cities. An exhaustive survey of the Nazi nightmare, of Germany's past and present, *Hitler* is a film accessible, both physically and intellectually, only to a few. Even for that limited number of viewers both willing and able to see the film, it does not always live up to frequently misguided expectations, for Syberberg's *Hitler* is in no way similar to Joachim Fest's contemporaneous documentary *Hitler – A Career* or to Leni Riefenstahl's infamous paean to Nazism, *Triumph of the Will*. Syberberg's film is rather an elaborate and evocative musing upon the origins and implications of Hitler and the Nazis and of what Syberberg refers to as the "Hitler in us," our individual guilt for the Nazi phenomenon. *Hitler, A Film from Germany* is a work of meditation and of mourning—*"Trauerarbeit,"* as Syberberg has called it. It attempts to reconcile the present with the past, to come to terms with *"the* subject of our century" by means of film, *"the* twentieth-century art form."

While Syberberg's *Hitler, A Film from Germany* has been more derided or ignored than praised and promoted by German film critics, in France and in England the film has been regarded as a cinematic masterwork. Similarly, in the United States the film's status as a *cause celèbre*, if not its financial success, has been insured by Susan Sontag's long essay in the *New York Review of Books* (21 February 1980), in which she wrote: "Syberberg's film belongs in the category of noble masterpieces which ask for fealty, and can compel it. After seeing *Hitler, A Film from Germany*, there is Syberberg's film—and then there are the other films one admires."

Syberberg was born in 1935 in Vorpommern, an area of pre–1945 Germany that is now part of Poland and that was also the home of Caspar-David Friedrich and Otto Runge—very visible, back–projected presences in Syberberg's most recent films. In 1947 Syberberg moved to Rostock in East Germany and then in 1953 to West Germany. He studied art history and German literature and graduated in 1963 after completing a well-regarded dissertation on Friedrich Dürrenmatt, whose frequently absurdist tragicomedies have obviously influenced Syberberg's formulation of visual images in his films. This period of university study Syberberg has described as "a hell of artistic inactivity" (F, 111), but this thorough humanistic education clearly differentiates Syberberg from many other West German filmmakers, with the notable exception of Alexander Kluge. This background has noticeably affected Syberberg's work as a filmmaker thematically, visually, and conceptually, for his is a cinema of ideas and allusions garnered from the entire German cultural heritage, beginning as early as the ninth-century *Muspilli*, an apocalyptic, poetic vision, quoted twice in *Hitler*. From 1963 to 1966 Syberberg worked for the Bavarian Television network producing a long series of short television films: "185 films of three to thirty minutes in length. (By way of comparison, the Oberhausen group made on the average each year one to two films approximately twelve to twenty minutes in length.) Sometimes it happened that three or four of my films were broadcast on the same day" (F, 111).

Since 1965 Syberberg has made thirteen feature-length films (in the context of Syberberg's work "feature-length" means anything from seventy-two minutes to the seven hours of *Hitler, A Film from Germany*). Seven of these films have been documentaries, and some of them have generated nearly as much attention and notoriety as the *Hitler* film. In 1965 Syberberg made a documentary about Romy Schneider, *Romy: Anatomy of a Face*, a film whose release the actress later prohibited. (Syberberg: ". . . her most beautiful film. The film of her life. Later destroyed by her" [F, 72.]) In 1969 he made a controversial documentary on a Bavarian soft-core pornomaker:

Sex-Business Made in Pasing. His most notorious documentary film, however, undoubtedly is *Winifred Wagner and the History of the House Wahnfried from 1914–1975* (1975). Winifred Wagner, the daughter-in-law of Richard Wagner and the matriarch of Bayreuth, was in charge of the Wagner Festspielhaus throughout the Nazi period. During the five-hour interview film she delineated for the camera the close, even intimate relationship of the Wagner family with Hitler, a bond which was common knowledge but publicly unacknowledged by the Wagner family. Accused by the Wagner family of invasion of privacy and exploitation of a vulnerable old woman, Syberberg at the very least brought into sharper focus the important debate over the interrelationship of art and politics and over the guilt through complicity of artists, musicians, and filmmakers during the Nazi period. In *Winifred Wagner* Syberberg provided the documentary underpinnings for the themes that also dominate his nondocumentary film constructions, in particular the film trilogy of which *Hitler* is the culmination. In the uproar surrounding *Winifred Wagner* Syberberg equated himself with the "seismograph being held responsible for the earthquake" and completely denies the charges of exploitation: "Where it was really important to her, she knew how to remain silent and knew very well when the camera was running" (F, 267).

Syberberg made his first nondocumentary film in 1968. (*Scarabea—How Much Earth Does a Person Need?*, based on a story by Tolstoy) and his second in 1970 (*San Domingo*, based on a story by Kleist). Syberberg's reputation as a filmmaker unquestionably rests, however, on the long film trilogy begun in 1972 with *Ludwig— Requiem for a Virgin King*, a cinematic meditation on the life of the eccentric nineteenth–century Bavarian king, the "mad" asethete who abandoned politics for a life of operatic artifice inspired by the works of Richard Wagner. The film was unavoidably compared to Visconti's *Ludwig*, which appeared at the same time. These comparisons led, surprisingly, to Syberberg's castigation by most West German critics but to almost universal acclaim by French reviewers in Paris, where the film became a long-running "art-film" success in much the same way as Herzog's *Aguirre* two years later.

Also in 1972 Syberberg produced an anomalous companion piece to *Ludwig* called *Theodor Hierneis, or: How One Becomes A Retired Royal Cook*. A one-actor film monologue, *Theodor Hierneis* tells virtually the same story as *Ludwig*, but tells it through the viewpoint of Ludwig's cook. Theodor Hierneis presents "the great world and the little, seen from below, from the kitchen, explained primarily

through a domestic's logic" (F, 22). Thus we find that the idyllic Wagnerian artificial lake which Ludwig had constructed on the roof of his Munich Residence "must have had a leak, because it was always dripping down on us so that we only went to bed with raised umbrellas" (F, 25). In its emphasis on the significance of everyday trivia for a comprehension of grand historical events and in its exploration of the macrocosm through the microcosm, *Theodor Hierneis* points to Syberberg's filmmaking methods and goals both in *Winifred Wagner* and in *Hitler, A Film from Germany*, where the viewer encounters as major figures Himmler's masseur, Hitler's valet, and Hitler's film projectionist.

The trilogy begun with *Ludwig* was continued in 1974 with *Karl May*, a three-hour "life" of Germany's most popular novelist of the late–nineteenth and early–twentieth centuries, who wrote utopian fantasies and adventure stories of the American West. "The film shows us in monologue-form the interior world of [Karl May] as a monstrous chamber-play, similar to the rules of a three-hour chamber-music work: 'The soul is a far land into which we flee'" (F, 39). By using a cast of performers associated with the Nazi film era—for example, Helmut Käutner and Kristina Söderbaum as Karl May and his first wife Emma—Syberberg emphasizes the continuity of nineteenth–century romantic idealism, the Nazi perversion of that idealism, and implicitly the unavoidable cultural schizophrenia of modern West Germany. *Ludwig* and *Karl May* have as a common thematic thread an exploration of the German political and cultural heritage that led to Hitler and the Nazi period. These are the subjects of the monumental conclusion of the trilogy, *Hitler, A Film from Germany* (1977).

In response to the predominantly hostile reception of his films in West Germany, Syberberg has come to regard himself as a total outsider in the German film community, a loner among misguided colleagues, market-oriented producers, and maliciously ignorant film critics. Understandably, perhaps, Syberberg feels a frequent need to justify himself and his own work. While many of the German filmmakers have been content to let their work speak for itself, giving theoretical explanations only in occasional interviews, Syberberg has produced an elaborate and explicit account of his own film aesthetic in his *Filmbuch*, first published in 1976, and in his introductory essay to the scenario of *Hitler, A Film from Germany*, published in 1978.

Like Werner Herzog, Syberberg conceives of film not as an imitation of life but as life itself. Film "is the new, fascinating, actual world of the cineaste, more important than life itself. Film has become its own world, the model by which people program their lives" (F, 93–94). Film, like dreams, like music, springs from the most profound level of the human spirit: "Film . . . is capable, by means of associations and their subconscious fabric, of creating entirely different connections and spaces: of the senses, of the mind, and of the soul. The elegance, rapidity, and beauty of this system are superior to all other arts, except for music. Film is born in the same cradle as psychology" (F, 87). Such a statement echoes similar assertions by Herzog and, for that matter, by Kluge: film is a visceral medium appealing to the viewer on a preintellectual, almost primal level.

For Herzog the basic power of film lies in the vibrancy and sensual appeal of its imagery, especially its visual imagery. Film derives its power from its ability to record and communicate essential and compelling images. At the heart of Syberberg's film aesthetic is the idea that film is more a creator than a recorder of human existence. Film is not a passive mediator but rather an active initiator through the unique elements of the medium: close-ups, montage, rapid changes of perspective. "There arise new systems of thought and feelings. . . . It becomes possible to cause the spectator to think in new combinations" (F, 13). Through the emotional and intellectual involvement of the spectator in the work of art, art becomes life. The ultimate potential of film to involve, to illuminate, and to reconcile arises from its ability to bridge the gap between art and life: "If we proceed from the idea that film is the continuation of life by other means, not, therefore, a mirror or reproduction, then it is clear that old aesthetic discussions such as 'here art, there life, reality or nature' do not come up" (F, 36). Even the documentary film, properly understood and exercised, becomes more than a recording of life: "Even the documentary film is . . . a continuation of life by other means, an individual form of reality with the help of realism. It is an artificial product created by the human hand and technology and its own kind of fantasy" (F, 86).

Underlying Syberberg's belief in the creative and existential potency of film is a related conviction that art "is the only way to survive" (F, 303). Film art can draw upon the same sources as science but transcends science by means of what Syberberg has called the "ethical means of artistic truth." Art, most particularly film art, can "take in, understand, rearticulate, and triumph over us and our history, up to this point humanity's bloodiest" (H, 18). The hyperbole of Syberberg's view of film and its ability to reconcile a nation with its bloody past may dismay, but the passionate conviction of Syberberg's essays is persuasive.

If Syberberg's assertions of the transrational power of the cinema are sometimes reminiscent of remarks by Herzog or Kluge, at other times he sounds like Straub in his insistence on the integrity of individual film components. "The props are equal to the actor; the music no longer is background; editing is directional rhythm. Noises are equal to the music, and motions of faces are taken seriously" (F, 11). The look of Syberberg's films is, to be sure, entirely dissimilar to the ascetic, static, and undramatic films of Straub. Syberberg's *Hitler,* for example, employs a structurally simple set or stage that is complexly and theatrically manipulated by means of props, costumes, and elaborate back projections. And one finds none of the fortuitous and obtrusive noise of Straub's "natural sound" in Syberberg's films. Straub's aesthetic is realist-reductionist; Syberberg's is surrealist–constructionist. However, in his unwillingness to subordinate sound to music or music to visual image or text to actor, Syberberg does in a way approximate Straub's purist use of film components.

Syberberg demonstrates a further similarity to Straub in his employment of musical texts, of music *as* text, and of musical structures in his films. Describing *Hitler, a Film from Germany,* Syberberg has said, "The entire ·thing has the character of a fugue with several intersecting lines and overlapping layers" (H, 24). He has described *Karl May* as "chamber music," and his *Ludwig* is a "requiem." Just as Straub has mentioned a "counterpoint" of sound and visual imagery in his *Chronicle of Anna Magdalena Bach,* so, too, Syberberg has said of *Ludwig:* "Image and sound are constantly checked for their parallel connection or contrastiveness in the sense of a musical counterpoint. . . ." The second half of this statement, however, shows the difference between Straub and Syberberg: ". . . montage stood at the cradle of film, editing is its heartbeat, and the reattainment of the aura of myth a high goal" (F, 12).

Straub's musical sources are Bach and Schoenberg. As might be clear from such neoromantic vocabulary as "heartbeat," "aura," and "myth," Syberberg's musical inspiration is Wagner. He has applied the Wagnerian concept of "total work of art" to film, the *"Gesamtkunstwerk* of our time," and has also referred to "my musical-epic film system." Syberberg resembles Wagner in his use of myth and legend as a means to elaborate upon contemporary themes, but his comprehension of the nature of music and film is also Wagnerian. Syberberg regards music and film as art forms equally capable of stirring the transrational human consciousness: "Music builds tunnels into the subconscious even of nations and eras. It succeeds where dialogue-argumentation fails" (F, 20).

For Syberberg music in film also implies film as music, not only as manifest in film structure (*Hitler* as "fugue" or *Ludwig* as "requiem") but as an integral part of a film's conception. Syberberg considers his film about Ludwig's cook to be proof that a "film as music" can exist "even without music . . . comprised of language and visual image only" (F, 20). In such a film as *Theodor Hierneis*, but also in *Hitler*, Syberberg says, the libretto/text is "performed by an actor as an instrument in the care of the director, here in the function of a conductor and a composer simultaneously" (F, 22). And the "requiem" in *Ludwig*'s subtitle Syberberg has defined as "language in monologues, in blocks, singly or in chorus, text-libretti. Rests, long takes, epic clarity, alienations, pathos and irony, the character of dreams and of visions . . . a relational and structural technique without chance in props, clothing, music, noises, etc" (F, 11).

The phrase "without chance" is most relevant for Syberberg's film style. The extreme length of his films may give an impression of undisciplined cinematic profusion, but in fact Syberberg's films are tightly controlled. Like the interlace of early Germanic art and epic, *Hitler, A Film from Germany* is a masterpiece of reiteration and elaboration. Shot entirely in a studio, so that extraneous sights or sounds never intrude upon the film's constructed universe, *Hitler* conveys Syberberg's "meaning" through its music, its overwhelming back projections, its lighting, its text, even its props, each of which bears connotation after connotation. Syberberg may be the most iconic of West German directors. Tables, chairs, dolls and other studiedly random objects, on the one hand, lend depth and contrast to the visual image by their simplicity and by their placement before the ornate back projections. On the other hand, they "are used—apart from their value as historical decoration—as signals of an intellectual and psychological sort or of functions derived from the story" (F, 40). Thus, for example, the artificial snow seen in *Karl May* and again in *Hitler* represents for Syberberg "the cold misery of everyday Germany" (F, 40). Or, in *Hitler* the recurrent model of Edison's Black Maria reminds us (*if* we recognize it as the first, primitive film studio) that we are watching a film, reminds us of film's origins and its potential. Syberberg's highly personal and characteristically mythologizing view is that "Edison's studio is the Holy Grail of cinema—we start with it and we end with it, it is something very magical" (SS, 230).

The excitement of Syberberg's films—if one can speak of excitement in such elaborately meditative and allusive constructions—is generated by a dialectic of contrapuntal film components rather than by rapid editing or virtuoso camera movement. *Hitler,* for example, is a languid film, one which dares to take its time in building its universe of images and ideas. Could Wagner, after all, have been told to hold his operas to ninety minutes? In *Ludwig* and *Hitler* a restriction of camera movement was demanded by the use of back projections, but such a restriction happily coincides with Syberberg's avowed intentions.

In describing *Winifred Wagner* Syberberg freely concedes that he created a "talking head" film without entertaining gimmicks. The cameraman was instructed "to move slowly in on her and her head, imperceptibly, so that the motion has an intensifying effect in the viewer's subconscious" (F, 257). In *Winifred Wagner* the visual image merely emphasizes the old woman's narrative as it is being told. In a fiction film such as *Hitler,* on the other hand, the visual image frequently *is* the narrative. The occasional grotesqueness of Syberberg's images seems derived from the theater of Friedrich Dürrenmatt: a naked old woman as Justice holding a scale laden with baby-doll heads and plastic penises is a precise visualization of the theme of Dürrenmatt's *Visit of the Old Lady,* for example.

More frequently Syberberg's visual imagery is reminiscent of Fassbinder. Both Fassbinder's *The Marriage of Maria Braun* and Syberberg's *Hitler* refer, for example, to Nazi racism through scenes of German women dancing with black American GIs. In Fassbinder's film this unspoken but obvious irony is built into the film's narrative; in Syberberg's it is made inescapably explicit by an isolated and extended shot of racially mixed couples dancing around Richard Wagner's tombstone to the music of a fox trot. Similarly, both in Fassbinder's *Bitter Tears of Petra von Kant* and in *Hitler,* department store mannequins appear. In Fassbinder's film they are used to reinforce narrative as constant but almost casual reminders of the shallowness of the characters' lives. In Syberberg's film the mannequins, in juxtaposition with other props, are themselves a visual narrative of the intertwining of present, past, and still earlier past that is the film's theme. The scenario describes: "A doll party. Mannequins from a department store of today with the clothing of the twenties, but with the show-window faces of today. On the projection screen: A Ludwig-stage-decoration from the French Baroque period" (H, 154).

Syberberg's ironic juxtapositions are not only visual. As Fassbinder in *Bitter Tears of Petra von Kant* juxtaposed the music of Verdi and the Platters, so has Syberberg created musical contrasts in *Ludwig*: "Musically two acoustic worlds of art bump against each other: that of

Wagner and that of ironically inserted popular and folk music" (F, 15). In *Hitler* the voices of the soundtrack are an incessant mixing of the voices of actors on–screen, of actors off–screen, and recordings of Hitler, Goebbels, and Nazi and Allied radio broadcasts from forty years ago. A recording of "Sieg Heil's" from a mass rally of the 1930s has been added to the soundtrack as the actor Peter Kern re-acts the mock-trial scene of the captured child-killer in *M* ("I can't help myself!"): a witty crystalization of the argument that the German people went "insane" under Hitler, an argument refuted by the parodical quality of its presentation. (Syberberg has written of "the chance to resolve unmentionable shock by means of laughter" H, 23.)

In his essay introducing *Hitler*, Syberberg summarized the theoretical underpinning of his film style: "I have made the aesthetically scandalous attempt to combine Brecht's teachings of the epic theater with Richard Wagner's aesthetic of music, to unite in film the epic system as anti-Aristotelian cinema with the laws of a new mythology" (H, 28). Syberberg's writings will never suffer from excessive clarity, but his basic point seems clear enough: his cinema is an attempt to combine the influences of Brecht and Wagner—*Siegfried* with alienation—spiced with Dürrenmatt's absurdity. Always, or so it seems, the New German filmmakers return to Brecht's theory of theater as the basis for their theory of the cinema.

Just as Brecht's theater is always political, so Syberberg's best-known films are political, though hardly revolutionary. They are intended not so much as acts of anger against the status quo as acts of sadness, pathos, and mourning. In his essays and less frequently in his films Syberberg decries the spiritual desolation and cultural barbarism of the post–1945 world, but the political system he wishes to confront in his films thus far is Nazism. *Ludwig, Karl May,* and, in its own way, *Winifred Wagner* are preparations for *Hitler, A Film from Germany.* Through the figures of Ludwig II, of Richard Wagner, of Karl May, and of Winifred Wagner these films delineate the relationship of German art, music, and literature to German politics and explore the culpability of German culture for the tragedy of German society. "Wagner and Karl May," Syberberg has written, "announce the approaching atrocities of Hitler" (F, 20). Syberberg's vision of Hitler rising from the grave of Wagner finds a reflection in the novels of Karl May; May's stories, his ideas, Syberberg writes, were "for May himself likeable and harmless as a self-redemption, but his works—pacifistically trivial and utopian, proletarian, surreal, full of comic book heroism—were a source for misunderstanding adherents" (F, 46).

Similarly, in the microcosmic life of Winifred Wagner Syberberg sees the past sixty years of German history. *Winifred Wagner and the History of the House Wahnfried from 1914–1975* has as its themes "art and politics, the famous aesthetizing of politics, here classically performed, very simply and through personal testimony. A woman with power . . . who can only justify herself by credibly testifying how she knew nothing about all of that. Politics for the unpolitical, demonstrated at its most important source, the sole predecessor of his ideology recognized by Hitler: Richard Wagner and his music" (F, 81).

If *Ludwig*, *Karl May*, and *Winifred Wagner* are also films about Hitler, so is *Hitler* concerned with much more than Hitler's twenty years as political leader and historical phenomenon. Syberberg's intention is not a retelling of history; it is a re-creation of the past as it exists in the present and as it conditions the future. The film's subject is Hitler but its theme is, as Syberberg puts it, "the Hitler in us." The film's unifying figure is the child (played by Syberberg's daughter), an image of the now and yet-to-be who wanders among the debris of the past, the child who represents, Syberberg says, "guilt" but also a "judging naivete" (H, 24). *Hitler, a Film from Germany* is "a child's world of dolls, full of stars and music, the stuff of a child's grand nightmare. . . . It is all like the clairvoyant vision of a child with closed eyes" (H, 32).

The child is the universal individual, both guilty and innocent, curious to know but afraid to see. *Hitler* is no documentary, no compilation of ultimately meaningless statistics. The point is not historical data but present human experience. The film looks not to Then but to Now. In the words of the Circusmaster in the film's first part, *Hitler* is "a film for us. It is a question of war and holocaust. Auschwitz as a battlefield of the race wars. It is a question of finding the cosmically guilty; and what would Hitler be without us? It is a question of the projection of the divine in mankind, of the starry heavens above us, and the moral law within me" (H, 82).

"The divine in mankind," "the moral law within me"—these are grandiose, Kantian concepts, but Syberberg never shrinks from even the grandest pretense. In his introduction to *Hitler*, he has written: "This film . . . moves between the axioms of chaos and systems of order, gods and underworld, God and hell, death and immortality, sacrifices, love, wars, creation and starry cosmos. Building stones of mythical worlds. In words, images, music, with the help of triviality" (H, 17). "Chaos," "creation," and "starry cosmos" convey the magnitude of Syberberg's vision, but his practice in *Hitler* is better defined by the phrase "with the help of triviality." The intention may be cosmic, but the specifics are often down–to–earth, even banal. And it is this polarity of intention and practice, of significance and signification, that is surely most responsible for the controversy surrounding Syberberg's film. Syberberg would find the world in a grain of sand, but not all others would agree to seeing it there. Syberberg's art is an accretion of layer upon layer of allusions which, arising from Syberberg's own mind, sometimes have a significance discernible only to Syberberg. Facile analogies and dubious connections are accepted by sympathetic viewers as an act of faith. To more hard-eyed, insistently objective viewers, on the other hand, these analogies and connections can often be more outrageous than convincing.

As he had done previously in his film about Ludwig's cook, Syberberg in *Hitler* frequently presents his historical theses in the garb of a catalogue-like accumulation of trivia. One of the most controversial sections of *Hitler* is a long monologue by Hitler's valet, who describes every possible detail (or so it seems) of Hitler's daily existence: his waking, his breakfast, his hats, his boots, his underwear, his brands of soap, shaving cream, skin cream. Syberberg's purpose here is multiple. On the one hand, he parodies our fascination with trivia concerning the famous, with the lives of Lincoln or Kennedy or Marilyn Monroe or Elvis Presley or even Adolf Hitler. On the other hand, he plays with the cliché that no man is a hero to his valet. On a third level, however, the valet's monologue or Himmler's dialogue with his masseur becomes ambiguous and controversial. Clearly we are being shown the humanity of Hitler and, by implication, the Hitler in humanity. This in turn implies a universal culpability for the crimes of Nazism and can be interpreted as an exoneration of Hitler. *Hitler, A Film from Germany* was released in the midst of discussions within West Germany concerning the abolition of the statute of limitations on war crimes. An exoneration of Hitler was, according to Syberberg, the least of his intentions ("Whoever fears here a re-selection of Hitler . . . has to be sick" H, 28). Rather, he is seeking an implication of all humanity in all the crimes of humanity, an idea which meets with a more positive response in Paris, London, or New York than in Frankfurt, Munich, or Berlin. An identification of specific guilt seems necessary in West Germany, while a universalization of responsibility appeals to liberal French, British, and American reviewers. Syberberg delivers an indictment not of just a few individuals, but of us all.

The valet's monologue also plays with Hannah Arendt's oft-quoted and oft-misleading formulation, "the banality of evil." Syberberg inverts this formulation, however, finding in "the evil of banality" the key to Hitler's success in Germany. What Arendt had apparently meant was the notion that the person next door might be a killer, that evil often wears the guise of mediocrity. Syberberg asserts that mediocrity itself is evil, a latent and almost primal capacity for harm that Hitler was able to evoke: "The banality of evil is taken seriously . . . but also the evil of banality. For in kitsch, in the banal, in triviality and its folksiness rest the last rudiments and nuclei of disappeared traditions of our myths. . . . Hitler knew how to activate that" (H, 18).

One of the great ironies of Syberberg's work is that he simultaneously denounces and invokes the German heritage of romantic irrationality ("the disappeared traditions of our myths"). His preoccupation with Germanic myths and legends, with romantic art and literature, with the music of Richard Wagner and the life of Ludwig II is both a criticism and a defense of these traditions and figures. Syberberg sees the irrational romantic spirit as the true German intellectual and spiritual identity which went astray, mutated, or was seduced during the Nazi era. The irrational, however, also offers the only means to spiritual reconciliation and redemption. The first sentence of his *Hitler* essay says: "In the voluntary relinquishing of its creative irrationality above all, and perhaps only here, did Germany truly lose the war" (H, 9). Again, a dubious and possibly even inflammatory statement, but Syberberg repeats his conviction that without irrationality, the creative irrationality lying at the heart of romantic genius, "Germany is nothing and dangerous, sick, without identity, explosive, and a wretched imitation of its possibilities" (H, 19).

In Syberberg's eyes at least, the irrational has been blamed unfairly for the Nazi catastrophe, for, as Syberberg shows by means of the speech of an SS officer in *Hitler,* the horror of Nazism and the "final solution" were actually a carrying out of rationality to an insanely logical extreme: "Our men taking part in the executions went through much more, remarkably, than their victims. From a psychological standpoint they went through something terrible. . . . To have gone through all that and, apart from a few human weaknesses, to have remained decent. That hardened us. That is an unwritten and never-to-be-written page of fame in German history" (H, 202).

Post-war Germany has eradicated irrationality but in the process has also eradicated the glories of its past—Hölderlin, Novalis, the early works of Schiller, folksongs, and fairy tales. But, Syberberg asks, "what would Einstein be without music, without German romanticism and classicism? We are living in a country without a homeland." Thus, no one should be surprised at the terrorism of contemporary West Germany. Is it not "the explosion of repressed German irrationality? . . . So much suppression of its own tradition and its own being had to evoke aggressions, radically and fanatically, in a German manner" (H, 15). A society which has given up irrationality may give up one kind of madness but it also gives up its wishes, its dreams, its very life.

Such remarks by Syberberg are certainly subjective, debatable, and even galling to those who do not accept the vague theoretical framework of Syberberg's arguments. Still, Syberberg's harshest detractor might well admire the subtly consistent and even rational arguments with which he turns his faith in the irrational into a justification for film and his filmmaking methods in *Hitler*. Histories give statistics, but only art can heal the wounds of the past. Film can be art, can partake of the curative realms of psychology, of music, of dreams. A film about Hitler should not be a documentary ("from statistics one learns no mourning" H, 14) but rather "a montage with the filmic means of the irrational. It is all there; the viewer must decide. Whoever wants it more directly, begins to lie, preparing new errors" (H, 27). In Syberberg's universe dreams, the irrational, film, and life itself are one and the same essence.

Syberberg's faith in film is somewhat surprising because he also implicates film in the responsibility for Hitler. A major figure in the second section of *Hitler* is Hitler's film projectionist, Ellerkamp, who tells us that "I am the man who knew Hitler's most secret wishes. His dream, that which he desired beyond the real world! Every day two to three films" (H, 145). That Hitler was an avid movie-watcher, especially before 1939, is well known, and the Nazi film industry is perhaps the most notorious example of art in the service of the state. The presence of the projectionist in *Hitler*, however, also functions as a reminder of the "Hitler in us." We too are viewing a film.

Beyond this analogy Syberberg alludes to a more startling hypothesis: after the beginning of the war, Ellerkamp says, Hitler watched only newsreels of the war, watched only the film that he himself produced. Echoing Ludwig, who attempted to make an opera of his own life, and Karl May, who says "I will write a drama, I am a drama, the drama of the human soul," and also Herzog's Aguirre, who says "I will direct history the way that others direct plays," the film projectionist says that Hitler "was really the greatest, the greatest filmmaker of all times" (H, 151). Thus, one comes again finally to the title of Syberberg's film: Hitler is not merely represented in a film from Germany; Hitler was and is a film from Germany.

Hans-Jürgen Syberberg's Hitler, A Film from Germany. *Courtesy of The Museum of Modern Art/Film Stills Archive*

Fire must be fought with fire. Only film, "the continuation of life with other means" (F, 12), can adequately mourn the past, can reconcile the present with the past, can help us acknowledge and thus subdue the destructive impulse, the Hitler, in each of us. *Hitler, A Film from Germany* is intended not as a story of a man but of mankind. Before making the film Syberberg described it as being "the Hitler in us. A world in us, a perfect inner-world projection, if it succeeds" (F, 305). The film has been made, its success is still debated.

Notes and References

Chapter One

1. Howard Thompson, *New York Times,* 22 September 1967, p. 57.
2. Bosley Crowther, *New York Times,* 25 September 1967, p. 56.
3. Allen Hughes, *New York Times,* 20 September 1968, p. 37.
4. Howard Thompson, *New York Times,* 27 September 1968, p. 98.
5. Raymond Sokolov, *Newsweek,* 21 September 1970, p. 98.
6. Paul D. Zimmermann, *Newsweek,* 18 October 1971, p. 108.
7. Roger Greenspan, *New York Times,* 9 October 1972, p. 38.
8. Andrew Sarris, "Films in Focus," *Village Voice* 19 (16 January 1974):49.
9. Andrew Sarris, *Village Voice* 18 (22 November 1973):77.
10. Vincent Canby, "The German Renaissance—No Room for Laughter or Love," *New York Times,* 11 December 1977, section D, p. 15.
11. Probably the best English-language introduction to German filmmaking during this period is Thomas Elsaesser, "The Postwar German Cinema," in *Fassbinder,* ed. Tony Rayns (London, 1976), pp. 1–16.
12. Figures are taken from *Film in der Bundesrepublik Deutschland,* ed. Hans Günther Pflaum and Hans Helmut Prinzler (Munich, 1979), p. 134.
13. For a more thorough exploration of the relationship between West German television and New German film and, more specifically, between WDR in Cologne and the Berlin *Arbeiterfilm,* see Richard Collins and Vincent Porter, "West German Television. The Crisis of Public Service Broadcasting," *Sight and Sound* 49 (Summer 1980):172–77, or "Westdeutscher Rundfunk and the Arbeiterfilm" *Quartelry Review of Film Studies* 5 (Spring 1980):233–51.
14. Volker Schlöndorff, *Die Blechtrommel. Tagebuch einer Verfilmung* (Darmstadt, 1979), pp. 114–15.
15. A compelling account of this kind of compromise, and of others, has been given by Klaus Eder in "Der Glaube ans grosse Geld," *Jahrbuch Film 79/80,* ed. H. G. Pflaum (Munich, 1979), pp. 100–107.
16. Norbert Kückelmann, a coinitiator with Kluge and Hans Rolf Strobel of the *Kuratorium junger deutscher Film.*

17.   Alexander Kluge, *Die Patriotin* (Frankfurt am Main, 1979), p. 280. Kluge went on to criticise the film subsidy system for its unresponsiveness to the different needs of the newer generations.

18.   More specific examinations of both groups can be found in *Quarterly Review of Film Studies* 5 (Spring 1980). See Marc Silbermann, "Cine-Feminists in West Berlin," pp. 217–32, and the previously mentioned article (note 13 above) by Collins and Porter on the *Arbeiterfilm*.

19.   The subsidy boards' preference for literature adaptations was lamented in various essays in *Die Zeit* and *Jahrbuch Film* during the late 1970s.

20.   Alfred Nemeczek, "Ganz schön heruntergekommen," in *Jahrbuch Film 78/79*, ed. H. G. Pflaum (Munich, 1978), p. 170.

21.   In *The Long Vacation of Lotte H. Eisner* (1979) by Sohrab Shahid Saless. Cited in *KINO. German Film* 1 (October 1979):2.

22.   Interviewed in *Filmfaust* 7 (March/April 1978):6.

23.   Reported in *Info: West Germany* I (April 1978):2.

24.   Schlöndorff, *Tagebuch*, p. 46.

Chapter Two

1.   All remarks attributed to Alexander Kluge in this chapter are taken from one of the following interviews; abbreviations are used to identify page references:

HKS   An interview with Ulrich Gregor in *Herzog/Kluge/Straub* (Munich, 1976), pp. 153–178.

FK   An interview with Frieda Grafe and Enno Patalas in *Filmkritik* 10 (September 1966):487–91.

K   An interview with Jan Dawson in *Kluge* (New York, 1977), pp. 26–42.

FM   An interview with Corinna Brocher and Barbara Bronnen in *Die Filmemacher. Der neue deutsche Film nach Oberhausen* (Munich, 1973), pp. 233–46.

2.   Wolfram Schütte, "Akte des Widerstands," in *Herzog/Kluge/Straub* (Munich, 1976), p. 21.

3.   Alexander Kluge, *Die Patriotin* (Frankfurt am Main, 1979), p. 40.

Chapter Three

1.   All quotations by Jean-Marie Straub and Danièle Huillet are taken from the following interviews; abbreviations are used to identify page references:

CC   An interview in *Cahiers du Cinema* 223 (August 1970):48–57.

E   Interviews by Andi Engel and by Geoffrey Nowell-Smith in *Enthusiasm* 1 (December 1975):1–31.

F   An interview by Frieda Grafe and Enno Patalas in *Filmkritik* 10 (November 1966):607–10.

FK   An interview by Wilhelm Roth and Hans Günther Pflaum in *Filmkritik* 17 (February 1973):65–78.

FM An interview by Barbara Bronnen in *Die Filmemacher. Der neue deutsche Film nach Oberhausen* (Munich, 1973), pp. 25–45.

HKS An interview by Karsten Witte in *Herzog/Kluge/Straub* (Munich, 1976), pp. 205–218.

2. A. H. Weiler, "German Newcomer's Three Films," *New York Times*, 24 February 1969, p. 30.

3. Quoted by Richard Roud in *Straub* (New York, 1972), p. 40.

Chapter Four

1. All remarks attributed to Volker Schlöndorff appeared in the following interviews or in his diary of the filming of *The Tin Drum*. Abbreviations are used to identify page numbers:

FC An interview by Barry and Greg Thomson in *Film Criticism* 1 (Winter 1976–77):26–37.

FK An interview in *Filmkritik* 10 (June 1966):307–309.

FM An interview by Corinna Brocher in *Die Filmemacher. Der neue deutsche Film nach Oberhausen* (Munich, 1973), pp. 73–88.

FR An interview by Thomas Thieringer in *Frankfurter Rundschau*, 7 February 1975.

KR An interview by Hans Höhn in *Kölnische Rundschau*, 1 December 1975.

T Volker Schlöndorff, *Die Blechtrommel. Tagebuch einer Verfilmung* (Darmstadt, 1979).

2. Melville has said of Schlöndorff: "We got on at once. Almost immediately I felt that I had met my spiritual son, and I still feel the same way about him today." *Melville on Melville* (New York, 1971), p. 89.

3. Schlöndorff has explained the intricacies of financing his early films in *Die Filmemacher*, pp. 80–84.

4. Quoted from an interview with Marjorie Rosen in *Millimeter* 4 (March 1976):38.

Chapter Five

1. From *Images at the Horizon. A Workshop with Werner Herzog.* Conducted by Roger Ebert. Edited by Gene Walsh (Chicago, 1979), p. 21. Herzog makes virtually identical statements in interviews with Lawrence O'Toole in *Film Comment* 15 (November/December 1979):48, and with Hans Günther Pflaum in *Herzog* (Munich, 1979), p. 68. Herzog has in fact been one of the most interviewed German directors; his accessibility and affability with the press and public is a significant characteristic of his directorial persona. Remarks attributed to Werner Herzog in this chapter are taken from one of the following sources; abbreviations are used to identify page numbers:

FM An interview with Barbara Bronnen in *Die Filmemacher. Der neue deutsche Film nach Oberhausen* (Munich, 1973), pp. 11–24.

FQ An interview/profile by Gideon Bachmann, "The Man on the Volcano: A Portrait of Werner Herzog," *Film Quarterly* 31 (Fall 1977):2–10.

H An interview with H.G. Pflaum in *Herzog* (Munich, 1979), pp. 59–86.

HG Alan Greenberg, *Heart of Glass*, including the scenario by Herbert Achternbusch and Werner Herzog (Munich, 1976).

HKS An interview with Kraft Wetzel in *Herzog/Kluge/Straub* (Munich, 1976), pp. 113–30.

I *Images at the Horizon* (see above).

NYT Letitia Kent, "Werner Herzog," *New York Times*, 11 September 1977, section D, pp. 19, 30.

S An interview/profile by Jonathan Cott, "Signs of Life," in *Forever Young* (New York, 1977), pp. 95–116.

SS An interview with David Overbey, "Every Man for Himself," *Sight and Sound* 44 (Spring 1975):73–75.

2.   Herzog's diary, written during this trip, was revised and published as *Vom Gehen im Eis* (Munich, 1978). Herzog has said of this diary, "I sometimes think that it is . . . even better than the films I have made" (H, 81).

3.   Chickens—along with monkeys, camels, and other beasts—are a recurrent Herzog obsession. "Chickens terrify me. . . . The most terrible thing is to look a chicken right in the eyes: it is stupidity that stares back at you, death and stupidity. . . . I don't believe in devils, I just believe in stupidity" (HKS, 115).

4.   Herzog at the Film Center of the Art Institute of Chicago, Illinois, 29 August 1977.

5.   There is no reason, Herzog maintains, for a filmmaker to record only literal truths, even in documentaries. He believes that "cinema verité" stays too close to the surface to convey essential truths. Thus he defends his writing the final title of *Land of Silence and Darkness*, which, he knows, the viewer will logically attribute to Fini Straubinger: "If a world war were to break out now, I wouldn't even notice" (H, 71).

6.   See Rudolf Hohlweg, "Musik für Film—Film für Musik," in *Herzog/Kluge/Straub*, pp, 45–51, for a description of how music is integrated into the structure of *Aguirre* and *Every Man for Himself.*

Chapter Six

1.   All remarks attributed to Rainer Werner Fassbinder in this chapter are taken from one of the following sources; abbreviations are used to identify page references:

C An interview with Norbert Sparrow in *Cineaste* 8 (Fall 1977):20–21.

F An interview with Wilfried Wiegand in *Rainer Werner Fassbinder* (Munich, 1975), pp. 63–90.

FC An interview with John Hughes and Brooks Riley in *Film Comment* 11 (November/December 1975):14–17.

FR An interview with Wolfram Schütte, "Feuilleton," in *Frankfurter Rundschau*, 31 January 1976.

K An interview with H.G. Pflaum in *Kino. Magazin für Film und Kultur* 3 (15 May 1980):27–41.

NT As cited by Arthur Lubow in "Cinema's New Wunderkinder," *New Times*, 14 November 1975, pp. 50–56.

R H.G. Pflaum and R. W. Fassbinder, *Das bisschen Realität, das ich brauche—Wie Filme entstehen* (Munich, 1976).

SS An interview with Tony Rayns in *Sight and Sound* 44 (Winter 1974/75):3–5.

2. Vincent Canby, "Rainer Werner Fassbinder—The Most Original Talent Since Godard," *New York Times*, 6 March 1977, section 2, pp. 1, 13.

3. Peter Cowie, ed., *International Film Guide* (London, 1976), pp. 61–73.

4. See Wilfried Wiegand's "Die Puppe in der Puppe: Beobachtungen zu Fassbinders Filmen," in *Rainer Werner Fassbinder* (Munich, 1975), especially pp. 42–46.

5. See "Der Ton," in Pflaum/Fassbinder, *Das bisschen Realität*, pp. 115–120.

6. Fassbinder's use of language, silence, and framing is described in greater detail in my "Forms of Communication in Fassbinder's *Angst Essen Seele Auf*," *Literature/Film Quarterly* 7 (Summer 1979):182–200.

Chapter 7

1. All quotations are taken from the following texts by or interviews with Wim Wenders; abbreviations are used to identify page numbers.

FC An interview with Carlos Clarens in *Film Comment* 13 (September/October 1977):42–46.

FK An interview with Walter Adler in *Filmkritik* 22 (December 1978):673–86.

SS An interview with Tony Rayns in *Sight and Sound* 44 (Winter 1974–75):2–7.

T Wim Wenders, *Texte zu Filmen und Musik* (Berlin, n.d.).

W An interview with Jan Dawson, in *Wim Wenders* (New York, 1976), pp. 4–24.

2. Wenders conspicuously denies, however, any links between his films—or those of Herzog or Fassbinder, for that matter—and the German films of the 1920s. "I do not believe that there is in . . . our films any tradition at all leading back to that period. Our films are new discoveries. Of necessity. Thank God." ("Sein Tod ist keine Lösung. Der deutsche Filmregisseur Fritz Lang," in *Jahrbuch Film 77/78*, ed. H.G. Pflaum [Munich, 1977], p. 164.)

3. "Sein Tod ist keine Lösung," p. 165.

Chapter Eight

1.   Abbreviations are used to identify page references in the following
sources of quotes attributed to Hans-Jürgen Syberberg:

      H   Hans-Jürgen Syberberg, *Hitler, Ein Film aus Deutschland*
           (Hamburg, 1978)

      F   Hans-Jürgen Syberberg, *Syberbergs Filmbuch* (Frankfurt am
           Main, 1976)

     SS   An interview with John Pym in *Sight and Sound* 46 (Autumn
           1977):227–30.

Selected Bibliography

WITH A FEW IMPORTANT EXCEPTIONS the following list contains only English-language literature on New German Cinema and its individual directors. For the most part reviews of single films have not been included.

General

1. Books and Special "New German Cinema" Issues of Periodicals
Gregor, Ulrich et al. *Herzog/Kluge/Straub*, Munich: Hanser, 1976. This, like all the volumes in Hanser Verlag's Reihe Film, is a very helpful introduction to its subjects. The book contains commentary, interviews, and complete filmographies.
Literature/Film Quarterly 7, no. 3 (Summer 1979). The first American special issue on New German Cinema, including an introduction and articles on Fassbinder, Herzog, Schlöndorff, and Wenders. Edited by James Welsh.
Pflaum, Hans Günther, and Hans Helmut Prinzler, *Film in der Bundesrepublik Deutschland*. Munich: Hanser, 1979. An indispensable introduction to New German Cinema, including short biographies and filmographies of 100 West German filmmakers.
Quarterly Review of Film Studies 5, no. 2 (Spring 1980). Thus far the best English-language introduction to New German Cinema, including a survey; articles on Fassbinder, Herzog, Kluge, and Wenders, on subsidies and financing, feminist films, *Arbeiter* films, and West German film archives; a chronological film list; and a bibliography. Edited by Eric Rentschler.
Wide Angle 3, no. 4 (1980). An arbitrary selection of articles on Brecht and film, Herzog, Fassbinder, Kluge, and Straub. Edited by Peter Lehman.

2. Periodicals
Baker, Rob. "'New German Cinema': A Fistful of Myths." *Soho Weekly News*, 23 March 1978, pp. 21–23.

Canby, Vincent. "The German Renaissance—No Room for Laughter or Love." *New York Times*, 11 December 1977, section D, p. 15.

Clarke, Gerald. "Seeking Planets That Do Not Exist." *Time*, 20 March 1978, pp. 51–53.

Dawson, Jan. "*Germany in Autumn* and *Eine Kleine Godard*." *Take One* 6, no. 12 (November 1978):14–15, 44–45.

———. "The Industry: German Weasels (Filmverlag Follies)." *Film Comment* 13, no. 3 (May/June 1977):33–34.

Denby, David. "The Germans Are Coming! The Germans Are Coming!" *Horizon* 20, no. 1 (1977):89–90ff.

Durgnat, Raymond. "From Caligari to 'Hitler.'" *Film Comment* 16, no. 4 (July/August 1980):59–70.

Eidsvik, Charles. "Behind the Crest of the Wave: An Overview of the New German Cinema." *Literature/Film Quarterly* 7, no. 3 (Summer 1979):167–81.

Elsaesser, Thomas. "The Postwar German Cinema." In *Fassbinder*, edited by Tony Rayns. London: British Film Institute, 1976, pp. 1–16.

Gregor, Ulrich. "The German Film in 1964: Stuck at Zero." *Film Quarterly* 18, no. 2 (Winter 1964):7–21.

Holloway, Ronald. "A German Breakthrough?" *KINO. German Film* 1 (October 1979):4–17.

———. "Who's Who in West German Film Industry: A Directory of Directors and Filmmakers Over the Period 1957–1977." *Variety*, 2 June 1977, p. 51ff.

Lubow, Arthur. "Cinema's New Wunderkinder." *New Times*, 14 November 1975, p. 55ff.

Manvell, Roger, and Fraenkel, Heinrich. "The Nineteen-sixties and the New German Cinema." In *The German Cinema*. New York: Praeger, 1971, pp. 124–33.

Overbey, David L. "From Murnau to Munich. New German Cinema." *Sight and Sound* 43, no. 2 (Spring 1974):101–3, 115.

Rentschler, Eric. "Deutschland im Vorherbst: Literature Adaptation in West German Film." *KINO. German Film* 3 (Summer 1980):11–19.

———. "Introduction. Critical Junctures Since Oberhausen." *Quarterly Review of Film Studies* 5, no. 2 (Spring 1980):141–56.

Sanford, John. "The New German Cinema." *German Life and Letters* 32, no. 3 (April 1979):206–28.

Sarris, Andrew. "The Germans Are Coming! The Germans Are Coming!" *Village Voice*, 27 October 1975, pp. 137–38.

Vogel, Amos. "A Nation Comes Out of Shell-Shock." *Village Voice*, 4 May 1972, pp. 87–88.

"Young German Film." *Film Comment* 6, no. 1 (Spring 1970):32–44.

About Individual Directors

I. Rainer Werner Fassbinder

1. Books
Iden, Peter et al., *Rainer Werner Fassbinder*. Munich: Hanser, 1975.
Rayns, Tony, ed. *Fassbinder*. London: British Film Institute, 1976.

2. Periodicals
Alvarado, Manuel. "*Eight Hours Are Not a Day*." In *Fassbinder*, edited by Tony Rayns. London: BFI, 1976, pp. 37–41.
Borchardt, Edith. "Leitmotif and Structure in Fassbinder's *Effie Briest*." *Literature/Film Quarterly* 7, no. 3 (Summer 1979):201–7.
Britton, Andrew. "*Fox and His Friends*: Foxed." *JumpCut* 16 (November 1977):22–23.
Canby, Vincent. "Rainer Fassbinder—The Most Original Talent Since Godard." *New York Times*, 6 March 1977, section 2, pp. 1, 13.
Cant, Bob. "Fox and His Friends: Fassbinder's *Fox*." *JumpCut* 16 (November 1977):22.
Combs, Richard. "*Chinese Roulette* and *Despair*." *Sight and Sound* 47, no. 4 (Autumn 1978):258–60.
Dawson, Jan. "The Sacred Terror: shadows of terrorism in the New German cinema." *Sight and Sound* 48, no. 4 (Autumn 1979):242–45.
———. "Women—present tense." *Take One* 7, no. 8 (July 1979):10–12.
Dawson, Jan, and Medjuck, Joe. "Misc: Fassbinder: A Year (or so) in the Life." *Take One* 4, no. 12 (July/August 1974):26.
Denby, David. "The Brilliant, Brooding Films of Rainer Fassbinder." *New York Times*, 1 February 1976, pp. 1, 13.
Elsaesser, Thomas. "A Cinema of Vicious Circles." In *Fassbinder*, edited by Tony Rayns. London: BFI, 1976, pp. 24–36.
Fassbinder, R. W. "Fassbinder on Sirk." Translated by Thomas Elsaesser. *Film Comment* 11, no. 6 (November/December 1975):22–24.
———. "Insects in a Glass Case: Random Thoughts on Claude Chabrol." Translated by Derek Prouse. *Sight and Sound* 45, no. 4 (Autumn 1976):205, 206, 252.
Farber, Manny, and Patterson, Patricia. "Rainer Werner Fassbinder." *Film Comment* 11, no. 6 (November/December 1975):5–7.
Franklin, James C. "The Films of Fassbinder: Form and Formula." *Quarterly Review of Film Studies* 5, no. 2 (Spring 1980):169–82.
———. "Method and Message: Forms of Communication in *Angst Essen Seele Auf*." *Literature/Film Quarterly* 7, no. 3 (Summer 1979):182–200.

Gilliatt, Penelope. "Current Cinema: Prodigy." *New Yorker*, 30 May 1977, pp. 104–5.

———. "Fassbinder." *New Yorker*, 14 June 1976, pp. 93–96.

———. "No Sadness That Art Cannot Quell." *New Yorker*, 28 March 1977, pp. 118–22.

Greenspun, Roger. "Phantom of Liberty." *Film Comment* 11, (November/December 1975):8–10.

Harrigan, Renny. "*Effi Briest. The Marquise of O* . . . Women Oppressed!" *JumpCut* 15 (July 1977):3–5.

Hughes, John. "Why Herr R. Ran Amok. Fassbinder and Modernism." *Film Comment* 11, no. 6 (November/December 1975):11–13.

Hughes, John, and Riley, Brooks. "A New Realism. Fassbinder Interviewed." *Film Comment* 11 (November/December 1975):14–17.

Iden, Peter. "Making an Impact. Fassbinder and the Theatre." In *Fassbinder*, edited by Tony Rayns. London: BFI, 1976. pp. 17–23.

Johnson, Catherine. "The Imaginary and *The Bitter Tears of Petra von Kant.*" *Wide Angle* 3, no. 4 (1980):20–25.

Kling, Vincent. "The Dynamics of Defeat." *1976 Film Studies Annual*. West Lafayette, Indiana: Purdue Research Foundation, 1976, pp. 157–66.

Leaming, Barbara. "Structures of Alienation." *JumpCut* 10/11 (June 1976:39–40.

Lellis, George. "Retreat from Romanticism: Two Films from the Seventies." *Film Quarterly* 28, no. 4 (Summer 1975):16–20.

Mayne, Judith. "Fassbinder and Spectatorship." *New German Critique* 12 (Fall 1977): 61–74.

McCormick, Ruth. "Fassbinder and the Politics of Everyday Life." *Cineaste* 8, no. 2 (1977):22–30.

Rayns, Tony. "Forms of Address." *Sight and Sound* 44, no. 1 (Winter 1974/75):2–7.

———. "Notes on Form and Syntax." In *Fassbinder*, edited by Tony Rayns, London: BFI, 1976, pp. 42–44.

Sarris, Andrew. "Can Fassbinder Break the Box-Office Barrier?" *Village Voice*, 22 November 1976, p. 57.

———. "Further Thoughts on Fassbinder." *Village Voice*, 11 July 1977, p. 39.

Sparrow, Norbert, "An Interview with Rainer Werner Fassbinder." *Cineaste* 8, no. 2 (1977):20–21.

Thomas, Paul. "Fassbinder: The Poetry of the Inarticulate." *Film Quarterly* 30, no. 2 (Winter 1976/77):2–17.

Thomsen, Christian Braad. "Fassbinder's Holy Whores." *Take One* 4, no. 6 (July/August 1973):12–16.

———. "Interview with Fassbinder (Berlin 1974)." In *Fassbinder*, edited by Tony Rayns. London: BFI, 1976, pp. 45–49.

Tyler, Ralph. "The Savage World of Rainer Werner Fassbinder." *New York Times*, 27 March 1977, section 2, pp. 15–16.

Wilson, David. "Anti-Cinema: Rainer Werner Fassbinder." *Sight and Sound* 41, no. 2 (Spring 1972):99–100, 113.

II. Werner Herzog

1. Books

Greenberg, Alan. *Heart of Glass*. Munich: Skellig, 1976.

Images at the Horizon. A Workshop with Werner Herzog. Conducted by Roger Ebert. Edited by Gene Walsh. Chicago: Facets Multimedia, 1979.

2. Periodicals

Andrews, Nigel. "Dracula in Delft." *American Film* 4, no. 1 (October 1978):32–38.

Bachmann, Gideon. "The Man on the Volcano: A Portrait of Werner Herzog." *Film Quarterly* 31, no. 1 (Fall 1977):2–10.

Benelli, Dana. "The Cosmos and its Discontents." *Movietone News* 56 (November 1977):8–16.

————. "Mysteries of the Organism: Character Consciousness and Film Form in *Kaspar Hauser* and *Spirit of the Beehive*." *Movietone News* 54 (June 1977):28–33.

Cleere, Elizabeth. "Three Films by Werner Herzog: Seen in the Light of the Grotesque." *Wide Angle* 3, no. 4 (1980):12–19.

Cott, Jonathan. "Signs of Life." *Rolling Stone*, 18 November 1976, pp. 48–56.

Eder, Richard. "A New Visionary in German Films: Werner Herzog." *New York Times Magazine*, 10 July 1977, pp. 24–26ff.

Eisner, Lotte H. "Herzog in Dinkelsbühl." *Sight and Sound* 43, no. 4 (Autumn 1974):212–13.

Finger, Ellis. "Kaspar Hauser Doubly Portrayed: Peter Handke's *Kaspar* and Werner Herzog's *Every Man for Himself*." *Literature/Film Quarterly* 7, no. 3 (Summer 1979):235–43.

Greenberg, Alan. "Notes on Some European Directors." *American Film* 3, no. 1 (October 1977):49–53.

Herzog, Werner. "Why Is There 'Being' At All, Rather than Nothing?" Translated by Stephen Lamb. *Framework* 3 (Spring 1976):24–27.

Horak, Jan-Christopher. "Werner Herzog's *Ecran Absurde*." *Literature/Film Quarterly* 7, no. 3 (Summer 1979):223–34.

Kael, Pauline. "Metaphysical Tarzan." *New Yorker*, 20 October 1975, pp. 142–49.

Kent, Letitia. "Werner Herzog." *New York Times*, 11 September 1977, section D, p. 19ff.

McCormick, Ruth, and Aufderheide, Pat. "Werner Herzog's *Heart of Glass*—Pro and Contra." *Cineaste* 8, no. 4 (1978):32–34.

O'Toole, Lawrence. "I Feel That I'm Close to the Center of Things." *Film Comment* 15, no. 6 (November/December 1979):40–50.

————. "The Great Ecstasy of the Filmmaker Herzog." *Film Comment* 15, no. 6 (November/December 1979):34–39.

Overbey, David L. "Every Man for Himself." *Sight and Sound* 44, no. 2 (Spring 1975):73–75.

Simon, John. "Cinematic Illiterates." *New York*, 20 October 1975, pp. 86–87.

Trojan, Judith. "*How Much Wood Would a Woodchuck Chuck. La Souf-rière.*" *Take One* 7, no. 2 (January 1979):11–13.

Van Wert, William. "Hallowing the Ordinary, Embezzling the Everyday: Werner Herzog's Documentary Practice." *Quarterly Review of Film Studies* 5, no. 2 (Spring 1980):183–92.

Vogel, Amos. "Herzog in Berlin." *Film Comment* 13, no. 5 (September/October 1977):37–38.

Walker, Beverly. "Werner Herzog's *Nosferatu*," *Sight and Sound* 47, no. 4 (Autumn 1978):202–5.

Young, Vernon. "Werner Herzog and Contemporary German Cinema." *Hudson Review* 30, no. 3 (1977):409–14.

III. Alexander Kluge

1. Books

Dawson, Jan. *Alexander Kluge and "The Occasional Work of a Female Slave."* New York: New York Zoetrope, 1977.

2. Periodicals

Dawson, Jan. "Alexander Kluge Interview." *Film Comment* 10, no. 6 (November/December 1974):51–57. (Also reprinted in *Alexander Kluge and "The Occasional Work of a Female Slave."*)

Franklin, James C. "Alienation and the Retention of the Self: The Heroines of *Der gute Mensch von Sezuan, Abschied von Gestern*, and *Die verlorene Ehre der Katharina Blum.*" *Mosaic* 13, no. 4 (Summer 1979):87–98.

Kay, Karyn. "Part-time Work of a Domestic Slave." *Film Quarterly* 29, no. 1 (Fall 1975):55–57.

Kluge, Alexander. "Excerpts from 'Big Business Bolshevik': The Genesis of *Strongman Ferdinand.*" Translated by Skip Acuff. *Quarterly Review of Film Studies* 5, no. 2 (Spring 1980):193–204.

———. "Selected Writings." Translated by Skip Acuff and Hans-Bernard Moeller. *Wide Angle* 3, no. 4 (1980):26–33.

Moeller, Hans-Bernhard, and Springer, Carl. "Directed Change in the Young German Film: Alexander Kluge and *Artists Under the Big Top: Perplexed.*" Wide Angle 2, no. 1 (1977):14–21.

IV. Volker Schlöndorff

1. Periodicals

Friedman, Lester D. "Cinematic Techniques in *The Lost Honor of Katharina Blum.*" *Literature/Film Quarterly* 7, no. 3 (Summer 1979):244–52.

Head, David. "'Der Autor muss repektiert werden'—Schlöndorff/Trotta's *Die verlorene Ehre der Katharina Blum* and Brecht's Critique of Film Adaptation." *German Life and Letters* 32, no. 3 (April 1979):248–64.

Phillips, Klaus. "History reevaluated: Volker Schlöndorff's *The Sudden Wealth of the Poor People of Kombach,*" *1978 Film Studies Annual.* West Lafayette, Indiana: Purdue Research Foundation, 1979, pp. 33–39.

Thomson, Barry and Greg. "Volker Schlöndorff: An Interview." *Film Criticism* 1, no. 3 (Winter 1976/77):26–37.

Zipes, Jack. "The Political Dimensions of *The Lost Honor of Katharina Blum.*" *New German Critique* 12 (Fall 1977):75–84.

V. Jean-Marie Straub/Danièle Huillet

1. Books

Roud, Richard. *Straub.* New York: Viking, 1972.

2. Periodicals

Bachmann, Gideon. "Nicht versöhnt." *Film Quarterly* 19 (Summer 1966):51–55.

Dermody, Susan. "Jean-Marie Straub and Danièle Huillet: The Politics of Film Practice." *Cinema Papers* 10 (September/October 1976):126–30.

Engel, Andi. "Andi Engel Talks to Jean-Marie Straub, and Danièle Huillet Is There Too." *Enthusiasm* 1 (December 1975):1–25.

Greene, Naomi. "Report from Venice: Cinema and Ideology." *Praxis* 2 (1976):249–56.

Huillet, Danièle. "Notes on Gregory's Work Journal." *Enthusiasm* 1 (December 1975):32–55.

Jenkins, Bruce. "The Counter-Cinemas of Straub/Huillet and Robbe-Grillet." *1976 Film Studies Annual.* West Lafayette, Indiana: Purdue Research Foundation, 1976, pp. 144–56.

Lellis, George. "Jean-Marie Straub's *Moses and Aaron.*" *Take One* 4, no. 12 (December 1975):37–39.

Magisos, Melanie. "*Not Reconciled.* The Destruction of Narrative Pleasure." *Wide Angle* 3, no. 4 (1980):35–41.

Nowell-Smith, Geoffrey. "After *Othon,* Before *History Lessons.*" *Enthusiasm* 1 (December 1975):26–31.

Rogers, Joel. "Jean-Marie Straub and Danièle Huillet Interviewed: *Moses and Aaron* as an Object of Marxist Reflection." *JumpCut* 12/13 (December 1976):61–64.

Straub, Jean-Marie, and Huillet, Danièle. "*Fortini/Cani*-Script." *Screen* 19, no. 2 (Summer 1978):11–40.

———. "Scenarios of *History Lessons* and *Introduction to Arnold Schoenberg's Accompaniment to a Cinematographic Scene.*" Translated by Misha Donat. *Screen* 17, no. 1 (Spring 1976):54–83.

Turim, Maureen. "*Ecriture Blanche*: The Ordering of the Filmic Text in *The Chronicle of Anna Magdalena Bach.*" *1976 Film Studies Annual.* West Lafayette, Indiana: Purdue Research Foundation, 1976, pp. 177–92.

Walsh, Martin R. "*Introduction to Arnold Schoenberg's Accompaniment to a Cinematographic Scene.* Straub/Huillet: Brecht: Schoenberg." *1976 Film Studies Annual.* West Lafayette, Indiana: Purdue Research Foundation, 1976, pp. 193–204.

———. "*Moses and Aaron*: Straub and Huillet's Schoenberg." *JumpCut* 12/13 (December 1976):57–61.

———. "Political Formations in the Cinema of Jean-Marie Straub." *JumpCut* 4 (November/December 1974):12–18.

Woods, Gregory. "A Work Journal of the Straub/Huillet Film *Moses and Aaron*." *Enthusiasm* 1 (December 1975):32–55.

VI. Hans-Jürgen Syberberg

1. Periodicals

Andrews, Nigel. "Hitler as Entertainment." *American Film* 3, no. 6 (April 1978):50–53.

Christie, I., ed. "The Syberberg Statement." *Framework* 6 (Autumn 1977):12–18.

Jaehne, Karen. "Old Nazis in New Films: The German Cinema Today." *Cineaste* 9, no. 1 (1978):32–35.

Landy, Marcia. "Politics, Aesthetics, and Patriarchy in *The Confessions of Winifred Wagner.*" *New German Critique* 18 (Fall 1979):151–66.

Pachter, Henry. "Our Hitler, or His?" *Cineaste* 10, no. 2 (Spring 1980):25–27.

Pym, John. "Syberberg and the Tempter of Democracy." *Sight and Sound* 46, no. 4 (Autumn 1977):227–30.

Sontag, Susan. "Eye of the Storm." *New York Review*, 21 February 1980, pp. 36–43.

VII. Wim Wenders

1. Books

Dawson, Jan. *Wim Wenders.* New York: New York Zoetrope, 1976.

Wenders, Wim, and Müller-Scherz, Fritz. *The Film by Wim Wenders: Kings of the Road (In the Course of Time).* Translated by Christopher Doherty. Munich: Filmverlag der Autoren, 1976.

2. Periodicals

Clarens, Carlos. "King of the Road. Wim Wenders Interviewed." *Film Comment* 13, no. 5 (September/October 1977):42–46.

Corrigan, Timothy. "The Realist Gesture in the Films of Wim Wenders: Hollywood and the New German Cinema." *Quarterly Review of Film Studies* 5, no. 2 (Spring 1980):205–16.

Covino, Michael. "Wim Wenders: A Worldwide Homesickness." *Film Quarterly* 31, no. 2 (Winter 1977/78): 9–19.

Dawson, Jan. "Filming Highsmith." *Sight and Sound* 47, no. 1 (Winter 1977/78):30–36.

Fox, Terry Curtis. "Wim Wenders Crosses the Border." *Village Voice*, 3 October 1977, pp. 42–43, 46.

Frisch, Shelley. "The Disenchanted Image: From Goethe's *Wilhelm Meister* to Wenders' *Wrong Movement*." *Literature/Film Quarterly* 7, no. 3 (Summer 1979):208–14.

Jaehne, Karen. "The American Fiend." *Sight and Sound* 47, no. 2 (Spring 1978):101–3.

Kael, Pauline. "Heart/Soul." *New Yorker*, 17 October 1977, pp. 173–79.

Kass, Judith M. "At Home on the Road." *Movietone News* 57 (February 1978):2–11.

Kauffmann, Stanley. "Wenders." *New Republic*, 29 January 1977, pp. 26–27.

Kinder, Marsha. "*The American Friend*." *Film Quarterly* 32, no. 2 (Winter 1978/79):45–49.

Lehman, Peter; Wood, Robin; and Lachmann, Edward. "Wim Wenders: An Interview." *Wide Angle* 2, no. 4 (1978):72–79.

Rayns, Tony. "Forms of Address." *Sight and Sound* 44, no. 1 (Winter 1974–75):2–7.

Schlunk, Jürgen E. "The Image of America in German Literature and in the New German Cinema: *The American Friend*." *Literature/Film Quarterly* 7, no. 3 (Summer 1979):215–22.

Simon, John. "Of Men and Justice: A Platonic Relationship." *New York*, 25 October 1976, pp. 90–92.

Welsh, James M. "Wim Wenders Bibliography." *Wide Angle* 2, no. 4 (1978):80–81.

Welsh, James M., and Kennan, Richard D. "Wim Wenders and Nathaniel Hawthorne." *Literature/Film Quarterly* 6, no. 2 (Spring 1978):175–79.

Filmography

THE FOLLOWING IS a list of New German films available in 16 mm. from American distributors during the winter of 1980–81. Other films will likely be available by the time this book appears in print. With the exception of *Germany in Autumn,* films are listed alphabetically by the filmmaker's last name.

DEUTSCHLAND IM HERBST [Germany in Autumn] (Pro-ject-Filmpro-duktion im Filmverlag der Autoren/Hallelujah-Film/Kairos-Film, 1978)
Direction and Screenplay: Alf Brustellin, Bernhard Sinkel, Rainer Werner Fassbinder, Alexander Kluge, Maximiliane Mainka, Edgar Reitz, Katja Rupé, Hans Peter Cloos, Volker Schlöndorff
Photography: Michael Ballhaus, Jürgen Jürges, Bodo Kessler, Dietrich Lohmann, Colin Mounier, Jörg Schmidt-Reitwein
Cast: Caroline Chaniolleau, Hildegard Friese, Hannelore Hoger, Lisi Man-gold, Katja Rupé, Angela Winkler, Franziska Walser, Heinz Bennent, Wolf Biermann, Hans Peter Cloos, Vadim Glowna, Helmut Griem, Dieter Laser, Horst Mahler, Enno Patalas, Walter Schmiedinger, Manfred Zapatka, the Collective "Rote Rübe"
Running time: 124 minutes
Premiere: March 3, 1978, Berlin
16mm rental: New Line Cinema

Walter Bockmayer

JANE BLEIBT JANE [Jane is Jane Forever] (Enten-Produktion/ZDF, 1977)
Screenplay: Walter Bockmayer and Rolf Bührmann
Photography: Peter Martin
Cast: Johanna König, Karl Blöhmer, Peter Chatel
Running time: 88 minutes
16mm rental: New Line Cinema

Uwe Brandner

ICH LIEBE DICH, ICH TÖTE DICH [I Love You, I Kill You]
Screenplay: Uwe Brandner
Photography: Andre Dubreuil
Cast: Rolf Becker, Hannes Fuchs, Nikolaus Dutsch, Monika Hansen
Running time: 94 minutes
16mm rental: New Yorker Films

Rainer Werner Fassbinder

KATZELMACHER (Antiteater-X-Film, 1969)
Screenplay: Rainer Werner Fassbinder
Photography: Dietrich Lohmann
Music: Peer Raben with themes by Franz Schubert
Cast: Hanna Schygulla (Marie), Lilith Ungerer (Helga), Elga Sorbas (Rosy),
   Doris Mattes (Gunda), Rainer Werner Fassbinder (Jorgos), Rudolf Wal-
   demar Brem (Paul), Hans Hirschmüller (Erich), Harry Baer (Franz), Peter
   Moland (Peter), Hannes Gromball (Klaus), Irm Hermann (Elisabeth),
   Katrin Schaake (Woman)
Running time: 88 minutes
Premiere: October 8, 1969, Mannheim.

GÖTTER DER PEST [Gods of the Plague] (Antiteater, 1969)
Screenplay: Rainer Werner Fassbinder
Photography: Dietrich Lohmann
Music: Peer Raben
Cast: Harry Baer (Franz), Hanna Schygulla (Joanna), Margarethe von Trotta
   (Margarethe), Günther Kaufmann (Günther), Carla Aulaulu (Carla), In-
   grid Caven (Magdalena Fuller), Jan George (Policeman), Marian
   Seidowski (Marian), Yaak Karsunke (Commissioner), Lilo Pempeit
   (Mother), Rainer Werner Fassbinder (Porno-buyer)
Running time: 91 minutes
Premiere: April 4, 1970, Vienna

WARUM LÄUFT HERR R. AMOK? [Why Does Herr R. Run Amuck?]
   (Antiteater and Maran-Film, 1969)
Codirector: Michael Fengler
Screenplay: Michael Fengler and Rainer Werner Fassbinder
Photography: Dietrich Lohmann
Music: Song by Christian Anders

Cast: Kurt Raab (Herr R.), Lilith Ungerer (His Wife), Amadeus Fengler
(Their Son), Franz Maron (R.'s Boss), Harry Baer/Peter Moland/Lilo Pem-
peit (R.'s Co-workers), Hanna Schygulla (Wife's School Friend), Herr and
Frau Sterr (Father and Mother), Peer Raben (R.'s School Friend)
Running time: 88 minutes
Premiere: June 28, 1970, Berlin

DER AMERIKANISCHE SOLDAT [The American Soldier] (Antiteater,
1970)
Screenplay: Rainer Werner Fassbinder
Photography: Dietrich Lohmann
Music: Peer Raben; song by Fassbinder and Raben, sung by Günther Kauf-
mann
Cast: Karl Scheydt (Ricky), Elga Sorgas (Rosa), Jan George (Jan), Margarethe
von Trotta (Chambermaid), Hark Bohm (Doc), Ingrid Caven (Singer), Eva
Ingeborg Scholz (Ricky's Mother), Kurt Raab (Ricky's Brother), Rainer
Werner Fassbinder (Franz)
Running time: 80 minutes
Premiere: October 9, 1970, Mannheim

WARNUNG VOR EINER HEILIGEN NUTTE [Beware of a Holy Whore]
(Antiteater-X-Film, Nova International-Rome, 1970)
Screenplay: Rainer Werner Fassbinder
Photography: Michael Ballhaus
Music: Peer Raben/Gaetano Donizetti/Elvis Presley/Ray Charles/Leonard
Cohen/Spooky Tooth
Cast: Lou Castel (Jeff, Director), Eddie Constantine (playing himself),
Hanna Schygulla (Hanna, Actress), Marquard Bohm (Ricky, Actor), Rainer
Werner Fassbinder (Producer), Ulli Lommel (Korbinian), Katrin Schaake
(Scriptgirl), Margarethe von Trotta (Production Secretary), Werner
Schroeter (Deiters, Photographer)
Running time: 103 minutes
Premiere: August 28, 1971, Venice

DER HÄNDLER DER VIER JAHRESZEITEN [The Merchant of Four
Seasons] (Tango Film, 1971)
Screenplay: Rainer Werner Fassbinder
Photography: Dietrich Lohmann
Music: Song by Rocco Granata
Cast: Hans Hirschmüller (Fruit Merchant), Irm Hermann (His Wife), Hanna
Schygulla (First Sister), Andrea Schober (Child), Gusti Kreissl (Mother),
Kurt Raab (Brother-in-law), Heide Simon (Second Sister), Klaus Löwitsch

(Harry), Karl Scheydt (Anzell), Ingrid Caven (The Great Love), Rainer
Werner Fassbinder (Zucker)
Running time: 89 minutes
Premiere: March 10, 1972, German television (ZDF)

DIE BITTEREN TRÄNEN DER PETRA VON KANT [The Bitter Tears of
Petra von Kant] (Tango Film, 1972)
Screenplay: Rainer Werner Fassbinder
Photography: Michael Ballhaus
Music: The Platters/The Walker Brothers/Giuseppe Verdi
Cast: Margit Carstensen (Petra von Kant), Hanna Schygulla (Karin Thimm),
Irm Hermann (Marlene), Eva Mattes (Gabriele von Kant), Katrin Schaake
(Sidonie von Grasenabb), Gisela Fackeldey (Valerie von Kant)
Running time: 124 minutes
Premiere: June 28, 1972, Berlin

WILDWECHSEL [Jail Bait] (Intertel, 1972)
Screenplay: Rainer Werner Fassbinder, based on the play by Franz Xaver
Kroetz
Photography: Dietrich Lohmann
Music: Ludwig van Beethoven
Cast: Jörg von Liebenfels (Erwin), Ruth Drexel (Hilda, His Wife), Eva
Mattes (Hanni, Their Daughter), Harry Baer (Franz), Rudolf Waldemar
Brem (Dieter), Hanna Schygulla (Physician)
Running time: 102 minutes
Premiere: December 30, 1972, Munich

ANGST ESSEN SEELE AUF [Fear Eats the Soul: Ali] (Tango Film, 1973)
Screenplay: Rainer Werner Fassbinder
Photography: Jürgen Jürges
Cast: Brigitte Mira (Emmi), El Hedi Ben Salem (Ali), Barbara Valentin
(Barbara), Irm Hermann (Krista), Rainer Werner Fassbinder (Eugen),
Karl Scheydt (Albert), Elma Karlowa (Frau Kargus)
Running time: 93 minutes
Premiere: March 5, 1974, Munich

FONTANE EFFI BRIEST [Effi Briest](Tango Film, 1972/74)
Screenplay: Rainer Werner Fassbinder, based on the novel by Theodor
Fontane
Photography: Dietrich Lohmann/Jürgen Jürges
Music: Themes from Camille Saint-Saens
Cast: Hanna Schygulla (Effi), Wolfgang Schenck (Baron Geert von Innstet-
ten), Karlheinz Böhm (Geheimrat Wüllersdorf), Ulli Lommel (Major
Crampas), Ursula Strätz (Roswitha), Irm Hermann (Johanna), Lilo Pem-

peit (Luise von Briest, Effi's Mother), Herbert Steinmetz (Herr von Briest, Effi's Father)
Running time: 141 minutes
Premiere: June 28, 1974, Berlin

FAUSTRECHT DER FREIHEIT [Fox and His Friends] (Tango Film/City Film, Berlin, 1974)
Screenplay: Rainer Werner Fassbinder
Photography: Michael Ballhaus
Music: Peer Raben
Cast: Rainer Werner Fassbinder (Franz), Peter Chatel (Eugen), Karlheinz Böhm (Max), Rudolf Lenz (Lawyer), Karl Scheydt (Klaus), Hans Zander (Springer), Christiane Maybach (Sister)
Running time: 123 minutes
Premiere: May 30, 1975, Munich

MUTTER KÜSTERS' FAHRT ZUM HIMMEL [Mother Küsters Goes to Heaven] (Tango Film, 1975)
Screenplay: Rainer Werner Fassbinder with Kurt Raab
Photography: Michael Ballhaus
Music: Peer Raben
Cast: Brigitta Mira (Mother Küsters), Ingrid Caven (Corinna), Karlheinz Böhm (Tillmann), Margit Carstensen (Frau Tillmann), Irm Hermann (Helene), Gottfried John (Niemeyer), Armin Meier (Ernst)
Running time: 120 minutes
Premiere: July 7, 1975, Berlin

SATANSBRATEN [Satan's Brew] (Albatros/Trio-Film, 1976)
Screenplay: Rainer Werner Fassbinder
Photography: Michael Ballhaus and Jürgen Jürges
Music: Peer Raben
Cast: Kurt Raab (Walter Franz), Margit Carstensen (Andree), Helen Vita (Luise Kranz), Volker Spengler (Ernst), Ingrid Caven (Lilly), Marquard Bohm (Rolf), Y Sa Lo (Lana von Meyerbeer), Ulli Lommel (Lauf)
Running time: 112 minutes

CHINESISCHES ROULETTE [Chinese Roulette] (Albatros/Les Films du Losange, 1976)
Screenplay: Rainer Werner Fassbinder
Photography: Michael Ballhaus
Music: Peer Raben
Cast: Margit Carstensen (Ariane Christ), Andrea Schober (Angela Christ), Ulli Lommel (Kolbe), Anna Karina (Irene), Macha Meril (Traunitz), Alexander Allerson (Gerhard Christ)
Running time: 86 minutes

DESPAIR/EINE REISE INS LICHT [Despair] (NF Geria/Bavaria/SFP, Paris, 1978)
Screenplay: Tom Stoppard, based on the novel by Vladimir Nabokov
Photography: Michael Ballhaus
Music: Peer Raben
Cast: Dirk Bogarde (Hermann Hermann), Andrea Ferreol (Lydia), Volker Spengler, Klaus Löwitsch, Alexander Allerson, Bernhard Wicki, Peter Kern
Running time: 119 minutes
American Premiere: New York Film Festival, 1978.

DIE EHE DER MARIA BRAUN [The Marriage of Maria Braun] (Albatros Film Michael Fengler/Trio Film/WDR, with the Filmverlag der Autoren, 1978)
Screenplay: Peter Märthesheimer and Pia Fröhlich
Photography: Michael Ballhaus
Music: Peer Raben
Cast: Hanna Schygulla (Maria), Klaus Löwitsch, Ivan Desny, Gottfried John, Gisela Uhlen, Elisabeth Trissenaar, Günter Lamprecht, George Byrd, Hark Bohm
Running time: 120 minutes
Premiere: February 20, 1979, Berlin

IN EINEM JAHR MIT 13 MONDEN [In a Year with 13 Moons] (Tango-Film, with the Filmverlag der Autoren, 1978)
Screenplay: Rainer Werner Fassbinder
Photography: Rainer Werner Fassbinder
Music: Peer Raben, Suicide, Roxy Music
Cast: Volker Spengler, Ingrid Caven, Gottfried John, Elisabeth Trissenaar, Eva Mattes, Günter Kaufmann
Running time: 129 minutes
Premiere: November 16, 1978, Munich

DIE DRITTE GENERATION [The Third Generation] (Tango-Film, with the Filmverlag der Autoren, 1979)
Screenplay: Rainer Werner Fassbinder
Photography: Rainer Werner Fassbinder
Music: Peer Raben
Cast: Volker Spengler, Bulle Ogier, Hanna Schygulla, Harry Baer, Margit Carstensen, Eddie Constantine

Running time: 111 minutes
Premiere: May 15, 1979, Cannes

LILI MARLEEN (Roxy Film/CIP Film/Rialto Film, 1980)
Screenplay: Manfred Purzer, Joshua Sinclair, Rainer Werner Fassbinder
  based on a novel by Lale Andersen
Photography: Xaver Schwarzenberger
Music: Peer Raben
Cast: Hanna Schygulla, Giancarlo Giannini, Mel Ferrer, Karl Heinz von
  Hassel, Erik Schumann, Hark Bohm
Running time: 116 minutes
With the exception of *Despair,* which is distributed by New Line Cinema,
  and *Lili Marleen,* which is distributed by UA Classics, all the films of
  Rainer Werner Fassbinder presently available in the United States are
  distributed by New Yorker Films.

Peter Fleischmann

JAGDSZENEN AUS NIEDERBAYERN [Hunters Are the Hunted]
  (Houwer-Film, 1968)
Screenplay: Peter Fleischmann, based on the play by Martin Sperr
Photography: Alain Derobe
Cast: Martin Sperr, Angela Winkler, Hanna Schygulla, Else Quecke
Running time: 88 minutes
16mm rental: Film Images/Radim Films

Hans W. Geissendörfer

JONATHAN (Iduna Films, 1969)
Screenplay: Hans W. Geissendörfer
Photography: Robby Müller
Cast: Jürgen Jung, Paul Albert Krumm, Hertha von Walther
Running time: 97 minutes
16 mm rental: New Yorker Films

DIE WILDENTE [The Wild Duck](Solaris-Film/Sascha/WDR, 1976)
Screenplay: Hans W. Geissendörfer, based on the play by Henrik Ibsen
Photography: Robby Müller

Cast: Jean Seberg, Bruno Ganz, Peter Kern, Anne Bennent
Running time: 105 minutes
16mm rental: New Yorker Films

Peter Handke

DIE LINKSHÄNDIGE FRAU [The Left-Handed Woman] (Road Movies
  Filmproduktion, 1977)
Screenplay: Peter Handke
Photography: Robby Müller
Music: J. S. Bach
Cast: Edith Clever, Bruno Ganz, Angela Winkler, Markus Mühleisen, Bern-
  hard Minetti, Bernhard Wicki, Rüdiger Vogeler
Running time: 113 minutes
16mm rental: New Yorker Films

Reinhard Hauff

DIE VERROHUNG DES FRANZ BLUM [The Brutalization of Franz
  Blum] (Bioskop Films/WDR, 1973)
Screenplay: Burkhard Driest
Photography: W. P. Hassenstein
Cast: Jürgen Prochnow, Burkhard Driest, Tilo Prückner, Eik Gallwitz
Running time: 104 minutes
16mm rental: New Yorker Films

MESSER IM KOPF [Knife in the Head] (Bioskop Films/Hallelujah/WDR,
  1978)
Screenplay: Peter Schneider
Photography: Frank Brühne
Cast: Bruno Ganz, Angela Winkler, Hans Christian Blech, Heinz Hönig,
  Hans Brenner
Running time: 108 minutes
16mm rental: New Yorker Films

Werner Herzog

LEBENSZEICHEN [Signs of Life] (Werner Herzog Filmproduktion, 1967)
Screenplay: Werner Herzog
Photography: Thomas Mauch with Dietrich Lohmann

Music: Stavros Xarchakos
Cast: Peter Brogle (Stroszek), Wolfgang Reichmann (Meinhard), Athina Zacharopoulou (Nora), Wolfgang von Ungern-Sternberg (Becker), Wolfgang Stumpf (Captain), Florian Fricke (Pianist), Werner Herzog (Soldier)
Running time: 90 minutes
Premiere: June 25, 1968, Berlin
16mm rental: New Yorker Films

LETZTE WORTE [Last Words] (Werner Herzog Filmproduktion, 1968)
Screenplay: Werner Herzog
Photography: Thomas Mauch with Dietrich Lohmann
Music: Cretan folk music
Cast: Inhabitants of Crete and Spinalonga
Running time: 13 minutes
Premiere: April 4, 1968, Oberhausen
16mm rental: New Yorker Films

MASSNAHMEN GEGEN FANATIKER [Precautions Against Fanatics] (Werner Herzog Filmproduktion, 1968)
Screenplay: Werner Herzog
Photography: Dietrich Lohmann, Jörg Schmidt-Reitwein
Cast: Petar Radenkovic, Mario Adorf, Hans Tiedemann, Herbert Hisel, Peter Schamoni
Running Time: 11 minutes
Premiere: March 28, 1969, Oberhausen
16mm rental: New Yorker Films

FATA MORGANA (Werner Herzog Filmproduktion, 1970)
Screenplay: Werner Herzog
Photography: Jörg Schmidt-Reitwein
Music: Händel, Mozart, Blind Faith, Francois Couperin, Leonard Cohen
Cast: Wolfgang von Ungern-Sternberg, James William Gledhill, Eugen des Montagnes; Narrators: Lotte H. Eisner/Wolfgang Bächler/Manfred Eigendorf
Running time: 79 minutes
Premiere: May 17, 1971, Cannes
16mm rental: New Line Cinema

AUCH ZWERGE HABEN KLEIN ANGEFANGEN [Even Dwarfs Started Small] (Werner Herzog Filmproduktion, 1970)
Screenplay: Werner Herzog
Photography: Thomas Mauch with Jörg Schmidt-Reitwein
Music: Florian Fricke and Spanish folk music
Cast: Helmut Döring (Hombre), Paul Glauer (Educator), Gisela Hertwig

(Pobrecita), Hertel Minkner (Chicklets), Gertraud Piccini (Piccini), Marianne Saar (Theresa), Brigitte Saar (Cochina), Gerd Gickel (Pepe), Erna Gschwendtner (Azucar), Gerhard März (Territory), Alfredo Piccini (Anselmo), Erna Smollarz (Schweppes), Lajos Zsarnoczay (Chapparo)
Running time: 96 minutes
Premiere: May 8, 1970, Cannes
16mm rental: New Line Cinema

LAND DES SCHWEIGENS UND DER DUNKELHEIT [Land of Silence and Darkness] (Werner Herzog Filmproduktion, 1971)
Screenplay: Werner Herzog
Photography: Jörg Schmidt-Reitwein
Music: J.S. Bach, Vivaldi
Cast: Fini Straubinger, Heinrich Fleischmann, Vladimir Kokol, M. Baaske, Resi Mittermeier; Narrator: Rolf Illig
Running time: 85 minutes
Premiere: October 8, 1971, Mannheim
16mm rental: New Yorker Films

AGUIRRE, DER ZORN GOTTES [Aguirre, the Wrath of God] (Werner Herzog Filmproduktion/Hessischer Rundfunk, 1972)
Screenplay: Werner Herzog
Photography: Thomas Mauch with Francisco Joán and Orlando Macchiavello
Music: Popol Vuh
Cast: Klaus Kinski (Don Lope de Aguirre), Helena Rojo (Inez de Atienza), Del Negro (Carvajal), Ruy Guerra (Ursúa), Peter Berling (Guzman), Cecilia Rivera (Flora, Aguirre's Daughter)
Running time: 93 minutes
Premiere: December 29, 1972, Cologne
16mm rental: New Yorker Films

DIE GROSSE EKSTASE DES BILDSCHNITZERS STEINER [The Great Ecstasy of the Sculptor Steiner] (Werner Herzog Filmproduktion, 1974)
Screenplay: Werner Herzog
Music: Popol Vuh
Photography: Jörg Schmidt-Reitwein with Francisco Joán, Frederik Hettich, Alfred Chrosziel, Gideon Meron
Cast: Walter Steiner
Running time: 45 minutes
Premiere: November 14, 1974, Munich
16mm rental: New Yorker Films

JEDER FÜR SICH UND GOTT GEGEN ALLE [Every Man for Himself and God Against All] (Werner Herzog Filmproduktion/ZDF)
Screenplay: Werner Herzog
Photography: Jörg Schmidt-Reitwein with Michael Gast and Klaus Wyborny
Music: Pachelbel, Orlando di Lasso, Albinoni, Mozart
Cast: Bruno S. (Kaspar), Walter Ladengast (Daumer), Brigitte Mira (Käthe), Hans Musäus (Unknown Man)
Running time: 109 minutes
Premiere: November 11, 1974, Dinkelsbühl
16mm rental: Cinema V

HOW MUCH WOOD WOULD A WOODCHUCK CHUCK (Werner Herzog Filmproduktion, 1976)
Screenplay: Werner Herzog
Photography: Thomas Mauch with Francisco Joán and Ed Lachmann
Music: Shorty Eager and The Eager Beavers
Cast: Ralph Wade, Alan Ball, Steve Liptay, Abe Diffenbach
Running time: 44 minutes
Premiere: September 1976
16mm rental: New Yorker Films

HERZ AUS GLAS [Heart of Glass] (Werner Herzog Filmproduktion, 1976)
Screenplay: Herbert Achternbusch and Werner Herzog
Photography: Jörg Schmidt-Reitwein with Michael Gast
Music: Popol Vuh and the Studio of Early Music
Cast: Josef Bierbichler (Hias), Stefan Güttler (Factory Owner), Clemens Scheitz (Adalbert), Volker Prechtl (Wudy), Sonja Skiba (Ludmilla), Brunhilde Klöckner (Paulin)
Running time: 94 minutes
Premiere: November 12, 1976, Paris
16mm rental: New Yorker films

LA SOUFRIÈRE (Werner Herzog Filmproduktion, 1976)
Screenplay: Werner Herzog
Photography: Jörg Schmidt-Reitwein, Ed Lachmann
Running time: 31 minutes
Premiere: March 1977, Bonn
16mm rental: New Yorker Films

STROSZEK (Werner Herzog Filmproduktion/ZDF, 1977)
Screenplay: Werner Herzog
Photography: Thomas Mauch and Ed Lachmann with Wolfgang Knigge and Stefano Guidi
Music: Chet Atkins, Sonny Terry
Cast: Bruno S. (Stroszek), Eva Mattes (Eva), Clemens Scheitz (Scheitz)
Running time: 108 minutes
Premiere: May 20, 1977, Munich
16mm rental: New Yorker Films

NOSFERATU—PHANTOM DER NACHT [Nosferatu, the Vampyre]
(Werner Herzog Filmproduktion/Gaumont, Paris, 1978)
Screenplay: Werner Herzog, based on the film *Nosferatu, a Symphony of Terror* by F.W. Murnau and the novel *Dracula* by Bram Stoker
Photography: Jörg Schmidt-Reitwein with Michael Gast
Music: Popol Vuh, Richard Wagner, Charles Gounod, Vok Ansambl Gordela
Cast: Klaus Kinski (Count Dracula), Isabelle Adjani (Lucy Harker), Bruno Ganz (Jonathan Harker), Jacques Dufilho (Captain), Roland Topor (Renfield), Walter Ladengast (Dr. Van Helsing)
Running time: 107 minutes
Premiere: January 8, 1979, Paris
16mm rental: Films Inc.

WOYZECK (Werner Herzog Filmproduktion, 1978)
Screenplay: Werner Herzog, based on the drama fragment by Georg Büchner
Photography: Jörg Schmidt-Reitwein with Michael Gast
Music: String Quartet Telč and Antonio Vivaldi, Benedetto Marcello
Cast: Klaus Kinski (Woyzeck), Eva Mattes (Marie), Wolfgang Reichmann (Captain), Willy Semmelrogge (Doctor), Josef Bierbichler (Drum Major), Paul Burian (Andres)
Running time: 81 minutes
Premiere: May 22, 1979, Cannes
16mm rental: New Yorker films
See also next entry.

Erwin Keusch/Christian Weisenborn

WAS ICH BIN, SIND MEINE FILME [I Am My Films—A documentary on the life and films of Werner Herzog] (Nanuk-Film, 1978)
Photography: Rene Perraudin and Martin Schäfer
Running time: 96 minutes
16mm rental: New Yorker Films

Klaus Kirschner

MOZART—AUFZEICHNUNGEN EINER JUGEND [Mozart—Chronicle of a Childhood] (Artfilm Pitt Koch/BR/Kuratorium, 1976)
Screenplay: Klaus Kirschner
Photography: Pitt Koch
Musical Advisor: Franz Beyer
Cast: Pavlos Bekiaris (Mozart, age 7), Diego Crovetti (Mozart, age 12), Santiago Ziesmer (Mozart, age 20), Marianne Lowitz (Mozart's Mother), Karl-Maria Schley (Mozart's Father), Ingeborg Schroeder (Nanerl, Mozart's Sister, age 11), Nina Palmers (Nanerl, age 17), Dietlind Hübner (Aloisia Weber)
Running time: 224 minutes
16mm rental: Unifilm Inc.

Alexander Kluge

ABSCHIED VON GESTERN [Yesterday Girl] (Kairos-Film, with Independent-Film, 1966)
Screenplay: Alexander Kluge, based on his short story "Anita G."
Photography: Thomas Mauch and Edgar Reitz
Cast: Alexandra Kluge (Anita), Hans Korte (Judge), Günther Mack (Pichota); Narrator: Alexander Kluge
Running Time: 88 minutes
Premiere: September 5, 1966, Venice
16mm rental: The Liberty Company

DER STARKE FERDINAND [Strongman Ferdinand] (Kairos-Film with Reitz-Film, 1976)
Screenplay: Alexander Kluge, based on his story "A Bolschewik of Capitalism"
Photography: Thomas Mauch and Martin Schäfer
Cast: Heinz Schubert (Ferdinand Rieche), Verena Rudolph (Gertie Kallmann); Narrator: Alexander Kluge
Running time: 97 minutes
Premiere: April 27, 1976, Bonn
16mm rental: The Liberty Company

Peter Lilienthal

ES HERRSCHT RUHE IM LAND [Calm Prevails Over the Country]
(FFAT/ZDF/ORF, 1975)
Screenplay: Peter Lilienthal and Antonio Skarmeta
Photography: Robby Müller
Cast: Charles Vanel, Mario Pardo, Eduardo Duran
Running time: 100 minutes
16mm rental: New Yorker Films

DER AUFSTAND [The Uprising](Proverbis Gesellschaft für Film + Fern-
sehen *et al.*, 1980)
Screenplay: Peter Lilienthal and Antonio Skarmeta
Photography: Michael Ballhaus
Cast: Augustin Pereira, Carlos Catania, Maria Lourdes Centano de Zelaya,
Oscar Castillo, Guido Saenz
Running time: 95 minutes
35mm rental: Kino International Corporation

Ulli Lommel

DIE ZÄRTLICHKEIT DER WÖLFE [Tenderness of the Wolves] (Tango-
Film, 1973)
Screenplay: Kurt Raab
Photography: Jürgen Jürges
Cast: Kurt Raab, Jeff Roden, Margit Carstensen, Rainer Werner Fassbinder,
Brigitte Mira
Running time: 85 minutes
16mm rental: Deutsch Films

ADOLF UND MARLENE [Adolf and Marlene](Albatros/Trio-Film, 1976)
Screenplay: Ulli Lommel
Photography: Michael Ballhaus
Cast: Kurt Raab, Margit Carstensen, Ulli Lommel, Ila von Hasperg, Andrea
Schober
Running time: 88 minutes
16mm rental: Deutsch Films

Wolfgang Petersen

DIE KONSEQUENZ [The Consequence] (Solaris-Film, 1977)
Screenplay: Alexander Ziegler and Wolfgang Petersen, based on the novel by
  Alexander Ziegler
Photography: Jörg Michael Baldenius
Music: Nils Sustrate
Cast: Jürgen Prochnow, Ernst Hannawald
Running time: 100 minutes
16 mm rental: Unifilm

Rosa von Praunheim

**NICHT DER HOMOSEXUELLE IST PERVERS, SONDERN DIE
  SITUATION, IN DER ER LEBT** [It's Not the Homosexual That's Per-
  verse But Rather the Situation in Which He Lives](Bavaria/WDR, 1970)
Screenplay: Rosa von Praunheim and Martin Dannecker
Photography: Robert Van Ackeren
Cast: Bernd Feuerhelm, Berryt Bohlen, Ernst Kuchling
Running time: 67 minutes
16mm rental: Filmmakers Cooperative

UNDERGROUND AND EMIGRANTS (Rosa von Praunheim/SFB/
  DAAD, 1976)
Screenplay: Rosa von Praunheim
Photography: Lloyd Williams, Ed Lieber, Scott Sorenson, Rosa von
  Praunheim
Running time: 89 minutes
16mm rental: Filmmakers Cooperative

TALLY BROWN NEW YORK (Rosa von Praunheim/WDR, 1978)
Screenplay: Rosa von Praunheim
Photography: Rosa von Praunheim
Running time: 90 minutes
16mm rental: Filmmakers Cooperative

ARMEE DER LIEBENDEN ODER AUFSTAND DER PERVERSEN
[Army of Lovers or Revolt of the Perverts] (Rosa von Praunheim, 1979)
Screenplay: Rosa von Praunheim
Photography: Rosa von Praunheim, Ben van Meter, Michael Oblovitz, John
  Rome, Werner Schroeter, Bob Schub, Nikolai Ursin, Juliana Wang, Lloyd
  Williams
Running time: 107 minutes
16mm rental: Filmmakers Cooperative

Frank Ripploh

TAXI ZUM KLO [Taxi to the Toilet] (Ripploh/Schier/Straub, 1980)
Screenplay: Frank Ripploh
Photography: Horst Schier
Music: "Flying Gay" by Hans Wittstadt
Cast: Frank Ripploh, Bernd Broaderup, Gitte Lederer, Hans-Gerd Mer-
  tens, Irmgard Lademacher, Beate Springer, Ulla Topf, Magdalena
  Montezuma
Running time: 92 minutes
16mm rental: Promovision International

Sohrab Shahid Saless

TAGEBUCH EINES LIEBENDEN [Diary of a Lover] (Provobis-Film/
  WDR, 1977)
Screenplay: Sohrab Shahid Saless
Photography: Manzur Yazdi
Music: Rolf Bauer
Cast: Klaus Salge (Michael Bauer), Eva Manhardt (Christel), Edith Hilde-
  brandt (The Mother), Ingeborg Ziemendorff (Frau Galinzky), Ursula Alexa
  (Saleswoman), Dorothea Moritz (Cashier), Gerhard Wollner (Police In-
  spector)
Running time: 92 minutes
16mm rental: The Liberty Company

Helke Sander

DIE ALLSEITIG REDUZIERTE PERSÖNLICHKEIT—REDUPERS
[The All-Round Reduced Personality—REDUPERS] (Basis-Film, 1977)
Screenplay: Helke Sander
Photography: Katia Forbert

Cast: Helke Sander, Frank Burckner, Ronny Tanner, Gesine Strempel,
Gislind Nabakowski, Joachim Baumann, Gisela Zies
Running time: 98 minutes
16mm rental: Unifilm Inc.

Volker Schlöndorff

DER JUNGE TÖRLESS [Young Törless] (Seitz/Nouvelles Editions de
Film, 1966)
Screenplay: Volker Schlöndorff, based on the novel *Young Törless* by Robert
Musil
Photography: Franz Rath
Music: Hans Werner Henze
Cast: Matthieu Carrière (Törless), Bernd Tischer, Marian Seidowsky,
Barbara Steele
Running time: 87 minutes
American premiere: New York Film Festival, 1967
16mm rental: New Yorker Films

MICHAEL KOHLHAAS—DER REBELL [Michael Kohlhaas] (Oceanic/
Houwer Film, 1969)
Screenplay: Edward Bond, based on the story by Kleist
Photography: Willi Kurant
Music: Stanley Myers
Cast: David Warner, Anna Karina
Running time: 100 minutes
16mm rental: Corinth Films

**DER PLÖTZLICHE REICHTUM DER ARMEN LEUTE VON KOM-
BACH** [The Sudden Wealth of the Poor People of Kombach] (Hallelujah
Films/Hessischer Rundfunk, 1970)
Screenplay: Volker Schlöndorff and Margarethe von Trotta
Photography: Franz Rath
Music: Klaus Doldinger
Cast: Reinhard Hauff, George Lehn, Margarethe von Trotta
Running time: 102 minutes
16mm rental: New Yorker Films

STROHFEUER [A Free Woman] (Hallelujah Films/Hessischer Rundfunk,
1972)
Screenplay: Volker Schlöndorff and Margarethe von Trotta
Photography: Sven Nykvist

Music: Stanley Myers
Cast: Margarethe von Trotta, Friedhelm Ptok, Martin Lüttge
Running time: 101 minutes
16mm rental: New Yorker Films

DIE VERLORENE EHRE DER KATHARINA BLUM [The Lost Honor of
Katharina Blum] (Bioskop/Paramount-Orion, 1975)
Codirector: Margarethe von Trotta
Screenplay: Volker Schlöndorff and Margarethe von Trotta, based on the
novel by Heinrich Böll
Photography: Jost Vacano
Music: Hans Werner Henze
Cast: Angela Winkler, Mario Adorf, Dieter Laser, Heinz Bennent, Hanne-
lore Hoger
Running time: 106 minutes
16mm rental: Films Inc.

DER FANGSCHUSS [Coup de Grâce] (Bioskop/Argos, 1976)
Screenplay: Genevieve Dormann, Margarethe von Trotta, Jutta Brückner,
based on the novel *Le Coup de grâce* by Marguerite Yourcenar
Photography: Igor Luther
Music: Stanley Myers
Cast: Margarethe von Trotta, Matthias Habich, Rüdiger Kirchstein, Matth-
ieu Carrière
Running time: 95 minutes
16mm rental: Cinema V

DIE BLECHTROMMEL [The Tin Drum] (Franz Seitz Film/Bioskop-Film,
Artemis Film/Hallelujah-Film/GGB 14. KG/Argos Films, Paris, with Jad-
ran Film, Zagreb, and Film Polski, Warsaw, 1979)
Screenplay: Jean-Claude Carrière, Volker Schlöndorff, and Franz Seitz,
based on the novel by Günter Grass
Photography: Igor Luther
Music: Friedrich Meyer and Maurice Jarre
Cast: Mario Adorf, Angela Winkler, David Bennent, Daniel Olbrychski,
Katharina Thalbach, Heinz Bennent, Fritz Hackl, Berta Drews, Tina
Engel, Mariella Oliveri, Charles Aznavour, Andrea Ferréol, Otto Sander
Running time: 145 minutes
Premiere: May 3, 1979
16mm rental: Films Inc.

Jean-Marie Straub/Daniele Huillet

MACHORKA-MUFF (Straub-Huillet/Atlas Film/Cineropa-Film, 1962)
Screenplay: Jean-Marie Straub and Danièle Huillet, based on the story "Bonn Diary" by Heinrich Böll
Photography: Wendelin Sachtler
Music: J.S. Bach, Francois Louis
Cast: Erich Kuby (Erich von Machorka-Muff), Renate Lang (Inn), Rolf Thiede (Murcks-Maloche), Günther Strupp (Heffling)
Running time: 18 minutes
Premiere: February 1963, Oberhausen

NICHT VERSÖHNT ODER ES HILFT NUR GEWALT, WO GEWALT HERRSCHT [Not Reconciled or Only Violence Helps Where Violence Reigns] (Straub-Huillet, 1965)
Screenplay: Jean-Marie Straub and Danièle Huillet, based on the novel *Billiards at Nine-thirty* by Heinrich Böll
Photography: Wendelin Sachtler, Gerhard Ries, Christian Schwarzwald, Jean-Marie Straub
Music: Bela Bartok, J.S. Bach
Cast: Henning Harmssen (Robert Fähmel at 40), Karlheinz Hargesheimer (Heinrich Fähmel as a Young Man), Heinrich Hargesheimer (Heinrich Fähmel at 80), Martha Ständer (Johanna Fähmel as an Old Woman), Ulrich Hopmann (Robert Fähmel at 18), Heiner Braun (Nettlinger), Ernst Kutzinski (Schrella at 15), Ulrich von Thüna (Schrella at 35), Danièle Huillet (Johanna Fähmel as a Young Woman)
Running time: 55 minutes
Premiere: July 4, 1965, Berlin

CHRONIK DER ANNA MAGDALENA BACH [Chronicle of Anna Magdalena Bach] (Franz Seitz Filmproduktion/RAI, Rome/IDI-Cinematografica, Rome/Straub-Huillet/Kuratorium Junger Deutscher Film/Filmfonds e.V./Hessischer Rundfunk/telepool, 1967)
Screenplay: Jean-Marie Straub and Danièle Huillet
Photography: Ugo Piccone, Saverio Diamanti, Giovanni Canfarelli, Hans Kracht, Uwe Radon, Thomas Hartwig
Music: J.S. Bach
Cast: Gustav Leonhardt (Johann Sebastian Bach), Christiane Lang-Drewanz
Running time: 94 minutes
Premiere: February 3, 1968, Utrecht

DER BRÄUTIGAM, DIE KOMÖDIANTIN UND·DER ZUHÄLTER [The Bridegroom, the Comedienne, and the Pimp] (Janus Film and Television/Straub-Huillet, 1968)
Screenplay: Jean-Marie Straub and Danièle Huillet, with portions of the play *Sickness of Youth* by Ferdinand Bruckner and poetry by Juan de la Cruz
Photography: Klaus Schilling and Hubs Hagen
Music: J.S. Bach.
Cast: Lilith Ungerer (Marie/Lilith), Rainer Werner Fassbinder (Freder/the Pimp), James Powell (James), Peer Raben (Alt/Willi), Irm Hermann (Désirée), Kristin Peterson (Irene), Hanna Schygulla (Lucy), Rudolf Waldemar Brem (Petrell)
Running time: 23 minutes
Premiere: October 10, 1968, Mannheim

LES YEUX NE VEULENT PAS EN TOUT TEMPS SE FERMER OU PEUT-ÊTRE QU'UN JOUR ROME SE PERMETTRA DE CHOISIR À SON TOUR (OTHON) [The Eyes Do Not Always Want to Close or Perhaps One Day Rome Will Permit Itself to Choose in Its Turn] (*Othon*) (Janus-Film/Straub-Huillet, 1969)
Screenplay: Jean-Marie Straub and Danièle Huillet, based on the play *Othon* by Pierre Corneille
Photography: Ugo Piccone, Renato Berta
Cast: Adriano Apra (Othon), Anne Brumagne (Plautina), Ennio Lauricella (Galba), Olimpia Carlisi (Camilla), Anthony Pensabene (Vinius), Jean-Marie Straub (Laco)
Running time: 82 minutes
Premiere: January 4, 1970, Rapallo

GESCHICHTSUNTERRICHT [History Lessons] (Straub-Huillet/Janus Film and Television, 1972)
Screenplay: Jean-Marie Straub and Danièle Huillet, based on the novel fragment *The Affairs of Mr. Julius Caesar* by Bertolt Brecht
Photography: Renato Berta
Music: J.S. Bach
Cast: Gottfried Bold (Banker), Johann Unterpertinger (Farmer), Henri Ludwig (Lawyer), Carl Vaillant (Poet), Benedikt Zulauf (Young Man)
Running time: 88 minutes
Premiere: October 10, 1972, Mannheim

EINLEITUNG ZU ARNOLD SCHOENBERGS BEGLEITMUSIK ZU EINER LICHTSPIELSZENE [Introduction to Arnold Schoenberg's "Accompaniment to a Cinematographic Scene] (Straub-Huillet, 1972)
Screenplay: Jean-Marie Straub
Photography: Renato Berta, Horst Bever

Music: Arnold Schoenberg
Cast: Günter Peter Straschek, Danièle Huillet, Peter Nestler, Jean-Marie
    Straub
Running time: 16 minutes
Premiere: April 9, 1973, Oberhausen

MOSES UND ARON [Moses and Aron] (Austrian Broadcasting/ARD/
    Hessischer Rundfunk/Janus-Film and Television/Straub-Huillet/RAI/
    ORTF/Taurus-Film, 1974)
Screenplay: Opera by Arnold Schoenberg
Photography: Ugo Piccone, Saverio Diamanti, Gianni Canfarelli, Renato
    Berta
Music: Performed by the Orchestra and Chorus of the Austrian Broadcasting
    under the direction of Michael Gielen, assisted by Bernard Rubenstein
Cast: Günter Reich (Moses), Louis Devos (Aron)
Running time: 110 minutes
Premiere: February 1975, Rotterdam

FORTINI CANI [The Dogs of Sinai] (Straub-Huillet/RAI/Sunchild, Paris/
    Polytel International/Artificial Eye, London/New Yorker Films, New York,
    1976)
Screenplay: Jean-Marie Straub and Danièle Huillet, based on the book *I cani
    del Sinai* by Franco Fortini
Photography: Renato Berta and Emilio Bestetti
Cast: Franco Fortini, Luciana Nissim, Adriano Apra
Running time: 85 minutes
All the films of Jean-Marie Straub and Danièle Huillet available in the United
    States are distributed by New Yorker Films.

Hans-Jürgen Syberberg

LUDWIG—REQUIEM FÜR EINEN JUNGFRÄULICHEN KÖNIG
    [Ludwig—Requiem for a Virgin King] (TMS Film Inc., 1972)
Screenplay: Hans-Jürgen Syberberg
Photography: Dietrich Lohmann
Music: Richard Wagner
Cast: Harry Baer (Ludwig), Hanna Köhler, Ingrid Caven, Ursula Strätz,
    Peter Moland, Peter Kern, Rudolf Waldemar Brem
Running time: 134 minutes
16mm rental: Zoetrope

KARL MAY (TMS Film Inc., 1974)
Screenplay: Hans-Jürgen Syberberg
Photography: Dietrich Lohmann

Music: Frederic Chopin, Franz Liszt, Gustav Mahler, *et al*
Cast: Helmut Käutner (Karl May), Kristina Söderbaum (Emma), Käthe Gold (Klara), Attila Hörbiger, Willy Trenk-Trebitsch, Mady Rahl, Lil Dagover
Running time: 187 minutes
16mm rental: The Liberty Company

WINIFRED WAGNER UND DIE GESCHICHTE DES HAUSES WAHNFRIED VON 1914–1975 [Winifred Wagner and the History of the House Wahnfried from 1914–1975] (Syberberg Filmproduktion, 1975)
Photography: Dietrich Lohmann
Cast: Winifred Wagner
Running time: 5 hours, shortened to 104 minutes for American distribution
Premiere: July 1976, Berlin
16mm rental: The Liberty Company

HITLER. EIN FILM AUS DEUTSCHLAND [Hitler. A Film from Germany] (TMS Film Inc. with WDR-Cologne, Ina-Paris, BBC-London, 1977)
Screenplay: Hans-Jürgen Syberberg
Photography: Dietrich Lohmann
Music: Gustav Mahler, Wolfgang Amadeus Mozart, Richard Wagner, Ludwig van Beethoven
Cast: Heinz Schubert, Peter Kern, Hellmut Lange, Rainer von Artenfels, Martin Sperr, Peter Moland, Johannes Buzalski, Alfred Edel, Amelie Syberberg, Harry Baer, Peter Lühr, Andre Heller
Running time: 405 minutes
Premiere: November 21–22, 1977, London
Distribution: Zoetrope

Margarethe von Trotta

DIE VERLORENE EHRE DER KATHARINA BLUM [The Lost Honor of Katharina Blum] (1975) Codirector, see listing under Volker Schlöndorff

DAS ZWEITE ERWACHEN DER CHRISTA KLAGES [The Second Awakening of Christa Klages] (Bioskop/WDR, 1977)
Screenplay: Margarethe von Trotta and Luisa Francia
Photography: Franz Rath
Cast: Tina Engel, Silvia Reize, Katharina Thalbach, Marius Müller-Westernhagen, Peter Schneider
Running time: 88 minutes
16mm rental: New Line Cinema

SCHWESTERN ODER DIE BALANCE DES GLÜCKS [Sisters or The Balance of Happiness] (Bioskop-Film/WDR, 1979)
Screenplay: Margarethe von Trotta with Luisa Francia and Martje Grohmann
Photography: Franz Rath
Music: Konstantin Wecker
Cast: Jutta Lampe, Gudrun Gabriel, Jessica Früh, Konstantin Wecker, Rainer Delventhal, Agnes Fink, Heinz Bennent
Running time: 91 minutes
Premiere: September 21, 1979
16mm rental: Cinema V

Wim Wenders

SAME PLAYER SHOOTS AGAIN (Wenders, 1967)
Screenplay: Wim Wenders
Photography: Wim Wenders
Music: Mood Music
Cast: Hanns Zischler
Running time: 12 minutes

SILVER CITY (Wenders, 1968)
Screenplay: Wim Wenders
Photography: Wim Wenders
Music: Mood Music
Running time: 25 minutes

ALABAMA—2000 LIGHT YEARS (Academy for Television and Film, Munich, 1969)
Screenplay: Wim Wenders
Photography: Wim Wenders and Robby Müller
Music: The Rolling Stones, Jimi Hendrix, Bob Dylan
Cast: Paul Lys, Werner Schroeter, Muriel Schrat, Christian Friedel, King Ampaw, Peter Kaiser
Running time: 25 minutes

SUMMER IN THE CITY (Academy for Television and Film, Munich, 1970)
Screenplay: Wim Wenders
Photography: Robby Müller
Music: Kinks, Loving Spoonful, Chuck Berry
Cast: Hanns Zischler, Edda Köchl, Libgart Schwarz, Marie Bardischewski, Gerd Stein, Helmut Farber, Wim Wenders
Running time: 120 minutes in American distribution

DIE ANGST DES TORMANNS BEIM ELFMETER [The Goalie's Anxiety at the Penalty Kick] (Filmverlag der Autoren/Osterreichischer Telefilm-Vienna, 1971)
Screenplay: Wim Wenders, based on the novel by Peter Handke
Photography: Robby Müller
Music: Jürgen Knieper
Cast: Arthur Brauss (Josef Bloch), Kai Fischer (Hertha Gabler), Erika Pluhar (Gloria T.), Libgart Schwarz (Anna), Marie Bardischewski (Maria)
Running time: 101 minutes

DER SCHARLACHROTE BUCHSTABE [The Scarlet Letter] (Filmverlag der Autoren/WDR/Querejeta, 1972)
Screenplay: Wim Wenders, Bernardo Fernandez, Tankred Dorst, based on the novel by Nathaniel Hawthorne
Photography: Robby Müller
Music: Jürgen Knieper
Cast: Senta Berger (Hester Prynne), Hans Christian Blech (Chillingworth), Lou Castel (Dimmesdale), Yeline Samarina (Hibbins), Yella Rottländer (Pearl), Rüdiger Vogler
Running time: 90 minutes

ALICE IN DEN STÄDTEN [Alice in the Cities] (Filmverlag der Autoren, 1974)
Screenplay: Wim Wenders and Veith von Furstenberg
Photography: Robby Müller and Martin Schäfer
Music: Can
Cast: Rüdiger Vogeler (Philip Winter), Yella Rottländer (Alice van Damm), Elisabeth Kreuzer (Lisa van Damm), Edda Köchl (Edda)
Running time: 110 minutes

FALSCHE BEWEGUNG [Wrong Move] (Solaris Film/WDR, 1975)
Screenplay: Peter Handke, freely adapted from *Wilhelm Meister's Apprenticeship* by J.W. von Goethe
Photography: Robby Müller
Music: Jürgen Kneiper
Cast: Rüdiger Vogeler (Wilhelm Meister), Hanna Schygulla (Therese), Hans Christian Blech (Laertes), Peter Kern (Landau), Nastassja Nakszynski (Mignon), Ivan Desny (Industrialist), Marianne Hoppe (Mother), Elisabeth Kreuzer (Janine)
Running time: 103 minutes

IM LAUF DER ZEIT [Kings of the Road] (Wim Wenders Produktion, 1976)
Screenplay: Wim Wenders
Photography: Robby Müller
Music: Axel Linstädt, performed by Improved Sound Ltd.
Cast: Rüdiger Vogeler (Bruno), Hanns Zischler (Robert), Elisabeth Kreuzer
(Cashier), Rudolf Schundler (Robert's Father), Franziska Stömmer
(Cinema Owner), Patrick Kreuzer (Young Boy)
Running time: 176 minutes

DER AMERIKANISCHE FREUND [The American Friend] (Wim Wen-
ders Produktion/Road Movies/Les Films du Losange/WDR, 1977)
Screenplay: Wim Wenders, based on the novel *Ripley's Game* by Patricia
Highsmith
Photography: Robby Müller
Cast: Bruno Ganz (Jonathan), Dennis Hopper (Ripley), Gerard Blain,
Nicholas Ray, Samuel Fuller, Peter Lilienthal, Daniel Schmid
Running time: 123 minutes
16mm rental: New Yorker Films

NICK'S FILM. LIGHTNING OVER WATER (Road Movies/Viking Film/
Wim Wenders Produktion, 1980)
Co-director: Nicholas Ray
Screenplay: Nicholas Ray, Wim Wenders
Photography: various
Music: Ronee Blakley
Cast: Nicholas Ray, Wim Wenders, Ronee Blakley
Running time: 91 minutes
With the exception of *The American Friend* (New Yorker Films), all the films
of Wim Wenders are distributed by Gray City, Inc.

Distributors' Addresses

The Liberty Company, 695 West 7th Street, Plainfield, NJ 07060

Cinema V, 595 Madison Avenue, New York, NY 10022

Corinth Films, 410 East 62nd Street, New York, NY 10021

Deutsch Films, 114 East 10th Street, New York, NY 10003

Film Images/Radim Films, 1034 Lake Street, Oak Park, IL 60301

Filmmakers Cooperative, 175 Lexington Avenue, New York, NY 10016

Films Inc., 440 Park Avenue South, New York, NY 10019

Gray City, Inc., 853 Broadway, New York, NY 10003

Kino International Corporation, Suite 314, 250 West 57th Street, New York, NY 10107

Libra Films, 150 East 58th Street, Suite 2104, New York, NY 10022

Monument Films, 352 Linda Lane, West Palm Beach, FL 33405

New Line Cinema, 853 Broadway, New York, NY 10003

New Yorker Films, 16 West 61st Street, New York, NY 10023

Promovision International, 105 East 15th Street, New York, NY 10003

UA Classics, 729 7th Avenue, New York, NY 10019

Unifilm Inc., 419 Park Avenue South, New York, NY 10010

Zoetrope, 916 Kearney Street, San Francisco, CA 94133

Index

223